Jeremy Black is one of the UK's most respected and prolific historians. He is Emeritus Professor of History at the University of Exeter and a renowned expert on the history of war. He is a Senior Fellow at the Foreign Policy Research Institute. His recent books include *Military Strategy: A Global History, A History of the Second World War in 100 Maps, Tank Warfare* and *The World of James Bond.* He appears regularly on TV and radio.

A BRIEF HISTORY OF

London

JEREMY BLACK

ROBINSON

ROBINSON

First published in Great Britain in 2022 by Robinson

5 7 9 10 8 6 4

A CIP catalogue record for this book
is available from the British Library.

ISBN: 978-1-47214-671-7

Typeset in Scala by Hewer Text UK Ltd, Edinburgh
Printed and bound in Great Britain by Clays Ltd, Elcograf S.p.A.

Papers used by Robinson are from well-managed
forests and other responsible sources.

Robinson
An imprint of
Little, Brown Book Group
Carmelite House
50 Victoria Embankment
London EC4Y 0DZ

An Hachette UK Company
www.hachette.co.uk

www.littlebrown.co.uk

For Emma, a London grandchild

Contents

·····················

Preface

For London today the emphasis is on transformation, whether with the impacts of the Covid pandemic of 2020–2, the consequences of a long-term rise in sea levels or the results of the country leaving the European Union in 2020. All suggest a period of international and domestic turmoil. This presents an opportunity for looking back, but with a distinctive perspective, that of London in its national and, even more, international contexts, rather than London to itself. Indeed, all those factors already mentioned are instances of such contexts. Thus, it is the interactions of London that will be considered, and notably so in order to address the question of why London became an international city, how it sustained that position and what is happening to it now.

This is as much about economics and culture as politics and society. It deals with migration, communications, empire and cultural energy, rather than the mechanisms of parish vestries. The history will be end-loaded: there will be enough to understand the earlier history, but the focus will be on the last half-millennium, the period in which London became a major trader with the trans-oceanic world and ruler of trans-oceanic colonies, while the English language became an increasingly important cultural medium, one centred on London.

Within that last half-millennium, the focus is on the period following the Great Fire of 1666. The first half-century was one of rebuilding and expansion, the creation of key institutions such as the Bank of England in 1694, the securing of parliamentary government, and a transformation in Britain's global position. As a simple multiple, however, of years by people, it is the last century that has to have the longest coverage. Moreover, the modernity that was, and is, always a major issue in the experience of London and response to it, both by Londoners and by others, was particularly apparent in a century of rapid change.

It is appropriate to remember a London childhood, not least fog, the sight of ruined trolleybuses and the plaintive cry of the rag-and-bone man, all past, and those I knew and who cared for me then. However, I would rather like at this point, December 2021, to thank the friends who have kindly given time and attention to reading drafts of this book, notably Peter Barber, Eileen Cox, Paul Double, Bill Gibson, Nigel Ramsay and Nigel Saul. They have greatly improved the book, but are not responsible for any remaining flaws. I have benefited greatly from the help of Duncan Proudfoot and Amanda Keats at Little Brown, and from Lucian Randall, as ever an exemplary copy editor. Lastly, this book is dedicated to Emma in the hope that the city will treat her kindly.

NOTE ON TERMS

City refers to the City of London and city to London as a whole.

Early London

The flames burned hard. They have left a distinct brown, burnt layer in the archaeological record of the first Roman London, almost everywhere in the built-up area to the east of the Walbrook, a tributary running down to the Thames. This was the devastation wreaked by Boudicca, Queen of the Iceni, in her war with the Romans in 60 CE, in the most traumatic episode in the city's early history.

Although the Romans were the first to create an urban settlement, they were not the first people to settle in the Greater London area. Instead, the long-term role of the Thames Valley as a communication route, the advantages of the riverside water meadows and the extent to which woodlands provided shelter for animals such as deer, had all attracted settlement long before the Romans arrived.

The tributaries of the Thames had provided plenty of water. In particular, Walbrook was clean and clear-flowing, and provided water all year round. As a result of these advantages, there was not only much animal life, but also, in part in order to pursue hunting, extensive pre-Roman human activity in the Palaeolithic, Mesolithic, Neolithic, Bronze and Iron Ages. Evidence, notably in the shape of remains of early hominids and finds of tool assembly, are supported by pollen and sediment studies, suggesting that, around 2000 BCE, there was a shift from nomadism and the hunting, gathering and slash-and-burn cultivation, to more defined agriculture, permanent settlement and fishing.

Thus, very briefly, we cover the bulk of human history in the London basin. This period, however, is not the history of a city, still less one with international – later, global – links. On the one

hand, there is no relevant 'deep history' of pseudo-mythic character and ancestry, but there was a key element that remains to the
present, that of physical placing. This was both very specific to the
site and in terms of the interaction of the latter with wider areas.
In each case, placing entails human decision and action, as later
with the development of bridges, embankments, tunnels and a
river barrage; but first must come a grasping of the possibility of
a site. Here a 'deep history' does come into play because this
understanding in part was a borrowing of what had earlier been
done by others.

There was to be a political dimension to this, but it was not
present from the outset. London itself was not a centre of tribal
polities and, in the Iron Age, that of the Trinovantes, with its
capital at Colchester, covered much of the territory north of the
Thames; although the concept of firm boundaries in this period is
not a helpful one and maps that suggest them are flawed.

Yet, although London was not a centre, there were Iron Age
settlements in the area, including at Crayford, Stratford and
Westminster. Discoveries include rich finds of Iron Age coins and
objects from the Thames foreshore at Putney and Barnes, as well as
ditches at Bermondsey. At the same time, despite the suggestion
that London was the site of a trading base prior to the Roman invasion of 43 CE, the balance of archaeological evidence implies otherwise. Instead, a settlement was probably established by the Romans;
dendrochronology on a timber drain revealed by archaeology
underneath No.1 Poultry has contributed to a date of about 47.

Roman London

London was established by the Romans at a strategic location on
the north bank of the Thames which, in the fashion of most
rivers, was much wider than today, as it remained until the
embankments were built from the mid-nineteenth century.
Moreover, with tidal marshes accordingly, the river was tidal to

---

Mythological Accounts

In Geoffrey of Monmouth's *Historia Regum Britanniae* [History of the Kings of Britain], finished in the mid-1130s, Aeneas of Troy's alleged great-grandson, Brutus, establishes human life in both Britain and London, with Brutus calling the latter New Troy. Repeated by William fitz Stephen in about 1173 and by Matthew Paris in about 1252, this story tells us more about later claims for an English identity separate to Normandy than about the true origins of London.

---

where the Romans built London. The low gravel banks of the north bank provided well-drained firmness for construction and a good site for the first bridge across the Thames. This communication node therefore linked a maritime route to the rest of the Roman Empire with roads within Britain, notably Ermine Street to York and Watling Street to Chester, roads that are the basis for modern routes, respectively the A10 and A5: the first stage of the latter is the Edgware Road.

After Boudicca's revolt was crushed in 60 CE, London was speedily rebuilt and repopulated, a testimony to the dynamism of Roman Britain and to the economic possibilities of London. The city quickly attracted not only foreign settlers but also the indigenous population. New buildings in the late first century CE included public baths and a wooden amphitheatre.

Not a legionary (leading military) base – for these were in or near frontier zones – London, however, developed as the key port. This made it more suitable as a city and governmental centre than the original official Roman capital, Colchester. This situation prefigured the relationship between London and Winchester in the eleventh century.

Different to the other major centres in Britain because it was a major port, London, however, was not one of the leading provincial cities of the Empire, north of, for example, the Alps, Lyons or Trier. In part, this was because Britain's economic and demographic weight in the Empire was less than that of France or Spain. Nevertheless, a city of considerable scale, London had large buildings, as well as a very large forum considerably more extensive than Trafalgar Square and, thanks to its commerce and role within the Empire, a highly cosmopolitan community. Roman London was the key point for the imperial colonisers, and trade and governance were organised accordingly.

Aside from the large suburb on the south bank, the standard Roman rectilinear-grid street plan in the main city, centred on forum and basilica, was an attempt to give shape to a more complex reality in which there were variations in land use by function and fashion, commerce and manufacturing. Indeed, differentiation by purpose and area has been a lasting character-istic of London, the purposes frequently dependent on external links.

One such was religion. It initially took the shape of the Olympian cults, including a temple of Jupiter, as well as that of Mithras, which left a third-century Mithraeum on the east bank of the Walbrook that was discovered in 1954. (The Mithraeum is now accessible at Bloomberg's European headquarters.) There is also evidence of worship of Egyptian gods, especially Isis, as well as the Phrygian goddess Cybele. Such practices reflected the extent to which cosmopolitan London included many from the other end of the Mediterranean. In relative terms, it was more cosmo-politan than is the case today. Although there is scant evidence for early Christian worship in London, Christianity provided cultural and institutional links with the Continent. In particular, a bishop of London attended the Council of Arles in 314.

Meanwhile the walling of the city with stone, enclosing the landward side from the 190s–210s, reflected the significance of London to the Romans. At just over two miles long, and about five metres high, the wall may well have required considerably more than one million cubic feet of ragstone, much of it presumably moved by boat from the quarries near Maidstone. Repaired and strengthened by bastions or towers, the wall and its gates, such as Aldgate and Ludgate, were a key feature of London's subsequent history and an enduring physical legacy from the Roman period. Furthermore, the Roman street plan, especially towards the Thames, has largely been preserved. A riverside wall which followed in the late third century provided protection against attack from the Thames, which was a reflection of the use of sea approaches by attackers.

Alongside building in stone, much was more cheaply built out of timber, which was readily available locally, and mud brick. This was a way to respond to the large number of settlers, most living in small, crowded houses, and thus in a dirty and noisy city. As with other periods of London life, there was a tension between city life and quality of life, one that was particularly acute in periods when numbers rose. Thus, the drains of Roman London could not readily cope with sanitation.

London remained important, being the capital of Roman Britain in the fourth century, and the sole mint and thus centre of liquidity; but the archaeological record from then is sketchy and coinage finds lower. At the same time, finds of coins minted in Roman London are quite common, testifying to its relatively high profile within the Empire and the extent to which its economy was integrated with the rest of the Empire. The distribution of late-Roman remains suggests that much of the western half of the walled city was more or less abandoned, with the main focus of continued settlement being to the east of the Walbrook stream. The city would have been affected by the growing crisis of an empire under pressure from 'barbarian' invaders, including a Saxon siege of London in 367–8, and the withdrawal of Roman troops in about 410.

AFTER THE ROMANS

The collapse of Roman patterns of government and trade, the major fragmentation of power and consumption, the recurrence of a subsistence economy and plague, all individually and even more collectively, hit hard at town life, especially after the mid-fifth century. Little, significantly, is known of London in the fifth or sixth century and the contradictions between written sources and archaeological evidence, both fragmentary, are significant. The Roman city seems to have been substantially deserted in part because, alongside its decline, the centre of remaining settlement moved west, along the banks of the Thames and also inland towards the Strand and Covent Garden.

Archaeological Evidence

Later building work, the destruction of material in centuries of cellaring, and the difficulty of excavating ephemeral timber structures before such methods were developed in the 1930s, affected the situation. In turn, the large-scale funding of rescue archaeology in London from 1973 greatly improved prospects. The excavations at No. 1 Poultry provided evidence of seventy-three Roman buildings and thousands of artefacts, including tools. In 2006, during restoration work at St Martin-in-the-Fields, archaeologists discovered a massive late-Roman sarcophagus complete with human skeleton, which appears to have been buried according to Christian practice. Excavations in Covent Garden in the 2000s produced finds from the early Saxon period of the late sixth or seventh century. It is probable that more work will produce additional valuable finds.

In turn, a revival in both Christianity and the volume of trade brought an increase in activity in the new Saxon settlement of Lundenwic to the west of the old walled city. This increase drew on the energy and wealth of the East Anglian and Kentish royal dynasties and on the developing importance of renewed links with the Continent. At the beginning of the seventh century, a church dedicated to St Paul was established in London as the seat of the bishop for the East Saxons, who dominated Essex and Middlesex. Like many other early Saxon churches elsewhere, the first St Paul's was sited within the former Roman city, in this instance on top of Ludgate Hill, the height of which is easy to overlook today. Small and built of timber, it burned down in 675 before being rebuilt – again in timber, which was plentiful in the region.

London was not a key political centre. Anglo-Saxon England indeed developed into a number of major kingdoms, but none of them centred on the city. As a result, Canterbury, the capital of Kent, which was one of these kingdoms, became the see of the Archbishop and not London.

As the centre of a bishopric, London was one of a number of towns. Yet, it was more important thanks to its role as a port and thus remained a key focus of both land and water routes. Settlement, however, continued to centre not on the area of the old Roman city but to the west of the River Fleet, around the Strand. Near Charing Cross, there was a reinforced embankment upon which ships were beached so that they could be unloaded. In the 730s, monk and pioneering historian of England, the Venerable Bede, described the city as 'a mart of many peoples'. Wool from the Cotswolds or woollen cloth was probably exported from London to France and the Low Countries, thus ensuring revenue. Canterbury lacked this commercial role and was affected anyway by the decline of the Kentish kingdom. Moreover, whatever the political consequences, London's role as a frontier town on the borders of several kingdoms and sub-kingdoms provided an opportunity for inter-state trade.

MERCIA, WESSEX AND THE DANES

In the eighth century, London came under the control of King Offa of Mercia, the Midland state, access to the city providing him with power in a wealthy area with much money, which enhanced the importance of London within Mercia. The dialect of the London area, like those of Oxford and the South Midlands, derives from Mercian forms of English. In turn, in the 820s and 830s, Mercia and Wessex – the Saxon kingdom dominating southern England – competed for control. The invading Vikings then came to the fore. Mounting attacks on London in 842 and 851, they probably established a garrison from 871.

King Alfred of Wessex's defeat of the Danes changed the situation and, in 886, he established control in London. The main settlement moved from Lundenwic, which lacked a defensive wall and had probably been devastated by the fighting. The legacy of Lundenwic included a number of churches, as well as the place name Aldwych (the 'old wic', or town) and a café today on the Aldwych called Lundenwic. Nevertheless, the ease with which wooden and wattle-and-daub constructions decayed helped to ensure that the site of the former Lundenwic reverted to open land. Meanwhile, the city had reverted to the old Roman site further east, while a significant suburb developed south of the Thames.

London was now part of Wessex's sphere of control and, as Wessex became the English state, so London's significance rose. A border city under Alfred, it benefited greatly from the rapid and complete driving back of the frontier with the Vikings. The consequent eroding of the distinction between Mercia and Wessex was very important to a changed status that saw London under Athelstan (r. 924–39) have eight moneyers, a number matched only by Canterbury and Winchester, the centres of government for church and state. In contrast, York was marginal. Of the single coin finds in England and Wales dating to 924–1135, London's mint produced the largest, the majority lying 75–125 kilometres from London, of which 64 per cent were found in eastern Kent, Norfolk, Suffolk, Cambridgeshire and along the Sussex coast. This suggests that London was a key purchaser of goods from a south-eastern hinterland, using, to this end, silver obtained by exports to the Continent.

London developed internally as well, with much of the medieval street system dating from this period and the population rising. Quays were built, including at Queenhithe and Billingsgate, while the Roman bridge was repaired. *'Cheap'*, the Anglo-Saxon word for 'market', left its mark at Westcheap and Eastcheap.

TENTH-CENTURY TURMOIL

Battling for London, 1014

'London Bridge is broken down,
Gold is won, and bright renown.
Shields resounding,
War-horns sounding,
Hildur shouting in the din!
Arrows singing,
Mailcoats ringing –
Odin makes our Olaf win!'

Ottar Svarte praised Olaf of Norway who came to the assistance of Athelred the Unready of England against invading Danish forces holding London Bridge. The Norwegian fleet attached cables to the bridge's piles and pulled it down.

Danish attacks in 994, 1009, 1013 and 1016 were beaten off, but with difficulty. Eventually victorious, king Cnut of Denmark and his sons ruled from 1016 until 1042. Cnut, who also ruled Denmark and Norway, found a governmental centre on the east coast of England to be more suitable than Winchester, the capital of Wessex. Without his predecessors' cultural, religious and historical ties to Winchester and what it represented, Cnut and his successors made London their military and governmental centre. This was a classic instance of the importance to London of broader political developments. It benefited from the resulting commercial links but also suffered from the Danish removal of bullion from the country. Harthacnut, Cnut's surviving son, died in 1042 at the wedding feast of a prominent Dane held in Lambeth, Tori the Proud, married to Gytha, daughter of the courtier Osgod Clapa. The dynasty of Wessex then returned in the person of Edward the Confessor. He became king by popular acclamation in London.

Meanwhile, the city benefited from the commercial growth of England and from the expansion of foreign trade, with German, French, Flemish and Scandinavian merchants all present in the early eleventh century. The wealth earned from wool exports proved the basis for an effective silver currency which, in turn, supported specialist crafts and assisted the process of government. By 1100, London had a population of between 10,000 and 20,000 people. Growth, including in Southwark, involved infilling and the development of new streets lined with timber houses. Property boundaries were fixed. Archaeological work in the 1990s at the eastern end of Cheapside has shown that the Poultry was built up with a row of buildings from the tenth century, followed by new streets. Surviving open spaces were filled in by 1200 with large stone properties in what was now a mercantile area.

Part of the growing wealth was spent on the church; on parish churches, monasteries, nunneries and hospitals. Much of the land surrounding the city was indeed granted to the church in late

Saxon times. Edward the Confessor rebuilt St Peter's monastery, or the West Minster, as a larger structure and also constructed the first royal palace on the site at what was Thorney Island, where the river Tyburn flowed into the Thames. The island is now part of the mainland, due to the embanking of the Thames. The first large Romanesque building in England, Westminster Abbey's new church, was dedicated in 1065 and Edward was buried there in 1066. Winchester had truly been replaced.

Like other towns, London benefited from the degree to which its life was not separate to that of rural areas, but part of it, not only for economic reasons but also for the cultural ones related to religion, and for governmental and political purposes. As a result, rural landowners also acquired an urban presence and property accordingly.

NORMAN CONQUEST

Unlike York and then Hastings, London was not a key site of battle in 1066 but, even more than York, it was a centre of strategic control. The crisis of 1066 very much showed London, and not Winchester, in this role. After being victorious over King Harold at Hastings on 14 October, William the Conqueror, Duke of Normandy, was beaten off at London Bridge and, as a result, had to cross the Thames to the west of the city. However, the weakness of the defeated Anglo-Saxon realm led to a speedy surrender and on Christmas Day William was crowned in Westminster Abbey. He issued a charter to London, promising to maintain its laws and customs as in Edward's reign; but what the conquering new order would bring in church and state, society and the economy, was uncertain.

2

Medieval London

....

Drama was to the fore at Smithfield on 15 June 1381 during the crisis of the Peasants' Revolt. Already London had been occupied, the Tower seized, prominent figures murdered and there had been a ransacking of places such as the palace at the Savoy of John of Gaunt, the king's uncle. In turn, Richard II met the main body of the rebels under Wat Tyler at Smithfield. During the meeting, William Walworth, mayor of London, believing that Tyler was threatening Richard, lunged forward and stabbed him in the neck, whereupon one of the king's knights despatched Tyler with a sword through the stomach. Astutely, Richard averted further violence by declaring himself the rebels' leader but, as soon as the rebels returned home, he revoked his promises and inflicted harsh punishments.

This was not the sole use of force nor explosion of violence in London. In particular, in the civil war of 1135–53, London's support for Stephen, nephew of Henry I, was very important to his eventual success over Matilda, Henry I's only legitimate child. Although she defeated Stephen at Lincoln, Matilda was driven from the city in 1141 thus preventing her coronation. In 1215, London backed the barons opposed to King John and the resistance of a royal force in the Tower was eventually ended, which helped lead the king to come to terms. Magna Carta was the outcome.

In 1264, the barons' victory under Simon de Montfort over Henry III owed much to support from London. In 1326, during the crisis that ended Edward II's reign, order in London collapsed and the Lord Treasurer, Walter de Stapledon, Bishop of Exeter, who had been left in charge as Keeper of London when Edward fled, was killed in Cheapside, having been dragged from St Paul's. In turn, London backed the revolt against the rule of Isabella and Mortimer in 1328–9, in large part because Mortimer was ignoring the city's political expectations.

In 1450, Jack Cade's rebellion in Kent saw London seized, as in 1381, unpopular officials killed, and Henry VI discrediting himself by running away. Eventually, the citizens restored order, while a royal pardon destroyed the cohesion of the rebels. In 1460, during the Wars of the Roses, a blockade forced the Lancastrian garrison in the Tower to surrender, while in 1471 a Lancastrian attack was repulsed by the citizens in hard fighting.

As it had been earlier, but even more so, London was a key site of control during these years. Battles were followed by an advance on London as with Edward IV, as the Earl of March, after the battle of Mortimer's Cross in 1469, and then, after the battle of Barnet, as king, receiving popular acclamation in 1471. Richard III's usurpation in 1483 focused on London. Its position as a key site of contention continued after the Wars of the Roses. In 1497, the Cornish rising focused on London, where Henry VII gathered an army and defeated the Cornishmen at nearby Blackheath.

It was not surprising that the standard image of London was of a walled city. Frequent conflicts made fortifications necessary.

GOVERNMENT

The political centrality reflected in these episodes was an expression of London's role as the site of legitimation and, as such, London's place reflected and encouraged a growing geographical fixity in the state. With constitutionalism and government expressed in a different fashion to today, the modern concept of a specific capital took a while to develop and the status of Winchester time to erode. As a result, there was an *ad hoc* character to

---

London in Maps

In Matthew Paris' Map of Great Britain of about 1255, London was acknowledged as the largest city by having the most elaborate towered and battlemented frame surrounding its name. In the larger Gough Map of about 1400, the roads from London, including to Bristol, Northampton, Norwich and Cornwall, largely followed Roman routes. Roads supplemented London's position as the leading port. London, the image of which in the Gough Map seems to have been redrawn in about 1470, again is the grandest of the marked cities, with its name and spires in gold leaf, other features in silver leaf and St Paul's and the Tower among the churches and fortifications shown.

London's governmental and political role, one that was seen in Westminster where the king heard mass in the abbey until the palace chapel was built in the mid-twelfth century. Westminster Abbey had great significance as the site of both coronations and ritual crown-wearing. London and Westminster were different parts of the same greater urban area, and this difference continued. Aside from being two miles apart, the City of London was a commercial centre and the site of citizen power, whereas Westminster was a royal and religious centre. This contrasted with Paris where the two sites were merged and royal power sat in the midst of economic power.

With the government ceasing to be peripatetic as well as a decline in the relative importance of the crown's French dominions, Westminster saw the fixing of governmental offices and royal residence. Moreover, as officials and records congregated in what became the centre of government, so the logic of treating it also as the centre of politics rose. Thus, while quasi-parliamentary bodies and, indeed, Parliament itself initially did not meet only in Westminster, the general settling of Parliament gathered pace from the 1470s. Earlier, the law courts became fixed in Westminster, with the Court of King's Bench and the Court of Common Pleas normally meeting there from the thirteenth century. A turning point came in the 1190s when Hubert Walter, Archbishop of Canterbury, the effective head of the government during the long absence abroad of Richard I, the Lionheart, both developed governmental practices and institutions that had a semi-permanent headquarters in Westminster and created an archepiscopal palace in Lambeth. In turn, Henry III focused more on London than his father, John, had done.

The growth of government activity created a major market for the merchants and artisans of London, but there was much more to the economic activity that took the population to over 30,000 by 1210, and about 80,000 or even 100,000 in the early fourteenth century, figures far greater than that for any other city in the British Isles. (The suggestion of a figure of 100,000 has met the rejoinder that it relied too heavily on extrapolations from very densely populated Cheapside.) As in later ages, migration was a major factor in maintaining the population, particularly from the South-East and East Anglia, but also from abroad, including from Normandy. Long-term economic growth, notably in the twelfth and thirteenth centuries, was significant as London benefited not only in population terms but also in marketing the resulting economy. Its ability to do so owed much to the enhanced communications of the period, both road and river, as well as to the network of local markets and fairs which was particularly strong in South-East England and East Anglia.

Within London, the infrastructure and sophistication of the city improved. Thus, William I (the Conqueror) built what became known as the White Tower of the Tower of London. The name was used after 1240 when Henry III had the Tower painted with whitewash. This was the key point in the defences, as it could be held against attack from within as well as without and thus served to overawe the City. There were smaller castles on the City's western side. To the south, in 1176–1209, the wooden bridge across the Thames was replaced by an impressive stone edifice with nineteen arches, high gateways and a superstructure including shops and houses, wooden buildings that proved fatal in a fire of 1212. This bridge underlined London's commercial significance.

Fire in 1087 led to the rebuilding from 1090 of St Paul's, which, when finished in 1314, was the longest cathedral (644 feet) in England, and had the highest spire (520 feet). St Paul's was as expressive of the new Norman order in religion as was the White Tower in military might. Due to delay by another fire in the 1130s, the Cathedral had Gothic as well as earlier Romanesque features.

The organisation and civic structure of the city developed and diversified. Thus, the provision of an effective water supply helped support the growth of population. Springs near Bond Street produced water that travelled via the 'Great Conduit' to Cheapside along a pipe installed from the 1230s. Regulations to ensure safety included the banning of thatch in the twelfth century, a step taken to prevent the risk of fire, confining dangerous crafts to single areas, building latrines, and the collection of waste. By the thirteenth century, the administration and maintenance of London Bridge had been entrusted to what became known as the Bridge House, and, by the mid-fourteenth century, it had been endowed with many rental properties to help it do so. Famines in 1257–60, 1315–17 and 1438–40 resulted in the building of the Leadenhall complex which included a public granary.

SOCIETY

As with the population of other cities, the smallest group consisted of the wealthy and prominent. The largest was the poor, many of them day-labourers, servants and paupers, who were very exposed to changes in the price of food, generally lived in inadequate housing and, as they could not afford much fuel, were often cold and wet in the winter.

Refuse

At the heart of the city, the Walbrook stream was little better than an open sewer and dumping ground, not least as a result of its use for leather tanning and butchering. As a consequence, there have been instructive archaeological finds. In 1288, the Walbrook had to be 'made free from dung and other nuisances' and, a century later, it was to be 'stopped up by divers filth and dung thrown in by persons who have houses along the said [water] course'.

In between, a third group enjoyed a more settled income than the poor but, individually and collectively, shared a precarious dependence on both the economy and the mischances of life. Many were artisans, their economic interest and social cohesion frequently expressed through fraternities of workmen. The most brutal display of chance was the Black Death, an epidemic of bubonic plague that killed between a third and a half of the population. Analysis of a 1346 tax assessment listing 370 people with goods worth at least ten pounds shows eleven dying prior to the plague, 106 during it, and 137 people in subsequent records. That left 116 unaccounted for, although some of them probably died of the plague without leaving a record, not least through not having had time to draw up wills. Later plague attacks possibly took the population down to about 40,000 by the 1370s.

Plague cut migration from rural areas, although with less crowding they were not so prone to infection as London, where rental values were put under pressure. As a result of the plague, London's bounds in 1550 were essentially still those of the 1170s. This contraction was also seen in rival English cities that did not enjoy London's considerable advantages of commerce and government.

Women were subordinate in government and the economy, but could still play a significant role. For example, many women were involved in the production side of the crucial Mercers company.

Dick Whittington

Already established in London as a Mercer by 1379, this youngest son of a Gloucestershire landowner went on to be Mayor in 1397–8, 1406–7 and 1419–20. He made much of his money by acting as Collector of Customs in London and Calais, in turn lending money to Richard II, Henry IV and Henry V. As part of the continual process of creating a heritage for the city, his tale of early poverty and a valuable rat-catching cat – now presented in Christmas pantomimes – did not emerge until the 1600s. Cats appeared in other European tales at the time. A large part of Whittington's earlier fame rested on his charitable benefactions. Such benefactions brought together religious duty, civic purposes and concern about social conditions.

ECONOMIC POWERHOUSE

The end of England's rise in population in the fourteenth century caused skill shortages that pushed up the cost of labour, encouraging a shift from grain production to the keeping of sheep for wool, which required less manpower. The export of wool had been fundamental to the national economy for centuries, and London's wool exports rose anew from the 1290s; now domestic clothiers were increasingly turning that wool into cloth for sale at home and abroad. Cloth finishing and exports brought much wealth to London, which was well placed to reach the markets in the Low Countries, notably Bruges, Ghent and Antwerp. They acted as entrepôts to the rest of Europe. By the close of the fourteenth century, more than half of the ships arriving in London were in some respect involved in trade with the Low Countries. This helped ensure exposure to their styles, notably in clothing, linens, earthenware, food and, eventually, books. Although the

Hanseatic merchants from northern Germany played an important role, the cloth trade from London came to be largely dominated by the Mercers' and Drapers' Companies. There were commercial links with the leading Italian and German cities, notably Cologne but, alongside the important presence of foreign merchants, there was an Anglicisation in trade and thus liquidity.

Providing a powerful aid to economic growth, regional and national communication systems improved, which helped internal and foreign trade and travel. The pilgrims of Geoffrey Chaucer's *Canterbury Tales* (c. 1387) have the Tabard Inn in Southwark as their meeting place for their journey to Canterbury. London-born to a family of vintners, Chaucer (c.1343–1400) was Comptroller of the Customs for London and then Clerk of the King's Works, a royal administrative role that related to London.

London's sway extended across the country. It both dominated the regional economy, that of the wealthiest part of England, and also increasingly created a national one, although provincial towns were relatively more important than is the case today. From the fifteenth century, even Kendal in distant Cumbria was served by regular packhorse trains moving goods as far as the capital. Every significant centre had such ties and the network of regular carriers' routes was instrumental in creating the national transport system. The improvement in land transport, including the replacement of fords by stone bridges, reduced the cost and unpredictability of transport, benefited London and fed business to its port facilities. Throughout its history, communications and systems of marketing and exchange of goods and services have been fundamental to London's relative position within England and Europe, key strands linking ancient Rome's roads with the nineteenth-century impact of steam and the current development of internet and related information, communications and commercial systems.

Moreover, as the relative wealth of the South-East within England grew, London benefited directly, not least as a source of goods and services and as a significant market for the economy of most of the region. Indeed, the regional dimension is a crucial element of London's history, one that looks to such later manifestations as large-scale commuting. Cities depend on their hinterlands, their prosperity and accessibility. The context of this dependence changed with the steam-powered transport revolution of the nineteenth century. Prior to that, the economics of the bulk supply of food and fuel were less favourable. In the Middle Ages, London drew supplies of grain, meat and wood from all over the South-East, while the city's mercantile credit was crucial to this production system. Goods were brought down the Thames Valley from Henley and, to a degree, beyond Oxford and by boat from the hinterland of East Anglian ports and then by sea (although the Thames route was adversely affected by economic difficulties after the Black Death). London's benefit included its development as a manufacturing hub – for example, metal working from the mid-fourteenth century – and service centre.

The growth of London's economy attracted people from elsewhere in England, and notably so from southern England. For example, many twelfth- and thirteenth-century Mercers came from East Anglia. Alongside permanent migrants, London had shorter-term residents, again reflecting its strength and diversity not only as a labour market but also as a site for activity. Thus, lay and ecclesiastical magnates spent time in London, including Southwark, their town houses providing bases for them to pursue their concerns, notably political influence. This presence, which became habit-forming, gave London greater centrality to national activity and revenue flow, not least as a place for their consumption of goods and services.

War disrupted trade and payments and added to insecurity. Yet, it could also benefit London, not least as it was well placed to

The Need for Wood

Providing the biggest market for wood in Britain, Londoners required it for heating and cooking, while the city's economy also depended on it for industrial and service activities such as metal working and baking and also for construction, including the tiles and bricks increasingly used from the fourteenth century. Most fuel came from wood, but charcoal and coal were increasingly significant from the late twelfth century, although coal use was hit by shipping costs and did not rise greatly until the late sixteenth century, when greater demand matched the lack of an ability to expand wood production. Firewood prices rose considerably from the 1280s, reflecting demand/supply pressures which were not helped by wood's bulk and therefore transport cost, which was eased by water transport. Access to this defined the supply zone. Wood traders and wharves, not only Woodwharf, reflected the supply system, with concentrated demand producing intensive production areas.

seek royal protection. There was also manufacturing for war, as with the growth in the production of longbows from the early fourteenth century. This led to the establishment of Livery Companies for bowyers (1363) and fletchers (1371). In turn, as an instance of the adaptability that was important to the London economy, firearms replaced this industry in the sixteenth century.

Paris was also a manufacturing, trading and service centre, but not to the same extent as London, which was on the tidal range in a way that the more inland Paris was not. This contrast was seen in the long-term character and development of the two cities, notably so in terms of economic activity and social structure.

At the same time as expansion, differentiation within London continued, not least as economic growth contributed to greater specialisation for the skilled portion of the workforce. The distribution of occupations reflected their particular needs, but also the guild system. Tax revenue per acre in 1332 was higher from wards near the river, such as Vintry, Dowgate and Bridge or in the centre, than further away. These were the wards where the wealthy lived, providing access to the shops and markets along and near Cheapside, and also to the quays and wharves along the river. The poor, in contrast, lived in the north and east.

Outside the City, but part of its economy, Southwark, a town in its own right, was affected by parallel demographic and economic trends, but its population, on average, was poorer and more transient, which posed challenges for poor relief. Southwark's population rose from over two thousand in about 1380 to maybe eight thousand by 1550, which made it one of England's significant towns.

Country Life

Much of the London area remained resolutely rural. Thus, Stepney, a manor of the Bishop of London, produced grain from the conventional unenclosed fields and had feudal labour services into the fourteenth century. The London market was seen in roadside market gardening and communities at Poplar and Whitechapel and the value of meadow land for grazing and hay. This market also helped bring prosperity to Romford, Hornchurch and Havering.

CITIZENSHIP

At the same time, a sense of identity was growing, notably from the twelfth century. In a society that referred to the past and was reverential of it, this process was based heavily upon precedent and the perceptions of history. Edward the Confessor had issued a writ confirming the laws and jurisdiction of the London guild of *cnihtas* (knights) and this was placed on the altar of the priory of Holy Trinity, Aldgate in 1125 as confirmation of the guild's gift of land and rights. A link can be drawn thence to the 1191 commune, which advanced claims for London's interests and, in turn, brought together Londoners of both English and Norse ancestry. A key and lasting element of the city's identity was that it took precedence over differences in ancestry and lineage and, instead, brought otherwise distinct groups into a commonality of shared identity and interest, and successfully so: by 1191, the distinction between Anglo-Saxons and post-1066 settlers was more or less obsolete. Pride in London's history and the conviction of its distinctive identity and importance played a role in this assertiveness and was also expressed in the laws and customs known as the 'London Collection', assembled during the period of opposition to King John in the early thirteenth century.

In a parallel process, various craft and mercantile guilds emerged, defined their roles, and, in multiple directions, asserted their economic and political interests, controlling local production and trade in a process involving regulation, lobbying, litigation and violence. These guilds, which were linked to the dense and varied texture of ecclesiastical foundations and activity, were to become the City Livery Companies. They were important to the creation in the Middle Ages of the distinctive features of government that were to provide the context for London's later development. These included a depth of governance that shared, and thus grounded, authority and responsibility. Accountability was eased by the stability in population of the later Middle Ages. Moreover, this accountability related to the lack of direct rule by the monarchy. The use of writing became more common, first with civic government in the fourteenth century, and then with the increase in the use of written documents by merchants and artisans.

Citizenship became an earned right, bestowed in return for membership of a guild (itself secured by patrimony, apprenticeship or purchase) and with payment through civic taxation; this citizenship was marked by taking the civic oath. In return, economic privileges and legal rights were granted, especially those of buying and selling property, trading and enjoying the protection of the courts. From 1319, would-be citizens had to gain the approval of those already practising their trade and citizenship was dependent upon support from existing trade associations. Citizens, moreover, did not have to pay the tolls charged on goods brought into the City across London Bridge.

Those excluded were called 'foreigners', irrespective of their place of birth, and most were confined to practising poorly paid occupations. Furthermore, there was also a tendency to regard marginal groups as presenting a threat to public health, order and morality, notably so prostitutes, beggars and vagrants and those thus defined. The City authorities and those of the particular wards often acted in concert. The use of almshouses only for the 'deserving poor' was an aspect of this exclusion. The suburbs, where authority was weakest, were a particular resort of marginal groups.

The governmental system developed apace, the city being divided into twenty-four wards by 1127, each with its own alderman, the modern complement of twenty-six wards being reached in 1550 when Bridge Without ward was added south of the Thames in what is now Borough. The achievement of autonomy by the Londoners under a mayor elected from among the aldermen rested on the strength of the local government offered by the ward system. Although each ward was headed by an alderman and the council – or court – of aldermen lent coherence to the city's government, the ward also had a wardmote or local forum. Local governmental structures and a political culture focused on cohesion helped limit social division within London; but many tensions remained, not least as a tendency towards oligarchy was unpopular among citizens.

A clear and strong government structure helped in the assertion of what could be presented as rights. In Magna Carta (1215), it was agreed that London was 'to have all its ancient liberties and free customs', and that the granting of aids to the Crown from the city would take place under strict conditions. The Mayor was one of twenty-five 'barons' sworn to see Magna Carta was maintained.

The rise of a national consciousness could lead to hostility towards those judged to be outsiders. Benefiting from royal favour, a Jewish community – possibly immigrants from Rouen, and based on Jews' Street (Old Jewry) was in place by 1130. The role of the Jews in helping to finance the Crown and other leading figures led, however, to growing criticism. In 1189 this resulted in a violent response, including the burning down of the London Jewry and anti-Semitic harassment culminated in Edward I's expulsion of the Jews from England in 1290. In 2001, archaeological work in Milk Street unearthed a Jewish ritual purification bath of about 1260.

There was less deadly hostility to other foreigners, notably Italians, Flemings and the French, although about forty Flemings were killed during the Peasants' Revolt and in 1469 there was, with the encouragement of Edward IV, an attack on the Steelyard, the depot of the Hanseatic League, while, as with the Grocers' Company, the foundation of Livery Companies owed much to the challenge from foreign merchants. The favour that the Crown showed towards alien workers and merchants, often as a result of the money and loans they provided, created resentment among their London rivals, underlining the extent to which the proximity of city and royal court could present problems as well as opportunities for Londoners. Partly as a result, the city frequently turned to those opposed to the Crown, for example to Simon de Montfort in the 1260s, the Lord Appellants in the 1380s, and Richard, Duke of York, in the 1450s. This linkage re-emerged in the late sixteenth and early seventeenth centuries as tension arose between monopolists linked to the court and other merchants opposed to their privileges.

The consciousness of London identity was shown by writers such as Robert Bale (c. 1410–73), Robert Fabyan (1470–1513), Richard Arnold (d. c. 1521) and Edward Hall (c. 1496–c. 1547), all writers of chronicles of London or work in which London was prominent. At the same time, there was no possibility that London would become an independent city state on the German or Italian pattern. Aside from the major role there of the royal government, there was also the extent to which London's prosperity depended on the rest of the country and to which prominent Londoners had a presence outside the capital. Thus, Richard Buckland (d. 1436) was not only a merchant stapler, fishmonger, shipowner and collector of customs in London, but also an MP and JP in Northamptonshire, while, as Victualler of Calais, he benefited from the war effort against France. His son-in-law, Robert Whittingham, was a prominent Londoner, Warden of the Drapers' Company and an Alderman, but also came to be a country gentleman and officeholder, with again a role in Calais. Hall, a Londoner, was the Common Serjeant and later Under-Sheriff but, educated at Eton and Cambridge, also served as MP for first Much Wenlock and later Bridgnorth.

The interrelationships of London with official and rural positions were readily apparent in these and other cases. They were paralleled by the multiple nature of commercial identities and interests. The combination made for dynamism and also a porosity of influence, both by and on London. The role of trade – notably, but not only, overseas trade – meant that any tendency to a rentier passivity was challenged by the opportunities for new profit and thus an enhanced position.

RELIGION

Medieval London was part of an international church. A departure point for pilgrims, notably to Canterbury, Santiago de Compostela and Jerusalem, it also saw crusading activity, particularly for crusader funds, and was a location for international Christian bodies such as the Knights Templar.

Meanwhile, in and around London the role of religion bore a clear institutional imprint. The archbishops of Canterbury and York and the bishops, notably those of Chester, Durham, Ely and Winchester, had presences in London with town houses, while the Bishop of London was not only important in the city but also had a wider presence as Dean of the Province of Canterbury. He also controlled a diocese that included Essex, Middlesex and much of Hertfordshire. As such, bishops helped appoint clergy and oversee the affairs of parishes, not least by ensuring that patronage rights were moved from lay to ecclesiastical bodies. Thirteen conventional churches and 126 parish churches in London and its suburbs were recorded by William fitz Stephen in the 1170s. The numbers held up and were greater than the fifty separate inns and taverns that have been listed for 1423–6, although most drinking establishments were probably smaller-scale.

Clerics were presented with plentiful opportunities and were an important part of London life, although competition ensured that many faced insecurity and low incomes. A significant amount of London's land was occupied by religious foundations, including the friaries whose houses occupied about 5 per cent, while they also owned much rental property. The Dominicans – the Black Friars – were the most significant. There was also a process of expansion in religious provision, as with the hospital of the Savoy, founded by Henry VII and finished in 1515, which included three chapels and twelve clerics. Providing accommodation for a hundred poor men, medical care and the distribution of food to the poor, the Savoy was also a place for intercession for the souls of the king and his family. The sole remains are the main chapel of the hospital which is now the Queen's Chapel of the Savoy. The absence of significant population growth in the later medieval period made it easier to provide for the destitute.

Alongside the religious confraternities – such as that of St Antonin founded by the Guild of Pepperers in 1345 – the guilds and the units of local government, the parish churches, many founded in the eleventh century, helped ensure a detailed pattern of belonging, with the churches serving as centres of identity for particular neighbourhoods. This sense of local identity, ringing out with church bells and maintained by frequent processions, linked the generations, with parish churches the venues for baptisms, weddings and funerals, helping to provide a sense of family coherence focused upon churches, which were key points for the face-to-face relationships that were central to community ones. The ritual observance crucial to Catholic practice contributed to this stability while the importance of this role helps explain the disruption caused by the Protestant Reformation.

Cooking

There is evidence of cookshops providing hot street food from the 1170s and by the 1300s there is evidence of their specialisations. This was a call on the wood burned in London and, for 1300, there is a recent estimate that 70,000 acres were required to provide the wood required for London. Such fast food was made possible, even necessary, by the developing world of work as well as the absence of ovens in many dwellings.

3

Tudor London

....

London was transformed in the sixteenth century by the Reformation and was increasingly affected by growing links with the world outside Europe. Alongside these two major developments, there was a significant growth in population and economic activity, as well as the creation of a new public culture in the shape of theatre. Thus, Shakespeare vies with Henry VIII as the most prominent Tudor resident of the London area, although their particular Londons were very different, Henry spending large amounts of time in Greenwich, Westminster and Hampton

---

'Evil May Day'

Begun the previous evening in the precinct of St Martin-le-Grand, the riot of 1 May 1517 provided a focus for wider tensions affecting many Londoners. Over two thousand citizens were reported to have rioted, attacking the homes and workplaces of foreigners. The brutal response included cannons being fired into the City from the Tower and the deployment of large numbers of armed retainers by the powerful Howard family, that of Thomas, 3rd Duke of Norfolk, after which the alleged ringleaders were executed for treason. The episode captured the anger spiked by the presence of about three thousand foreigners in London, notably its eastern wards. They were prominent in trade, weaving, dyeing, tanning, cooperage, brewing and much else, and it was this that created a focus for hostility. This, however, was the last eruption on such a scale.

Court, but avoiding the Tower. Aware of his dignity, Henry would not have recognised nor appreciated his depiction by Shakespeare and John Fletcher in the play performed as *All is True* in 1613, later published as *Henry VIII*.

Reformation

London played a key part as a centre for early Protestantism, not least because of its citizens' roles in printing and in trade with northern Europe, where Protestantism began. Although there were many supporters of traditional Catholicism in and near London, notably in Westminster, the city was still the centre of change. Moreover, the key areas of violent opposition to the Reformation – notably Yorkshire in 1536 and Cornwall in 1549 – were at a distance. The first victim of action against Protestants under the Catholic Mary I (r. 1553–8) was burned at Smithfield in 1555; London, Kent and Sussex had a disproportionately high number of Protestant martyrs, being geographically nearest to continental Protestantism and also most exposed to royal power and attention. Indeed, the triangle of London, Canterbury and Windsor represented the focus of the politicisation of religion in the critical Reformation period from the 1530s. In that area, conformity was far easier to enforce and nonconformity far harder to conceal.

After William Caxton (c. 1422–c. 1491) established the first English printing-house within the precincts of Westminster Abbey in 1476, an enterprise moved to the City after his death, London became the centre of publication and benefited from the rising number of individual readers. Attempts to establish printing further afield initially failed. London was also a place where Protestant works published on the Continent were brought into England, sometimes legally, sometimes illicitly. At the same time, it was not just London but, increasingly, its hinterland that was influential.

London changed as a result of the Reformation. Twenty-three religious orders had estates in or adjoining the city and their seizure by Henry VIII in 1536–40, in the dissolution of the monasteries, provided plentiful opportunities for the expansion of the built-up area. There had been earlier instances of moves against ecclesiastical institutions, such as the suppression of the Knights Templar in 1312, but nothing on the scale of the Reformation. Shrines were smashed, monasteries, nunneries and chantry chapels seized, dissolved and destroyed or repurposed, fraternities brought to a close and clerics who were judged suspect were executed. The establishment of Protestant worship and religiosity, in turn, brought London the definition of new associations including Dutch and French churches for foreign Protestants.

SOCIETY

The physical expansion of London reflected its rise in population, after modest growth in the fifteenth century, to approximately 50,000 in 1500, a population similar to that of Roman London in the third century. It lagged behind Paris, Naples, Milan, Venice, Granada, Prague and Lisbon, but the population rose to about 200,000 in 1600, about 375,000 to 400,000 in 1650, and about 500,000–600,000 in 1700, which was then nearly 10 per cent of a substantially larger English population. In contrast, Norwich, the second-largest city in 1600, had about 15,000 inhabitants.

This growth was more impressive given the high death rate in the densely packed city. The toll was heavy, as seen in the poetry of John Donne, Dean of St Paul's, whose wife Ann died in 1617 after giving birth to a stillborn child. Suffering was a frequent subject of his poetry and his last sermon took the theme of 'Death's Duel'. The high death rate was countered by migration to London. This was different to the situation from around 1800, when immigration generally supplemented indigenous growth. While expanding, the city remained compact and densely built-up. Thomas Platter, a Swiss visitor, noted in 1599, 'The city of London is not only brimful of curiosities, but so popular also that one simply cannot walk along the streets for the crowd.'

Aside from competition for land, accentuating boundary disputes, London's numbers put acute pressure on housing, employment and poor relief, at the same time as they added to the labour force that contributed to expanded production, as in brewing and glassmaking. House-building itself became a major source of work, one that was notable, given that the rate of increase in the population was greater than it would be in the twentieth century and followed a period when there had been no such growth. Each migrant, from abroad or, more commonly, from within England represented an individual decision that life might be better in London. For many, however, this hope proved illusory, as rural penury often translated into urban poverty. Moreover, urban degradation was more pernicious because of the absence of the community support that could be more present in rural parishes.

The major growth in population made the capital a more important market but also posed a range of acute problems for its authorities. These also led to a disorientating perception of a past characterised by stability and order and a present consisting of disruption, dissolution and foreboding. That prefigured the situation in subsequent periods of rapid population growth. Rootlessness was a perception that underlay concerns about what was presented as vagrancy, but alongside anxieties about the mass of disorderly individuals there were more pointed fears about the multifaceted challenge to the law-abiding. This notably came from criminal gangs, seduction and venereal disease, heresy and treason. The surveillance, policing and punishment deployed accordingly, in turn became fresh fields of tension and anxiety and they were evaded and defied. Neighbourhoods were contested, with the situation more challenging at night. This danger forced forward responses such as the deterrence offered by watch patrols, as in Shakespeare's *Much Ado About Nothing* (1598–9), which, though set in Messina, had clear resonances of London.

The social system was not only a troubling challenge but also an important advantage and was more fluid in towns: mobility was greater and social control laxer, which were part of London's lasting character. There was acute social differentiation in the city, but this was not expressed in traditional terms of deference, as that in rural England generally was. In practice, the sense of opportunity in London surpassed the reality; but it contributed, nevertheless, to the feeling of flux, one captured by playwrights. In particular, the emphasis on citizens, for example in Shakespeare's *Richard III* (1592–3) and *Julius Caesar* (1599), reflected their significance in London where, by the 1590s, two-thirds to three-quarters of the adult male residents were citizens.

Developing Areas

Alongside the expansion of the built-up area, buildings within the City were constantly being renewed. It was relatively easy to clear, alter or improve the medieval wooden and mud structures and opportunities for redevelopment were offered by both prosperity and fire. Each could lead to the clearing of crowded tenements. The overall urban structure of the City, with its property boundaries, city walls and liberties (areas of particular jurisdiction), was retained through most of this redevelopment and a contrast developed between the City and the suburbs.

To the west, Westminster increasingly became the West End, with Henry VIII's development of Whitehall and St James's Park followed by the aristocracy taking over the town palaces of the bishops, and gentry spending the parliamentary session near Westminster. The 'new men' who benefited from the Tudors built with ambition: Lord Protector Somerset built Somerset House on the south side of the Strand only for that to be stopped when he was executed in 1552. The rise in litigation, the centralisation of political patronage, the emergence of a London season and the servicing of all these activities, contributed to the development of Westminster, which preceded the later town-building to the west in the century from the creation of Covent Garden in the 1620s. By 1639, Westminster had a population of about 35,000. Many were poor, finding work episodic and thus depending on relief. To the east, Wapping was drained by a Dutch engineer in the reign of Henry VIII and Wapping and Tower Hamlets were shown in the vignette map of London on the Anglian Figura map of about 1536–7.

There was also expansion on the South Bank of the Thames. Long-established as a southern suburb, Southwark – part of Surrey and outside the jurisdiction of the City, with a reputation as a disorderly competitor – became something of a 'Wild South' with scant law or regulation. Much of the area contained low-grade housing, while land availability made Southwark attractive to entrepreneurs and it became home to rings for bull- and bear-baiting, and then also to theatres. Expansion downriver included anchorages, shipbuilding yards, and the large palace at Greenwich built by Henry VII in about 1500.

In addition to the more defined suburbs, the Greater London area extended to include a broader range of impact and influence that economically and emotionally became part of London. The economic links included the provision of food, hay and gravel, healthy weekend homes for businessmen, opportunities for craftsmen, and sites for recreation and socialising. As early as *The Singularities of London* (1578), an early guidebook, foreign visitors were being recommended to go to view London from Highgate if they truly wanted to understand it.

The failure of the Crown to implement an integrated approach to the suburbs ensured that their governance and authority were fragmented, as was that of London as a whole, a situation that remained the case until the Greater London Council was established in 1965. Thus, Westminster remained separate. There, because of opposition from the Crown and the Dean and Chapter to a borough government, a Court of Burgesses, established in 1585 and nominated by the Dean, had less power than the City of London Corporation. To contribute to the mélange of clashing power there were also in Westminster the Middlesex JPs, a High Steward appointed by the monarch and the vestrymen of the individual parishes, as well as the local gentry who could be reluctant to heed appropriate authority. This interaction both challenged and was crucial to stability.

The area that was most regulated was the City, under the Mayor and Corporation. It was able to call on a network of control in order to enforce regulations, as with the recoinage early in Elizabeth's reign, during which the Mayor instructed the Livery Companies to send representatives into every market in order to ensure that the new coins were taken. The companies served as ways to regulate but also to link, the latter role including the City and the suburbs, which helped contain differences. Guild politics, indeed, also proved a way to register, but also contain, differences, contributing to a metropolitan community, as compromise was a way to deal with the large-scale disruption of economic and religious change. At the same time, concern about the suburbs remained strong, as part of a wider sense of anxiety about change and uncertainty.

PROSPERITY AND POVERTY

The commercial entrepôt between England and the wider world, the prime site of consumption and a major centre of manufacturing, London benefited from the growing prosperity of England. London money financed activity across the country, providing investment, credit and demand, as well as philanthropy, with the Livery Companies therefore enjoying a national range.

Visitable History: Bruce Castle

Bruce Castle, Tottenham, an imposing building, is a brick-built, sixteenth-century manor house, later remodelled, that houses a museum covering the histories of Haringey and the Royal Mail. There was an earlier house on the site. The current house was owned by the Comptons in the sixteenth century and sold by the indebted Richard, 3rd Earl of Dorset to Hugh, 1st Lord Coleraine, who choked to death on a turkey bone in 1667. The central tower and Jacobean features were retained when the house was modernised in the early eighteenth century. Sold, in turn, by the family in 1792, the house, having been a suburban retreat for an aspiring city businessman, became a progressive school in 1827 with Rowland Hill as headmaster; he was later the first head of the Post Office. The school closed in 1891 and was bought by Tottenham council, providing the first public park in the borough in 1892 and opening as a museum in 1906. A similar story of transition can be seen elsewhere, for example Lauderdale House in Highgate and (without the park) Sutton House.

London also helped mould a national economic market. By 1600, provincial manufacturers and merchants were typically opening London offices and engaging in regular trade with the capital. Although much manufacturing was in London, in part using raw materials sourced elsewhere, the city was also a market for industry that was based elsewhere. Thus, Maidstone developed papermaking and brewing for the London market. The city was also a key market for food and fuel from across the country, particularly so for areas from which they could be transported by water. In particular, the development of North-Eastern coal production and the related trade from the Tyne freed London from dependence on nearby wood and enabled its rising population to rely on a mixture of fuel from a distance and food from nearby, with much of Middlesex's woodland cleared for market gardening and the extraction of gravel. Other major European cities, notably Paris, were unable to rely on this mixed system, which became increasingly effective with use. Coal duties were a source of revenue and were later used for the purchase of open space, notably Epping Forest in 1878.

Yet, London was also a very challenging place in which to live. About a quarter of the city's population died as a result of plague in 1563. Moreover, the former royal palace of Bridewell was acquired by the City in 1553 as a house of correction in an important attempt to restructure social welfare. The unemployed able-bodied were made to work, with some also sent in chain-gangs to clean streets and ditches and others later sent or sentenced to be indentured servants to Virginia.

The condition of the majority of London's population aroused governmental and journalistic attention, albeit in a different form to that of the close of the nineteenth century. This condition caused both material deprivation and lower life expectancy. Marginalised by the strains of hard work and poverty, the poor also had only a limited role in the more intense level of public politics and culture developing in London in the late sixteenth century. Instead, public patronage, and the opportunities of the marketplace, ensured a continuing focus on those with money, with other sources of authority and patronage weakened, at least relatively so. Already, the Reformation had undermined earlier patterns of cultural control, providing, for example, new opportunities for playwrights. As a result, Londoners could see themselves depicted on the stage, as in Ben Jonson's comedy *Bartholomew Fair* (1614), set at the four-day fair that was held annually at Smithfield from 1133 to 1855 to provide both trading opportunities and recreation. The play's cast includes Zeal-of-the-Land Busy – a Puritan – the pimp Whit and Justice Overdo and the action is rumbustious. This was very different to the *Survey of London* (1598) by John Stow (c. 1525–1605), a Merchant Taylor with antiquarian interests. This ward-by-ward topographical history provided more detail than earlier works and also captured the strong sense of place within London. His monument in St Andrew Undershaft church encompasses an effigy wielding a real quill pen that is frequently renewed.

London's reputation among those who did not live there was varied. It was at once a place of glamour, excitement and attraction, and also of filth, squalor, degradation and immorality; the stuff of ballads and folk songs. It saw expansion and anxiety, prosperity and poverty – all more vividly etched than anywhere else in the country. Certainly, the awareness of London grew greatly in England during the Tudor age, a process encouraged by print and Protestantism. London seemed very much both the source of the high rate of sweeping change across the country and of the words, ideas and images through which change was defined, asserted and debated. Provoking dislike and suspicion, resentment of London's dominance was far from rare.

This dominance was also seen in the economy, with London continuing earlier trends both as a market and as a source of products and capital. That in turn, was, as before, in part a consequence of the city's role as England's crucial economic intermediary with the overseas world. Its expansion in this produced and directed greater demand elsewhere in the country – for example, in the Norwich sailcloth industry from the 1580s; and such responses further helped focus economic links while also fostering and financing demand elsewhere for London goods and services.

Continuity and change were not incompatible. Thus, in the sixteenth century, London added to its dominance of woollen cloth exports, notably to the Low Countries and Germany by means of the Merchant Adventurers Company, new trades, especially those carried on by the Levant Company and then the East India Company. Given monopoly privileges by the Crown, these companies in turn provided it with money, including loans. Subsequently, trade with the Caribbean and North America was to follow. City companies were also to be involved in the colonisation of Ulster.

There was also an increasingly significant global role. London was the base for joint-stock commercial organisations which could raise investment and share risk from a wide range of partic016ipants, such as the East India, Hudson's Bay, and Levant Companies. Opportunities for trade also increased because of the movement of anchorages from Queenhithe and Billingsgate downriver to Deptford, Wapping and Ratcliffe, a move that provided more space. Improving shipbuilding and ship repair facilities, London's first dry dock was built at Rotherhithe in 1599, followed by another, for the expanding East India Company, at Blackwall in 1614–17. By 1617, London was a presence in India, Virginia and Bermuda, as well as in more familiar places.

In turn, this expansion, which helped to rework transformative networks of exchange, brought activity and wealth into London. Indeed, rather as there was to be a symbiotic relationship between the development of naval power and Britain's rise to greatness, so also with London and greatness. Thus, alongside the emphasis on 'the ancient order' by Livery Companies and others, there was very much an agenda and energy of change, one seen in particular in new global links.

The Tax Burden

'Every year I have heard an exceeding outcry of the poor that they are much oppressed by the rich of this city, in plain terms of the common council ... the burden is more heavy upon a mechanical and handicrafts poor man than upon an alderman.'

Complaint about regressive taxation,
Richard Stock, Paul's Cross sermon, 1603

4

The Seventeenth Century

....

'In the country the christenings exceed the burials, yet in
London they do not. The general reason of this must be
that in London the proportion of those subject to die until
those capable of breeding is greater than in the country . . .
or else we must say that London is more unhealthful, or
that it inclines men and women more to barrenness, than
the country.'

John Graunt, *Natural and Political Observations
made upon the Bills of Mortality* (1662)

'London Under the Tudors' cannot be followed by a chapter
entitled 'London Under the Stuarts' because, from 1641 to 1660,
London was the centre of resistance to that family, eventually as
the capital of republican governments, while Charles I was
executed in the city in 1649. As a political maelstrom, the
English Revolution did not leave the equivalent to its later
French namesake: the Tower was not stormed and destroyed as
the Bastille was to be in 1789. Nor were the eleven-mile-long
fortifications erected by the Parliamentarians in 1642–3 retained:
in the event, they never needed to be used against Royal attacks.
Nor was London attacked by foreign forces, as Paris was to be in
1814 and 1815.

Nevertheless, the Civil War was a key period in a tumultuous age for London, one that included the Gunpowder Plot
(1605), the Plague (1665), and the Great Fire (1666). The last
– unanticipated – brought much more change to the fabric of
the city and launched a new panorama. Instead, the period
needs to be divided into three: first, the continuation of the

Elizabethan age, then the mid-seventeenth century crisis and, lastly, the creation and development of a new city.

The Gunpowder Plot

In 1601, Robert, 2nd Earl of Essex failed in his coup attempt in London, being beheaded soon afterwards. Just four years later, and very differently, a small group of Catholic conspirators managed to smuggle 800 kilograms of gunpowder into the cellars under the Houses of Parliament, planning to blow it up when the new king, James I (r. 1603–25; James VI of Scotland), opened the session on 5 November. The conspirators hoped that the destruction of the royal family and the Protestant elite would ignite rebellion and lead to the overthrow of the Protestant establishment. There was no sense that the Reformation could not be reversed – as it indeed, had been in England under Mary I (r. 1553–8) and in a few other parts of Europe. The plot, however, was exposed because of an attempt to warn a Catholic peer, William, 4th Baron Monteagle. Captured in the cellars, Guy Fawkes was tortured to force him to reveal his co-conspirators and was then executed.

The early seventeenth century has left in London two splendid sites that capture wealth and style. The Banqueting House was intended by James I to be the nucleus of a massive new palace at Whitehall. Fearful of assassination (which was altogether separate from his paranoia about witches), he disliked the colonnade in the previous hall on the site and was ready to spend lavishly to further his palatial plans, doing so at Somerset House, Richmond and St James's. The Banqueting House, an explicit statement of the divine right of monarchy, was built in 1619–22 by Inigo Jones (1573–1652, the Londoner son of a Welsh clothworker living in Smithfield). He introduced a Palladian architectural style to England, while the Banqueting House offered a setting in which Londoners and others could see the king and royal family eat in public (as previous monarchs had done), with tickets sold accordingly. Painted by Rubens in the early 1630s, the ceiling was commissioned by Charles I and displayed *The Apotheosis of James*. Meanwhile, the Russell family transformed the former garden of Westminster Abbey into Covent Garden (i.e. the convent's garden), a key stage in the city's expansion to the west. Here the large, open piazza was surrounded by brick houses, as also seen in the new square at Lincoln's Inn Fields. In addition, completed in 1613, the 'New River' project brought even more benefit, with its canal, reservoir, and metropolitan system of wooden mains (pipes) providing fresh water. It demonstrated the openness of London to talent as the key entrepreneurs in the project were Welsh. Another form of entrepreneurship was the establishment of the first taxi rank in 1634: Captain John Bailey began with four hackney carriages (horse-drawn carriages) based in the Strand.

In his *London and the Country Carbonadoed and Quartered into Several Characters* (1632), Donald Lupton (d. 1676), a miscellaneous writer, referred to London as 'a great world' with 'so many worlds in her'. These included the criminal worlds that were discussed by Thomas Dekker (c. 1572–1632), a Londoner who became a playwright, not least in his *The Belman of London* (1608) and *Lanthorne and Candle-Light* (1609), in which swindlers and confidence men were presented as playing a well-developed role. Dekker's comic play *The Shoemaker's Holiday* (1599) deals with class tensions and shows the communal feelings of the artisanal shoemakers, one of whom, Simon Eyre, becomes Mayor. This was a frequent strand in London life. It had pantomime possibilities, but could also take a more sombre turn, as in George Lillo's play *The London Merchant* (1731). Alongside the cosmopolitan opulence and royal and aristocratic patronage, there was

Puritanism, with its distinctively sober and pious lifestyle that proposed a set of values against which the royal court seemed corrupt. James I tried to hold the ring, his visit to St Paul's Cathedral in March 1620 reflecting the possibility of maintaining the nexus of Crown, Church and popularity, but Charles I (r. 1625–49) was to find this impossible.

John Taylor, London's 'water poet'

A Thames waterman, Gloucester-born John Taylor (1578–1653) was unusual, as a pamphleteer and poet, in being one of the poor. Competition between watermen and coachmen emerges from his works, as does anger with the move of the theatre companies from the south bank of the Thames to the north in 1612.

MID-CENTURY

Although there were always those who supported him, Charles I's policies and attitude did not commend him to most Londoners who benefited from the extent to which, despite royal efforts, ideas circulated freely. Hostility was apparent in the late 1620s and 1630s. In May 1640, there were public protests against William Laud, Archbishop of Canterbury, including attacks on Lambeth Palace and on the prisons where detained protestors were held. As a consequence of the strength of Puritanism in London, the attempt to enforce High Church Laudian ideas was very controversial. This authoritarianism compounded the offensive nature of Laudian ceremonial and doctrine, not least its stress on the sacraments and its favour for church services that emphasised the cleric, not the congregation. Puritanism, in contrast, provided an identity across London, one that was not limited by parochial boundaries.

Moreover, Charles pressed the City hard for loans and gifts to help him deal with his finances, including ruling without Parliament from 1629. Mindful of the shared interests of Crown and London's oligarchical elite, the City authorities provided funds including, in 1637, purchasing a new charter that confirmed established privileges.

Yet, accumulated grievances generated serious strain and, when Charles' rule faced crisis over his total failure to suppress opposition in Scotland in 1639–40, London saw much opposition, not least as a centre of clandestine, hostile publication. The MPs elected locally in 1640 to the 'Long Parliament' were Puritans and about fifteen thousand Londoners signed a petition presented to Parliament in December 1640 that called for an end to bishops. Judged undesirable by Royalists, such pressure resulted in criticism of London opinion as sectarian, unruly and lacking social quality, charges that were contested in the capital. In 1641, London crowds played a vocal and vigorous role in an atmosphere of mounting crisis, although they took more than one view, Charles being greeted when he entered London that November.

The fretful Charles eventually resorted to the use of force, arriving in Parliament on 4 January 1642 with troops in order to seize his leading opponents, who had already fled to the City by river, the most convenient way thence from Westminster. The House of Commons followed, sitting in the Guildhall for a week while, as part of the politicisation in which existing and new bodies clashed and redefined roles, the City's Common Council elected a Committee of Safety charged with defending the City and by-passing the Court of Aldermen, among whom Charles still had supporters – notably those who were members of the privileged companies with royal charters, such as the Levant Company. In contrast, merchants who were in trade without such monopolies, such as those working with North America (after the dissolution of the Virginia Company in 1624), as well as interlopers, looked to Parliament.

There was no chance of Charles seizing his opponents in the City and when, on 5 January 1642, he appeared at the Guildhall to ask the Corporation for help in bringing his opponents to trial, he found scant support. As he departed, the crowd made its hostility clear, while Sir Richard Gurney, the Mayor, a merchant who was a past Master of the Clothworkers Company, was assaulted. Rumours that evening of a Royalist attack led, despite Gurney's opposition, to the mobilisation of the Trained Bands and much of the population, in defence of the City.

London's Role

'The plague of war which now wastes this nation, took its beginning in and from the City of London.'

Peter Heylin, 1643

As both sides prepared for war, Charles left London on 10 January 1642 to raise funds and out of fear for his safety and, especially, for that of his wife, Henrietta Maria, in the face of the ugly and threatening demonstrations in Whitehall. His departure weakened the Royalists in London, and the Common Council in March 1642 established its ability to take decisions without the support of the Mayor (who soon after was sent to the Tower) and aldermen.

That November, Charles, now at the head of an army, advanced on London after the battle of Edgehill, but, on what was a key date in London's history, he was checked at Turnham Green on 12 November by a larger Parliamentary force, many of them Londoners. This was an advance on London that was very different from that mounted by rebel forces, such as those of the Cornish in 1497 or Wyatt's rebellion in 1554 (an attempt, based in Kent, to block Mary's Spanish marriage, that was thwarted first at London Bridge and then Ludgate).

Charles retreated to establish his capital at royalist Oxford, while London, in turn, was fortified, an area far larger than that encompassed by the medieval walls being included in the eleven-mile-long defence system. It was never besieged during the war and, unlike most other urban centres, was unscathed. London's major support was important to Parliament's victory. The contrast with Oxford was clear, not least in money, manpower, industry, trade, organisational strength and publications. In 1643, the attempt to negotiate peace fell foul of radicals in London as well as Charles' folly.

After repeated defeats, notably at Naseby in 1645, Charles surrendered in 1646; but the victors totally fell out, the army occupying London in 1647 in defiance both of Parliament and of the war-weary Presbyterians who, as a result of consistent electoral support, were dominant on Common Council. The troops wanted their arrears paid and were concerned about Charles and Parliament's views on Church organisation. Following victory in a renewed civil war in 1648, particularly at Preston, the army was responsible for the execution of Charles on 30 January 1649 outside the Banqueting House in Whitehall. Charles walked through the House under the glorious painted ceiling by Rubens he had commissioned, before proceeding to his execution. Ironically, in the winter of 1647–8, Charles had planned a major redevelopment of the palace at Whitehall that would have incorporated the Banqueting House.

The execution increased Royalist denunciations of London which, to Henry Leslie, Bishop of Down in 1649, was 'the great city, spiritually Sodom, where our Lord was crucified'. The end of the monarchy was accompanied by the removal of the royal presence in the capital, including royal coats of arms and other devices. The statues of Charles and his father at the west end of St Paul's were demolished, as was that of Charles at the Royal Exchange.

London was distinctive in this trial and execution, but not in opposition to monarchy. The young Louis XIV was challenged by the *Fronde* in Paris, while risings in the 1640s also overthrew government authority in Barcelona, Lisbon, Naples, Moscow and Constantinople. Capital cities posed major problems for government, not least as they brought together elite and popular opposition. In London, it was not the background that was unique, but the solution.

London's support for the Parliamentary cause in the Civil War made it easier to preserve the essentials of its political and social structures. Thus, radical attempts to make the Common Council more representative of the freemen than of the liveries of the guilds were resisted successfully. London, however, had more influence during the regime of the Rump Parliament in 1648–53 than under Oliver Cromwell in 1653–8. A Huntingdonshire gentleman, he had no particular affinity for the city while the Rump, in contrast, made commercial protection a key plank of its policy and built up the navy to this end. This greatly helped London's commercial position as part of a broader attempt to boost national trade. Of particular long-term importance were the protectionist Navigation Acts of 1650 and 1651 which were designed to target the Dutch.

Coffee Houses

Trade led to a major change in London's social scene with the opening of the first of its coffee houses, in St Michael's Alley, Cornhill, in the early 1650s, established by a trade with Turkey and using coffee from Mocha, Yemen, supplied by Daniel Edwards. One member of the initially hostile public referred to 'this newfangled, abominable, heathenish liquor'. The premises were run by Edwards' exotically named Armenian servant, Pasqua Rosée. Within a decade, there were over eighty coffee houses in London.

Cromwell's Protectorate turned out less favourable to London's commerce, as it waged a war with Spain that hit trade as well as resulting in a serious financial burden. By the time of Cromwell's death in 1658, social tensions and disaffection were both grave. Meanwhile, he had made one important change to the composition of the city's population when, in 1656, he acquiesced to the return of Jews to England. By 1662 there was a synagogue with a congregation of a hundred in Creechurch Lane. The original synagogue would be replaced in 1701 by Bevis Marks.

From 1659, the political instability of the Interregnum after the death of Cromwell – not least due to the weakness of his son and short-term successor, Richard – combined with the strains created by government policies, had led much of the capital's populace to support a return to monarchy. Moreover, the leaders of the city's Presbyterians preferred monarchy on terms to both the Independents and the related religious sectarianism which had expanded greatly in London in the 1640s and 1650s with the collapse of episcopal authority. In 1660, George Monck, the army commander in Scotland, marched south into England, occupied London without difficulty and restored a moderate Parliament. This recalled Charles II, the eldest son of Charles I.

Cromwell's corpse was exhumed and hanged at Tyburn, the traditional place of execution for common criminals. A new Bear Garden was built in Southwark after the Puritan prohibition of bull- and bear-baiting was lifted; and maypoles destroyed under Cromwell were replaced. The following year, an attempt by 'Fifth Monarchists', led by Thomas Venner, a millenarian cooper, to seize the City on behalf of 'King Jesus' was defeated by the City's forces supported by troops under Monck, by then the Duke of Albemarle. A Devonian, Monck was in charge of London's government during the Plague of 1665, maintained order during the Great Fire of 1666 and died in Westminster in 1670, being buried in the Abbey.

London Celebrates

The Surrey-born John Evelyn (1620–1706), who lived in Deptford from 1652, wrote in his diary:

> 'On 29 May 1660, Charles II entered London with a triumph of ... horse and foot, brandishing their swords and shouting with inexpressible joy; the way strewed with flowers, the bells ringing, the streets hung with tapestry, fountains running with wine; the mayor, aldermen and all the companies in their liveries, chains of gold, banners; lords and nobles, everyone clad in cloth of silver, gold and velvet; the windows and balconies all set with ladies, trumpets, music and myriads flocking the streets ... I stood in the Strand and beheld it and blessed God. And all this was done without one drop of blood ... it was the Lord's doing.'

John Evelyn was a member of the group that in 1660 founded the London-based scientific group the Royal Society. His pamphlet *Fumifugium; Or The Inconvenience of The Air and Smoke of London Dissipated* (1661) was not only a political text but also a criticism of air pollution in the city, for which he blamed coal and proposed that industries that used a lot of it be moved, notably brewers, lime-burners and soap-boilers. In addition, chandlers and butchers were to be expelled from London. In 1652, Lodewijck Huygens, a Dutch visitor to Windsor Castle, could see London's smoke, which had earlier spoiled his view from the top of St Paul's.

PLAGUE AND DISEASE

This reimposition of royal and ecclesiastical control was to unravel over the following three decades but, in the meanwhile, Londoners were offered brutal reminders of the vulnerability of human society. St Paul's had lost its steeple to lightning in 1561 and much of the roofing was destroyed in the subsequent fire, but that was as nothing to what was to come in the 1660s. Indeed, there was no major fire between 1212 and 1663.

Smashing hopes that bubonic plague was in decline, the brutal and rapidly spread Great Plague of 1665 hit London hardest. Plague epidemics had already made major impacts in 1603, 1625 and 1636. The last outbreak greatly increased the death rate by five to six times and killed over 60,000 people in total. These epidemics usually began in the northern suburbs of London rather than the docks. As deaths mounted in 1665, helped by a long, hot summer, red crosses were painted on the doors of infected houses in a fruitless attempt at isolation. City records indicate that some 68,596 people died during the epidemic, although the actual number of deaths is suspected to have exceeded a hundred thousand out of a total population estimated at 460,000. The authorities could not keep up, while the diarist Samuel Pepys was told by his parish clerk, 'There died nine this week though I have returned but six.' Moreover, the recording did not work well for Quakers or poor transients. Dead paupers were thrown into large burial pits such as one at Tottenham Court.

Many fled the city, including the wealthy, most doctors and a large number of the parochial clergy. This was a serious issue as, in response to the crisis, many of the churches were thronged. London's economy was also ruined. Public places were closed, sports banned, a 9 p.m. curfew was imposed and fairs were prohibited. Beginning in April, the attack did not abate until the November frosts. The Great Plague led the royal court to move to

Oxford, but this provided a demonstration of London's importance, for there was no way in which Oxford could serve as a viable capital other than as a crisis measure.

In 1665, it was easy to interpret the Great Plague as divine displeasure. It could not be foreseen that this was to be the last major outbreak. Mutations in the rat and flea populations were probably more important in preventing a recurrence of plague than clumsy and erratic public health measures or alterations in human habitat thanks to construction of brick, stone and tile which would in large part come about due to the Great Fire of 1666.

Smallpox, which killed Mary II (the wife of William III) in 1694, was to replace plague as the most feared disease, although without epidemics comparable to those of the plague. Immunity to smallpox was low, not least because a more virulent strain began to have an impact in the second half of the seventeenth century. Both the virulence and the case-fatality rate of smallpox continued to rise thereafter. As smallpox was airborne, it was far more contagious than plague had been, although the fatality rate was lower. Smallpox was most serious in London, where the disease became endemic as well as epidemic. This situation proved particularly deadly for infants and children. Smallpox was particularly easily transmitted in the family or household groups as proximity was important. It was also socially selective, as the poor lived at a higher population density than the wealthy. In addition, smallpox viruses remained viable for up to a year and could be contracted via clothing or bedding. The poor were less able to afford to destroy clothing and bedding after a death and this increased their vulnerability to smallpox; they were also less likely to be able to wash their hands after defecating and urinating, which increased the chances of ingesting contaminated food and contracting gastric infections. Inoculation against smallpox – especially the Suttonian method, variolation, from about 1768, and, from 1796, the safer alternative of vaccination – were not yet in place to lessen the chance of attack. Both acute diarrhoea and dysentery were also killers.

FIRE

Soon after the Great Plague, further calamity was visited on the capital with the Great Fire, which raged for four days from 2 September 1666. It began in Thomas Faryner's bakehouse in Pudding Lane, near London Bridge, either as a result of failure to extinguish an oven properly or because the temperature inside the bakehouse was so high that the flour dust in the air spontaneously combusted. Anti-Catholic propaganda blamed the fire on the Catholics, while the Protestant Dutch saw it as divine judgement on their English enemy. The context was a densely populated city where regulations were widely ignored, and there was much poor building to cope with the rising population. Moreover, highly flammable goods in warehouses, such as tobacco, did not help the impact of building in wood.

The strength of the fire, fanned by the strong easterly winds, was such that it was able to cross the Fleet River, and this spread destroyed early hopes that the fire would be only minor. Partly as a result of these hopes, the necessary measures to create effective firebreaks by pulling down houses were not taken until later on. Charles II and his brother, James, Duke of York (later James II), took an active role in fighting the flames, filling buckets and encouraging the fire-fighters, and there was success in preventing the spread of the flames, not least by the use of gunpowder to create firebreaks, saving the Tower; but the blaze swept on, defying the generally inadequate responses. It was only finally stopped on the night of 4–5 September when the wind dropped, which permitted fire-fighters to rally and dowse the fires, although fires under the rubble remained for some time.

The fire left the City devastated, destroying St Paul's, the Guildhall, the Royal Exchange, eighty-seven churches, forty-four livery halls and about 13,200 houses, burning 373 of the 448 acres within the City walls and another sixty-three acres to the west. Far more damage was inflicted than occurred in the Blitz of 1940–1 although, in contrast to the thousands killed in those attacks, only five people definitely died in the Great Fire. In practice, however, many poor people probably died as fire swept through places like Bridewell. Because Parish Clerks' Hall was burnt down, no bills of mortality were produced for some weeks and it was difficult to work out who was dead and who had fled. As autumn nights drew in, the homeless camped in fields in Islington and Moorfields, while mercantile and other activities were relocated.

REBUILDING

In the aftermath of the fire, Charles issued a declaration promising that London would be rebuilt better and would 'rather appear to the world as purged with the Fire . . . to a wonderful beauty and comeliness, than consumed by it'. More particularly, he declared that a handsome vista would be created on the riverbank by banishing smoky trades. John Evelyn, Peter Mills, Christopher Wren, Robert Hooke, Richard Newcourt and Valentine Knight produced plans for rebuilding London to a more regular design, the pattern followed in other leading European cities, and one that reflected the favour of the period for dramatic long streets and rectilinear town plans. Evelyn urged the value of zoning, especially the long-established idea of the removal of noxious trades from areas of habitation, while Wren proposed a City with two central points, the Royal Exchange and St Paul's. Ten roads were to radiate from the former, while a piazza in front of St Paul's was to be the focus of three key routes in the western part of the City, which was laid out in a grid dependent on the major through-routes, with piazzas or rond-points playing a key organisational role. The river was to be faced by a 'Grand Terras'. Wren's plan influenced John Gwynn's 1776 proposal for a replanning of the entire city. Evelyn was also interested in piazzas, while Hooke (who later became City Surveyor) and Newcourt each proposed a regular grid.

Resources and will were lacking, while the existing property rights of individuals made up the chief stumbling blocks to organised planning. Yet, more positively, these rights stimulated the rebuilding. The need for a rapid rebuilding, not least to prevent merchants staying in the West End, was paramount and, with the government impoverished by war with the Dutch, this rebuilding involved tapping the resources that could be readily raised by property owners. This, however, ensured that many faced serious debt. Despite the work of the Fire Courts, which adjudicated competing claims to land, there was no equivalent to the commissioners empowered by Parliament to organise the planning and rebuilding of Warwick after the devastating fire of 1694, an expedient that proved particularly successful in that case. Instead, the Rebuilding Acts for London of 1667 and 1670 were far more restricted in their scope. Nevertheless, they dispensed with the requirements of the trade guilds to aid rebuilding and also sought to limit the danger of a new fire by stipulating that buildings should have no projecting windows and should have at most four storeys. Houses were to be built out of brick and to be uniform in their frontages; and these regulations acted as the model for large-scale urban building elsewhere in England. The fire also greatly encouraged taking out insurance policies and the resulting insurance companies developed their own fire services, albeit without providing the necessary unitary provision.

In London, existing property rights ensured that boundaries did not change in the rebuilding. Existing roads were also preserved. The opportunity was taken, nevertheless, to reduce the number of parishes, while numerous streets were widened. The sole new street, however, was King Street and, on from that, Queen Street, which created a new route from Guildhall to the river. Designed by Wren and Hooke, the 202-foot-high Monument to the fire followed in 1677 and remains an impressive legacy with its viewing platform. Inscriptions at the base originally blamed Catholics for the blaze. The new Royal Exchange, an Italianate building with arcades, built in 1669 by Edward Jarman, was, in turn, to be destroyed by fire in 1838.

Praise for St Paul's

'Out of the ashes, this Phoenix is risen and by Providence designed by you.'

John Evelyn of Wren

Wren, as King's Surveyor of Works, had to be content with designing the dramatic new St Paul's, much of which was built in the 1700s, becoming the key work in the English Baroque. He was also responsible for designing fifty-one London churches, all in use by 1696, for long a highpoint of London's architectural heritage although, challenged by Victorian redevelopment and German bombing, only twenty-three survive. The churches affirmed the established Church in the face of Nonconformist/Dissenter tendencies. Finally completed in 1710, but in use from 1697, St Paul's towered over the City and thus provided a key point in vistas from elsewhere in London and from the suburbs, but the absence of any coherent plan to the rebuilding ensured that St Paul's could no more provide a clear centre to the new London than any of the other buildings in the city.

Nevertheless, the rebuilding, which may have cost close to six million pounds, left a city that was considerably more attractive visually than that on display after the air attacks in World War Two. The plan for the canalisation of the River Fleet to provide space for more wharves failed, however, and the canal became a sewer which was to be covered over in 1733. The canal and the rebuilding of the churches and public buildings were financed by a coal tax. Beyond the reach of the Great Fire, much of medieval and Tudor London survived the seventeenth century, but this did not amount to much within the walls, as the print by Hollar in 1669 made clear.

It took time for London to be repopulated. Eighty thousand people had fled and, by the end of 1672, a quarter had still not returned. The lower cost of living in the Middlesex suburbs, which stimulated the spread of built-up area, was cited as a reason: taxes in the City were higher and had indeed further become so as a consequence of the costs in London attendant on new churches, paving and drains. As a result, in 1673, the City – mindful that over three thousand of its new houses were unoccupied – took steps to ease the burdens on new freemen. Yet, there was a reluctance in the City to understand the extent to which Londoners now had alternative living spaces and, indeed, that citizenship was not the only way to gain the benefits and pleasures of London life.

The City's loss of control over the identity, and thus interests, of London and Londoners was to become a more prominent theme in succeeding decades. This theme – the distinction between the City proper and a far bigger London – remains highly significant to this day, not least with two mayors, albeit with the key distinction now being the Greater London Authority area and the wider region. There is the additional problem, apparent from the time of the foundation of the London County Council and, more clearly, the Greater London Council and Greater London Authority, that the size of an expanded London authority brought pretensions and divisions that ensured strong clashes between it and some of the constituent boroughs.

In a fresh mark of the threat posed by fire, the Inner Temple was hit hard in 1677, while the royal palace in Whitehall, one of the largest in Europe, burned down in 1698, with only the Banqueting House saved. William III did not rebuild Whitehall as a royal palace, and, from then, the centre of government in

Whitehall diverged from the royal residence which, instead, became Kensington or St James's. No new royal residence was built at Whitehall, where the administration had moved from the ruined palace to the undamaged sports facilities, such as the tennis court and cockpit, on the other side overlooking St James's Park, supposedly on a temporary basis until Whitehall Palace was rebuilt. The Parliament buildings were unaffected.

MORALITY IN LONDON

London was not only a site of battle with fire and the elements. To moralists, there was also the challenge of laxity, more specifically a sexual permissiveness that was a reaction to Puritan zeal. Engine, a maid in Edward Ravenscroft's play *The London Cuckolds* (1681), explained:

> 'This employment was formerly named bawding and pimping, but our Age is more civilised and our language much refined. It is now called doing a friend a favour. Whore is now prettily called Mistress. Pimp; friend. Cuckold-maker; gallant. Thus the terms being civilised the thing itself becomes more acceptable. What clowns they were in former ages.'

Characters like Engine helped explain the attacks on the alleged profanity and immorality of the stage, for example by the non-juror cleric Jeremy Collier in his pamphlet *A Short View of the Immorality and Profaneness of the English Stage* (1698), which led to government pressure on the London playhouses the following year. Cambridgeshire-born Collier became an encyclopedia compiler and died in London.

The sense of London as uniquely sinful was to be a frequent theme of moralists, one that has continued to the present. Prostitution, indeed, was one of the major industries and, more generally, there were also possibilities for adventures and independence with the anonymity that the city offered and that moralists deplored. Intimate personal information from and about individuals became more common in the eighteenth century, but there is no reason to doubt that what it indicates was equally pertinent for the seventeenth. Two clear themes were the dangers posed by the venereal disease of Londoners and a contrast between metropolitan vice and rural activities. Thomas Steavens noted in 1741:

'I was indiscreet enough to desire the employment of Miss Sally Clerk, a young lady who sells oranges at Drury Lane Playhouse; and she cruel enough to consent to it, in short an unnatural flame on my side, and a still more unnatural one on hers had made such a bonfire of my body that I was obliged to apply to mercury.'

As a reminder of the harshness of life, a Dutch visitor in 1662 witnessed the treatment of a woman convicted of murdering her husband, a crime treated with great severity and scant consideration of provocation:

'We saw a young woman, who had stabbed her husband to death ... being burned alive ... She was put with her feet into a sawn-through tar barrel ... A clergyman spoke to her for a long time and reproved her and said the prayer. Then faggots [sticks] were piled up against her body ... and finally set alight with a torch ... and soon it was ablaze all round.'

Far less harshly, just over half of the thieves committed to Bridewell in 1642–58 were women who, rather than their clients, were also those blamed for prostitution, while women were largely excluded from coffee houses – as they were from many activities – as, indeed, were the poor. In practice, however, there were women involved in responsible economic positions. For example, in the 1690s and 1700s, Elizabeth Hervey was the London agent of her family's cloth manufacturing business in Taunton. Such activity, however, was of limited interest to commentators who found London a tempting stage for the culture wars of the age.

THE EXCLUSION CRISIS

In the 1670s, despite Charles' public devotional commitment at the Chapel Royal, there was much disquiet about the morality of the royal court, and virulent suspicion that its laxity extended to tolerance of Catholics. George Larkin's pro-government *Publick Occurrences Truly Stated* referred to 'the confiding coffee-houses, where the grave men puff out sedition'. Anxieties led, in 1678, to the controversy over what was called the Popish Plot. An adventurer, Titus Oates, claimed that there was a Catholic plot to assassinate Charles – who had no legitimate children – and replace him with his Catholic brother, James. The mysterious murder of Sir Edmund Godfrey, the London magistrate who took Oates's evidence, and whose body was found in Primrose Hill, as well as the discovery of suspicious letters in the possession of James's former private secretary, Edward Colman, inflamed concerns and helped the plot to become sensational news. Colman was executed as a traitor, as were a dozen others.

In a political atmosphere made frenetic by rumour and hard-fought elections and with rival Dissenting and Anglican identities providing much of the dynamic for contention, the Popish Plot became the Exclusion Crisis (1678–81), an attempt to use Parliament to exclude James from the succession and to weaken Charles' government. London was a centre for support for Dissenters, for anti-Catholicism and for Exclusion, support associated with the Whigs, a political party that looked to the same groups and tendencies that had opposed Charles I: Whig common councillors tended to represent parishes that had a strong Nonconformist tendency, one looking back to Puritanism. Following a pattern that in many respects went back to the Reformation, the differing religio-political groups were based in specific neighbourhoods. Spreading news, London was the centre of newspaper activity and postal services.

The Whigs' royalist opponents were termed Tories, and they argued that Exclusion threatened the social order and might, indeed, cause another civil war. The association of London with the Whigs led Charles to summon the new Parliament to Oxford in 1681, which returned to the geographical politics of the Civil War. Oxford proved a propitious setting for Charles on that occasion, but was not again to play such a role. Indeed, Parliament was never again to meet outside London, even during the air and rocket attacks of the twentieth century and talk in the early twenty-first century of it moving out of the capital has proved to be nothing more substantial.

The cause of Exclusion failed in 1681, in Britain rather than London, in part because most of its supporters did not wish to push it to the point of violence, but also because Charles was more skilful than his father and retained control of Scotland and Ireland. As a reminder of the diversity of opinion, Tory crowds turned out in force in support when James returned to London, burning effigies of Jack Presbyter and of the Whig leader the Earl of Shaftesbury. Royal control over town corporations, especially London, was strengthened and this control was used to remove political opponents. In 1683, the charter of the City was abrogated and, with it, the Whigs' position undermined. This served both Charles and the London Tories. Moreover, the Whig newspapers were stamped out. There was also a crisis in London's governance, with the City authorities forced to default on their debts in 1683 as a result of long-standing cumulative deficits. Control over London helped ensure that Charles, in the last years of his reign, held sway over his kingdom.

As a reminder that politics was often overshadowed, the great freeze of 1683–4 led to a frost fair, Evelyn noting, 'Streets of booths were set upon the Thames ... all sorts of trades and shops furnished and full of commodities. Coaches plied from

Westminster to the Temple, and from several other stairs to and fro, as in the streets; sledges, sliding with skates, a bull baiting, horse-and-coach races, puppet plays and interludes, cooks, tipling and other lewd places, so that it seemed to be a bacchanalian triumph, or carnival on the water.' Moreover, the extent to which political issues fired up everyone and in a consistent fashion may be doubted.

James II's more dogmatic and inflexible stance totally squandered the legacy left him. Indeed, James (r. 1685–8) helped ensure that opposition to his policies for autocracy and Catholicisation drew together much of the political nation. London played a major role in this opposition, as James's attempt to use the formal levers of power repeatedly clashed with a strongly held sense of loyalty to national and Protestant liberties and local interests. In 1685, Henry Compton was suspended as Bishop of London for refusing to suspend John Sharp, Rector of St Giles-in-the-Fields, who had criticised Catholicism from the pulpit.

Huguenot Arrivals

The local and national situation seemed more threatening and urgent in 1685 as Louis XIV's abrogation of Protestant rights in France led to a flood of Huguenot refugees into London. The Huguenots, who rose to take up about 8–10 per cent of the city's population by 1690, were to be important to London's character, settling in particular to the east, especially in Spitalfields, where they played a major role in manufacturing, notably in silk weaving. Their arrival expanded the city physically in this direction. Other Huguenot areas of settlement included Soho, Leicester Fields, Chelsea and Wandsworth. By the late 1690s, there were forty-five Huguenot churches in London, about a quarter of them in Spitalfields, with others in the City and to the west. The Huguenots dramatised the issue of immigration, but there were other migrant flows into the city. One major stream was that of

Scots and in 1665 the Royal Scottish Corporation, a charity to support needy Scots in London, received its charter.

There were tensions in the short term as a result of the Huguenot influx, notably pressure on housing and competition for jobs, especially with lower-paid workers and the Companies of Silkweavers and Cabinet-makers, and these tensions led to some discrimination and violence, including riots in 1675 in part due to the pressure on silk workers created by the use of new looms. The Huguenots were accused of working for lower wages. Yet, broadening the industrial base, their new skills and techniques helped in the development of a damask and brocade industry in Spitalfields, while papermaking and work with gold and silver also all benefited. They were a major part of the labour force involved in manufacturing, a force larger than that taking part in trade.

In the long term, the Huguenots were to integrate well into London society. That they were Protestants ensured that they could be absorbed into the established culture far more readily than was the case with later Jewish and Muslim immigration. Nevertheless, the Huguenots, in the short term, made London more differentiated than the rest of the country, in part because they accentuated the cosmopolitan character of the city. Alongside new ideas, unfamiliar foods were introduced, including caraway seeds, garlic, oxtail soup and pickles. Their Protestantism was not that of the Church of England, although some preferred it to Nonconformity and, by an Act of 1708, Huguenots who conformed to the Church of England were automatically naturalised. Many of the Huguenots looked to Amsterdam, a key site in their diaspora. Indeed, intellectual and cultural links with the Low Countries were to increase as a result both of the Huguenot immigration and of William III of Orange, the key political figure in the United Provinces (Netherlands), who became king in 1689. There was to be no comparable linkage between London and Hanover while the Hanoverian dynasty was on the British throne from 1714 to 1837.

THE GLORIOUS REVOLUTION

James's pressure on Protestant London was demonstrated in the winter of 1687–8 when the questions about favouring tolerance for Catholics which the king put to all parliamentary candidates and magistrates were also put to members of the Livery Companies: 3,500 members were expelled for failing to agree. Meanwhile, Catholic schools were founded in London, a Benedictine (Catholic monastic order) house was established in Clerkenwell and Catholic priests in the city sought to recruit Anglicans, all contributing to a sense of menace. The birth of a Prince of Wales on 10 June 1688, later the Jacobite claimant 'James III', suggested that the new pro-Catholic order would be lasting, rather than a temporary interlude before James's Anglican daughters, the childless Mary and then Anne, succeeded him.

On 30 June, London was the centre of a massive demonstration of opposition to James, when the acquittal of the Seven Bishops (Archbishop Sancroft and six bishops), tried in Westminster Hall for refusing to support royal wishes on religious tolerance by reading the Declaration of Indulgence, was greeted by a great outpouring of public joy, including a large number of bonfires. The City clergy had been very active and effective in supporting the bishops and persuading Nonconformists not to back James's concessions to them. The importance of London in public opinion was emphasised by the way both James and his opponents sought to win popular opinion by publishing tracts and books. In turn, the acquittal was to be memorialised when the Palace of Westminster was rebuilt following the fire of 1834, as E. M. Ward's fresco was included in the Commons North Corridor.

In November 1688, James's nephew and son-in-law, William III, invaded with a Dutch army, in order to protect Protestantism and traditional liberties and to ensure that Britain lined up against Louis XIV, with whom the Nine Years' War was beginning.

Compton, the suspended Bishop of London, was one of the 'Immortal Seven' who had invited William to invade. Landing at Brixham, William marched on London, control over which again proved crucial. James deployed his forces at Salisbury, but his nerve failed and the resistance dissolved. In turn, William refused to halt his march on the city in order to allow negotiations to proceed – as the Tory leaders would have preferred – and James fled the capital. With William still outside London, fear of the London mob and of complete anarchy encouraged the Archbishop of Canterbury and leading peers to take control of the city.

Captured and returned to London, James was finally driven from the city by Dutch pressure. Moreover, James's captors had to encourage him to flee a second time, leaving him unguarded. The report in the *London Courant* of William's arrival at St James's Palace linked demonstrations of support with the ideology of the new order. The Prince arrived:

'attended by a great number of persons of quality in coaches and on horseback, while multitudes of people of different ranks crowded the highways, echoing their joy from all hands in the loudest acclamations of welcome, which was more entirely testified by the cheerfulness and serenity that sat in all peoples countenances, to whom either true religion or liberty are of any value, all such ascribing their deliverance from popery and slavery to the courage and conduct of his Illustrious Highness, next to the providence and power of the Almighty. Nor were the exterior testimonies of ringing of bells, bonfires at night etc. wanting to testify a general satisfaction at the coming of His Highness.'

London was the place of the Convention called in 1689 to settle constitutional issues. James's flight enabled William and Parliament to claim that James had deserted the realm and abdicated the throne, and Parliament, in 1689, offered the crown to William and his wife Mary. They were crowned by Compton. William's success was such that, in 1715, the Jacobites initially planned to repeat his scheme to seize power with a landing by James II's son, 'James III' (the 'Warming-Pan Baby'), in the south-west of England, where there was to be a major rising, followed by a march on London.

THE NEW ORDER

The new political order from 1688–9, the Revolution Settlement, was one that suited powerful London interests as well as an increasingly defined and potent self-image of the city as a modern, commercial centre. In particular, the establishment of the Bank of England in 1694, with its central role in public finances, provided a key junction between government and capital and one in which London acted as the focus for, and anchor of, national financial activity.

This role matched the theatrical accounts of London as a city of energy and flux. In his successful play of 1696, *The Relapse*, John Vanbrugh referred to London as 'that uneasy theatre of noise'. This theatre, however, could have a violent side, as in 1711–12 when the young gentlemen of the 'Mohock Club' brawled and were said to slit the noses of victims, among other brutal activities. A major attempt to improve public order occurred in 1697 when the sanctuary privileges of the Alsatia, a red-light area of Whitefriars, east of the Temple, were abolished, although it took a long time to make the area orderly. Cultural panics were part of London's history, as they were of other major cities.

The Revolution Settlement produced a very different political world to that of James II, one that centred on London. Whereas Parliament had not met for most of the period 1682–8, there was now the creation of Parliamentary monarchy with a practical requirement for annual sessions of parliament and, after the passage of the Triennial Act of 1694, of elections at least every three years. Moreover, the lapsing of the Licensing Act in 1695 led to the end of the control over the number of printers by the Stationers' Company and of pre-publication censorship; this was followed by the expansion of the press. Some of the new papers spread London's influence across England. Papers such as the *Flying Post*, *Post Boy* and *Post Man*, all of which first appeared in 1695, were published on Tuesdays, Thursdays and Saturdays, when the post coaches left London. At once, this postal service enabled the new papers to meet both metropolitan and provincial demand and to establish their claim to be national voices. The first British daily paper, the *Daily Courant*, appeared in London in 1702. No other British city followed with a daily until the following century.

The improvement of the road system facilitated the spread of London's influence. In 1663, the earliest turnpike trust was created, while the first section of the London–Norwich road was turnpiked under an Act of 1696. The trusts were authorised bodies of local businessmen and landowners who obtained individual Local Acts of Parliament to raise capital to repair and improve a road or network of local roads and to charge tolls to finance this process. The creation of a national turnpike network had to wait until the mid-eighteenth century but, in the meanwhile, communication links had already improved, in part driven by the needs of serving the London market, by both land and water. In turn, the growth of the London-focused transport network had significant commercial and economic implications. In 1702, a visitor to Helston in Cornwall noted, 'Where we dined was the Royal Oak Lottery which one could hardly have expected to have found in a country town so remote from London.'

London also benefited from the improvement of its river links. That of the Thames – for navigation between Oxford and London – had a major impact upon the supply of food, wood and other commodities to the capital. Similarly, the Wey navigation, between the Thames and Guildford (1653) – the first major river navigation involving extensive new cutoffs – was predicated on the booming and profitable trade in grain and timber from west Surrey to London.

Political attention and contention were focused on the competition between Whigs and Tories for office, but this competition also related to a host of issues in dispute, including religious toleration, Church government and foreign policy. The London press ventilated these issues, as did the developing world of the coffee house. Most of the contention was peaceful, but the attack by Tory, High Church mobs on Low Church meeting houses in London in the Sacheverell Riots in 1710 indicated the possibility of violence: Henry Sacheverell was very much a London celebrity, part of a number of London clerics with a public reputation.

Sociability was also related to politics and, in the 1710s, London's political clubs supervised electoral efforts. Events in London, moreover, provided important episodes for the public politics reported and debated in the press. Thus, the elections of London's MPs were seen as of particular significance, while the Common Council elections also attracted attention that extended to foreign commentators, as with the French envoy dwelling in 1716 on Tory victories in the Common Council elections.

These were also years of large-scale and difficult war waged with France from 1689 to 1697 (the Nine Years' War) and from 1702 to 1713 (the War of the Spanish Succession), which led to unprecedented government expenditure. This put considerable pressure on the London money market, as did the need to finance military operations abroad and thus transfer metal money abroad. War encouraged the growth of London, both the formal military organisation of government in London and the informal military support systems organised from the City. The *Observator* newspaper of 10 June 1702 commented on the public's interest in the war:

''Tis an easy matter to pull down pallisades, to attack half-moons, bastions, and counterscarps, in the coffee-houses of London and Westminster, and to bomb citadels and castles with quart bottles of wine in a tavern, where there is seen no smoke but that of tobacco, nor no shot felt but when the reckoning comes to be paid.'

Such commentary was socially and politically subversive. In Delarivier Manley's novel *Secret History of Queen Zarah and the Zarazians* (1705):

'Apprentice boys assume the air of statesmen before they have learned the mystery of trade. Mechanics of the meanest rank plead for a liberty to abuse their betters, and turn out ministers of state with the same freedom that they smoke tobacco. Carmen and cobblers over coffee draw up articles of peace and war and make partition treaties.'

THE MONEYED INTEREST

More critically, London was seen as the centre of a moneyed interest that many regarded as disruptive. In his pamphlet *The Conduct of the Allies* (1711), Jonathan Swift offered the classic Tory critique of financial activity and speculation, specifically 'undertakers and projectors of loans and funds' seeking 'to create a moneyed interest'. This Tory presentation of London drew on Cavalier and Anglican disquiet about the city during the seventeenth century and, in many respects, was the latest iteration of the critique associated with the Exclusion Crisis. However, there was an additional dimension due to what would subsequently be termed the Financial Revolution, namely the development of the money market and of related practices and institutions, notably the Bank of England. The funded national debt, guaranteed by Parliament and based on the Bank, enabled the borrowing of hitherto unprecedented sums and at low rates of interest.

To critics, however, this new system led to a moneyed interest that was seeking political power as well as the social displacement of landed society and the ideological replacement of its associated culture. The criticism drew on tensions between ideas of virtue and those of commerce, specifically the asserted incompatibility of civic humanism with the moneyed interest. This was very much an image of London as a threat. Moral and paternalistic attitudes towards wealth clashed with the reality of new money. Indeed, in 1696, as an alternative to the Bank of England, there was a politically pointed (and unsuccessful) attempt to found a Land Bank using landed wealth as a credit source.

Reprising the complaints about usurious London merchants in the Tudor century, London was seen by critics as a site and source of false values – financial, political and sexual. It was where everything was for sale, as with the notice in the *London Journal* of 27 November 1725 for Thomas Rogers, 'Agent for Persons that buy or sell merchandises, estates etc.' who was willing to meet customers at the Rainbow coffee house to discuss the purchase and sale of estates. Indeed, bankers bought status and land. For example, Sir Richard Child, later 1st Earl Tylney, had Wanstead House built in 1714–20; it was demolished in 1822. James Brydges, 1st Duke of Chandos, who made his money as Paymaster General, built a magnificent house at Canons, but, with the exception of the Baroque chapel, the house and contents were auctioned and dismantled for building material soon after Chandos' death in 1744: the cost had proved too great and an estate praised by Alexander Pope survives now only in the name of a tube station (Canons Park) and in part as the site of a girl's school, the North London Collegiate School.

In some respects, the critique of London was anachronistic, as commercial values and the money economy were scarcely new; London merchants had been buying country estates close to London from at least the late fifteenth century and intermarriage between merchant society and the nobility had increased from the 1590s. In this and other respects, social divisions were permeable and status was open to negotiation and adjustment. Indeed, as far as cultural values and control over land were concerned, the disruption attendant on the Reformation was far more acute than that linked to the Financial Revolution. Yet, the link between money and power appeared to critics to be closer than ever before, and the speculation associated with financial assets appeared to challenge reality and value.

Within London, there was a different but related development, as the guilds, which had become brotherhoods of wealthy merchants by the sixteenth century, increasingly became associations of the wealthy (and worthy), committed to charity, education and clubability, but lacking any real accountability. This transformation removed an important, employment-linked, vertical strand in the city's socio-political fabric and contributed to a well-founded Tory critique from within London of the Whig dominance of the City world of money and privilege.

From both within London and from outside the city, there was also concern about the metropolis as the destination of immigrants. After the Huguenot influx came that of German Protestants fleeing Catholic persecution, especially in the Palatinate, the source of the 'Poor Palatines'. By 1709, over 13,000 Palatine refugees had reached London. About 6,500 were housed in army tents on Blackheath, about 5,100 in the navy's ropeyards at Deptford and 1,400 in the warehouses of Sir Charles Cox, a Southwark brewer and MP.

TRADE

Alongside the importance of London to Britain's governance and politics came its growing role in a developing global economy. As far as Britain was concerned, trans-oceanic voyages began first from Bristol, but London came to play the key role, in trade, finance and, more generally, in the commerce and culture of the British Atlantic. The stage reflected these new links. In Shakespeare's *All is True* (1613, later *King Henry VIII*), a London porter wonders why there is so much noise: '. . . have we some strange Indian with the great tool [penis] come to Court, the women so besiege us?' Ironically, the Globe theatre was burnt down during the first production of the play as a result of the thatch catching light after cannon were fired to mark an entry by the actor playing the king. In Philip Massinger's London-set play *The City Madam* (c. 1632), the villain is ready to sell his sister-in-law and nieces to the heroes who are disguised as 'Indians' seeking women for sacrifice.

London's commercial role had vile aspects, notably in the trans-Atlantic slave trade, in which the English participated from the sixteenth century. The Company of Adventurers of London Trading to the Ports of Africa (the Guinea Company), which was granted a monopoly by James I in 1618, only traded to the Gambia in 1618–21 before abandoning the unprofitable trade. Another group of Londoners dominated the Scottish Guinea Company, founded in 1634, which operated on the Gold Coast, but the Company had only limited success. Their role was a reminder of the role of London capital in many concerns. The Company of Royal Adventurers Trading into Africa, chartered in 1660 and reformed as the Royal African Company in 1672, was more successful in this cruel trade, and London dominated Britain's slave trade until the 1710s, when it was superseded by Bristol which, in turn, was to be superseded by Liverpool. The regulatory framework that had maintained London's control was dismantled in 1698 by the Ten Per Cent Act; named because the merchants had to pay a 10 per cent duty to maintain the Company's forts. As a result, the African trade was freed from the control of the Royal African Company, whose position had been undermined after the Glorious Revolution led to a decline in government support. The Ten Per Cent Act legalised the position of private traders, and made shifts in the relative position of ports far easier, helping lead to the rise of Bristol at the expense of London.

As another instance of the issues caused by London privileges and the need to circumvent them that government confronted, the army in the 1690s was rearmed, with matchlock muskets and pikes replaced by flintlocks equipped with socket bayonets. To circumvent the monopoly of the London gunmakers, which acted as a drag in a situation made urgent by the Nine Years' War, the Ordnance Office employed their Birmingham counterparts.

The company structure, however, was preserved for trade with South and East Asia, as well as in the case of the Hudson Bay Company, which was also controlled from London. The East India Company, founded in 1600, came to form the basis of Britain's Indian empire. A joint-stock concern, the Company reflected the strength and sophistication of London's commercial and financial circles and it contrasted with the far greater state direction of most continental trading companies. In 1609, James I came to the launch of the Company's ship *Trade's Increase*. Joint-stock companies also operated within the British Isles, the London Lead Company extracting lead from the Pennines in the 1660s.

London's commercial position reflected the dynamism of its traders. The value of London's imports from the East India Company and the English plantations nearly doubled from the 1660s to the end of the century, while the percentage of London's total imports by value from these areas rose from 24 to 34 per cent in the same period. Such statistics reflected the rise in direct trade over using intermediary traders – especially the Dutch – and intermediary ports. This rise was a result of mid-century legislation, the Navigation Acts of 1650 and 1651, which were reprised in the Navigation Act of 1660 and the Staple Act of 1663, which in effect created a national monopoly as the form of commercial regulation, thus limiting companies with royal monopolies. London's role in the British economic system was enhanced by the prohibition of exports direct from the colonies to foreign markets with, instead, the requirement that goods be exported to England or one of its colonies. Entrepreneurs also benefited from the absence of local tariffs.

Shipbuilding, another activity in which Thameside concerns played the major role in this period, was helped by legislation in

1660 stipulating that all foreign-built ships in English ownership be registered. Two years later, the purchase of Dutch ships (the principal source of imported craft) was hindered when an Act decreed that ships of foreign build not registered by that date were to be deemed alien and to be subject to alien duties.

Peter the Great of Russia came to Deptford on the Thames (where the Howland Dock was begun in 1660), as well as to the United Provinces, to see shipbuilding in progress, as he searched for foreign models for the industry he intended to establish. Shipbuilding reflected the powerful role of the Thames not only in shaping London and in its transport links, within and outside the city, but also in its economy. In an echo of Venice, as Antonio Canaletto's painting of *The River Thames on Lord Mayor's Day* (1747–8) indicates, the river was also very important to the city's image and played a ceremonial role, in this case showing an annual riverine procession of the City's leaders.

Helped in part by Dutch investment after the Glorious Revolution of 1688–9, which both constituted an important aspect of growing Anglo-Dutch co-operation and reflected the openness of the city's commercial culture, London's role in the multi-centred trading system was becoming more prominent. Direct trading required more capital resources and expenditure and a more sophisticated organisational structure, but this trading enabled the British – essentially in the shape of London merchants – to bear the bulk of the transaction costs themselves and also to take much of the profit. This process can be seen with Indian trade, largely financed with returns for bullion that could be obtained only from profits on other trades; for example, the export of light draperies to the Mediterranean and of sugar to Hamburg. The profitability of these trades, and the role of the Anglo-Dutch link, helped provide a financial strength that underlined London's importance economically and politically. Thus, following a pattern that has remained the case to the present, London benefited from being an emporium, such that – far from being compartmentalised – the British trading system had important financial as well as economic inter-dependence. Indeed, British re-exports rose from £2.13 million in 1700 to £3.23 million in 1750, as imported goods – such as tobacco from the Chesapeake or sugar from the West Indies – were re-exported to continental Europe, notably to entrepôts such as Hamburg and Livorno.

The importance of trade led to the appearance in London of specialist newspapers as part of the process of adding depth, sophistication and diversity to the mercantile sphere. Insurance and long-term credit benefited from the increase in the accessibility of information. In 1696, Edward Lloyd, a coffee-house keeper, published a tri-weekly, *Lloyd's News*, containing many shipping stories. During Anne's reign, other relevant newspapers included *Proctor's Price-Courant*, the *City Intelligencer*, *Robinson's Price-Courant* and *Whiston's Merchants Weekly Remembrancer*.

Imports also affected the material culture and structures of sociability in London, as with teapots and coffee houses and the patterns of behaviour linked to the consumption of chocolate, coffee and tea. New codes of conduct were thereby set in London; for example, differences between men and women in their consumption of the new drinks. In turn, London audiences saw themselves depicted on stage in these contexts, as with John Philip's play *The Inquisition* (1717), the action of which opened in Child's coffee house. Exports, meanwhile, took London goods across the world. When Peter Macskásy, a landowner in Transylvania (modern Romania), died in 1712, his effects included 'a pair of London summer gloves'.

INDUSTRY

London also remained an important centre of manufacturing, especially in the luxury trades and in cloth finishing, both high-value activities. Other industries included shipbuilding, needle-making and industries focused on serving the growing population of the city, such as slaughterhouses, brewing, sugar-boiling, soap-boiling, glue-making, kilns and the production of tobacco pipes, in large part from Dorset ball clay. The Bear Garden in Southwark was replaced by a glassworks in the 1680s. Commercialisation was seen in the case of Oliver Cromwell's wife, Elizabeth, who wished to brew her own ale in Whitehall, only to accept a new London ale. The difficulty of moving and preserving products such as beer and meat contributed to the location of these industries in the London area, with animals walked by drovers to Smithfield where they were slaughtered. Variety was to be a distinctive characteristic of London's manufacturing until its marked decline in the late twentieth century. This variety contributed to the employment provided and skill required. In the seventeenth century, wages rose and London was the high-wage centre of the country.

The regulatory environment was shown with the Glorious Revolution, which ended the monopoly of the London Guild of Distillers in 1690 and was followed by a major rise in the distillation of gin, seen as a patriotic alternative to French brandy, on the import of which restrictions were imposed. Gin production in London existed before William III came to the throne, but became very much more popular thereafter, and a deadly Gin Craze followed in the early eighteenth century, one that was brutally depicted by Hogarth.

On a longstanding pattern, manufacturing helped ensure considerable pollution. Tanning – which required leather treatment with urine and faeces – soap-boiling and glue-making – all aspects of the processing of dead animals – were noxious. In turn, this pollution helped affect the geography of the city, reflecting and contributing to the lack of appeal of particular areas. The dominant westerly (from the west) airstream meant that the East End was less attractive than its western counterpart, although residents in the latter suffered lower air quality when easterly winds prevailed. Many of the noxious industrial processes were located south of the Thames; for example, the tanneries. There were also lime kilns in Limehouse and Bankside. Such industries also affected others, requiring clean air or water. By the 1680s, the dyers were moving from Southwark to Crayford as they dried the finished cloth in the open and could not afford the proximity of industries producing noxious fumes.

London Brewing

Long-established, brewing greatly expanded in the eighteenth century due to the production of porter, a generously hopped, dark-brown beer aged in the brewery and named after the porters who popularised it. The drink made the fortune of Samuel Whitbread. Major brewers of porter included Truman's Black Eagle Brewery in Spitalfields. Redemption's Fellowship Porter is a modern example. London's porter brewers developed the technology of production, notably with thermometers and large storage vats. Stout and India Pale Ale (exported to India) were brewed in London.

Industrial sites both revealed specialisation and yet were also flexible as energy sources, especially water power, and premises could be used for other purposes. This was particularly seen with the Wandle, one of the southern tributaries of the Thames: a centre of water-powered grain milling in medieval and, even more, Tudor times, this valley also became the setting, from Croydon to Wandsworth, of a greater range of industries, including the printing and dyeing of textiles. Just as there was residential differentiation within London, so there was also industrial diversity. This was not only a matter of pollution. To the east of the City, there were new industries such as silk weaving, as well as other manufacturing that benefited from a cheaper and less working-regulated environment than that in the City. Nevertheless, industry continued in the latter, including printing.

London's role grew within a developing national economy. London merchants directed production elsewhere; for example, the Norwich textile trades. The first shipload of Cheshire cheese reached London in 1650 and, by 1664, more than fourteen cheese ships were sailing from the North-West, and by the 1680s over fifty. Return cargoes from London helped to transform the regional economy, both in the North-West and elsewhere. Cheese, a food not dependent on immediate consumption, also came to London from Somerset via Bristol. From the 1670s, grain for London (as well as oats for its horses) came by means of coastal shipping from along England's coast. Feeding the city's growing numbers depended on agricultural expansion in England, as food was not, on the whole, imported, and also on greater organisational efficiency. The bulky nature of food and the problems of cost and preservation involved in transporting it ensured that Kent and the Thames Valley were key sources of crops, fruit and vegetables in London. Hops and malt were produced in Kent and East Anglia to provide the beer and ale that was more crucial than today due to the lack of clean water, the difficulty of providing fresh milk and the restrictions on, and cost of, wine imports. Animals came from further afield due to the practice of droving: walking them to near London, fattening them up on nearby meadows, and slaughtering them to provide fresh meat. Cattle and sheep were driven from as far as Scotland and Wales, while geese and turkeys walked from East Anglia.

As another instance of the city's role as the focus of production and trade within the country, coal from the North-East of England continued to be shipped from Newcastle. By 1682, 70 per cent of the coal shipped from the River Tyne went to London. When the Scots invaded England in 1644, one of their objectives was to secure coal supplies for their Parliamentary allies in

London, as Newcastle was then under the control of the Royalists. Thus, the Scottish capture of the city that year was very important to London. The use of coal, all of which had to be imported, contributed to the extent to which Londoners were part of a trading economy. They were market-dependent, buying processed or transported products, such as bread and coal, rather than those they could forage locally.

Across the period, water was particularly favoured for the movement of heavy or bulky goods and this was significant for London, which had access to both maritime and river routes. For example, cloth at the start of the eighteenth century was generally taken from Stroud by Thames barge from the transit point of Lechdale. London was also the focus of wagon routes, not least because many cross-country routes were poorly developed. London's organisational strength was important in ensuring that merchants across England sent goods there to be distributed elsewhere in the country.

IMAGES OF LONDON

By the end of the period, London, which had benefited visually from the rebuilding after the Great Fire, was also displaying clear signs of confidence in the naval success and imperial destiny of the country. In part, this was a matter of London's place as a setting for the projects of government. For example, the naval role was celebrated in the Royal Hospital for Seamen for which the Tudor palace at Greenwich had been rebuilt. By 1663, Charles II had decided on a major programme of works. The initial construction was carried out by John Webb, but the scheme was transformed into the hospital for the navy, appropriately situated near the Thames. Executed by Wren, who was also responsible for the Royal Hospital in Chelsea for ex-servicemen, the result was a masterpiece of English Baroque architecture. In 1708, James Thornhill was commissioned to paint the Great Hall and by 1712 he had provided a triumphant ceiling work, proclaiming British power. William III and Anne were shown bringing peace and liberty to Britain and Europe. The subsequent painting at the end of the hall made reference to naval success and power, a list of naval victories appearing as part of the group portrait of the Hanoverian royal family.

Very differently, the extent to which London was changing, while yet retaining traditional features, was captured in Marco Ricci's painting *A View of the Mall from St James's Park* of about 1710. The Mall was a promenade where fashionable society went to see and be seen, to intrigue, to flirt and to proposition. The park contained three avenues for pedestrians and, in the 1700s, Queen Anne's gardener, Henry Wise, planted 350 limes to provide shade. In his painting, Ricci has Wren's St Paul's in the distance and shows London society on display, but this is also a world with cattle grazing in order to provide the city with milk. Elizabeth Cromwell had herself kept cattle there. The large number of women depicted in Ricci's painting reflected the extent to which many public places were not segregated. An additional take on the scene may be provided by Bird Cage Walk in the park being a major centre for homosexual sex.

Another theme was the growth of a public, entrepreneurial culture defined by the market, a culture that had flowered in the Elizabethan and Jacobean theatre but then been hit hard by politics. Public concerts became more frequent, those organised by John Banister in 1672 being the first such to be advertised. The role of advertising was enhanced by the expansion of the press from the 1690s and this, in turn, helped normalise the sense that music was performed for, and paid for by, the public. Henry Playford, who succeeded his father as an active publisher of music, broadened his position in the music market with a tri-weekly concert in 1699 at a coffee house where his music could be sold. He also established a club for music practice. In his preface to the fourth edition of *The Second Book of the Pleasant Musical*

Companion published in 1701, Playford linked improvement and sociability, both key themes in London's culture:

'The design therefore, as it is for a general diversion, so it is intended for a general instruction, that the persons who give themselves the liberty of an evening's entertainment with their friends, may exchange the expense they shall be at in being sociable, with the knowledge they shall acquire from it.'

Meanwhile, spatial differentiation was becoming more apparent with the development of the West End, which was very different. for example, to that of Shadwell in the late seventeenth century. This differentiation was also a cultural one, captured repeatedly in plays across the period that portrayed a rivalry between citizens and gentlemen. The former could be criticised for greed or praised for industry and honesty and the latter praised for nobility or criticised as vicious seducers, especially eager for the wives of merchants. The Whig playwright Nicholas Rowe, in *The Tragedy of Jane Shore* (1714), presented a city merchant acting an honourable part in opposition to a vicious nobleman. London recorded and propagated these tensions and each of these images contributed to the impression it created, both for its citizens and further afield.

5

The Eighteenth Century

....

'With what face can these men who at present govern the capital of Great Britain presume to breathe the spirit of patriotism when their whole conduct is nought but the most unparalleled scene of detestable corruption and mal-administration?'

Anonymous, *City Corruption and Mal-Administration Display'd* (1739)

'At present, every trader in any degree of credit, every broker and attorney, maintains a couple of footmen, a coachman and a postilion.'

Tobias Smollett, *Humphry Clinker* (1771)

London dominated the public gaze. In mid-century, Antonio Canaletto, with his splendid canvases, used talents developed to depict Venice in order to show the resplendent glories of modern London, as Marco Ricci had done earlier in the century. A modern pride in London was expressed in Canaletto's views, with recent or new buildings, such as St Paul's Cathedral, Greenwich Observatory, Somerset House, Westminster Bridge and the new western towers of Westminster Abbey playing a prominent role. This pride was also expressed in John Rocque's map of 1746 and in the presentation of London as a superior Paris.

A less grand view, but one that accurately captured the city's expansion, was offered by Richard Wilson in his *Westminster Bridge Under Construction* (1744), with the blue openness of the River Thames and the sky being spanned by the new bridge. Canaletto's *A View of London and the River Thames* of about

1746–7, produced for Prince Lobkowicz, who had visited the city in 1745, similarly depicts work on the bridge, which obviously impressed contemporaries.

In 1700, London had more than half a million citizens, more than all other English towns put together and, by 1800, over a million. Although London's share of the national population did not rise over that hundred-year period, it had become the most populous, and wealthiest, city in Europe or the Americas (and the third most populous in the world) and it was over ten times larger than the second city in England. Indeed, in 1805, George III – who had a markedly conservative view about social values and structures – referred to 'the overgrown metropolis'. London's growth from 1650 to 1750 – from about 400,000 to about 675,000 – was such that it could have absorbed about half the surplus of births over deaths from the rest of England. This surplus increased in part because Poor Law relief helped to limit the demographic consequences of poor harvests.

At the same time, although large, London was compact, especially north to south and, more specifically, not yet suffering from the congestion and sprawl of the following centuries. Yet, the

---

Depopulating the Countryside

'. . . another occasion of depopulating the country is the continual, immoderate growth, as well as the mortality, of the City of London. It is now almost twenty years since my good old landlord died; and he was used in his time to compare the kingdom to a rickety child, who has such an unequal conflux of humours to his head, as to weaken his body. But what would he have said, had he lived to see the many streets and buildings that are lately added.'

The West-Country Farmer (1731)

eighteenth century saw considerable expansion, notably in Mayfair, Marylebone, Spitalfields, Whitechapel, Lambeth and Kennington and also further afield; for example, in Highbury. As a result, frequent coach services brought commuters into the City and Westminster by the end of the century. Beyond continuous suburbia came the separate villages that were increasingly part of London, such as Hampstead and Wimbledon.

With is market gardening, brickfields, schools and other activities serving London, Hackney was part of the in-between world of outer London, where settlements on or close to the outskirts of the city were greatly affected by its life. They were not only economically linked, but also places where Londoners could pursue leisure, as in Blackheath, where cricket matches were played in front of big crowds from the 1730s and annual archery tournaments were staged by 1770. Proximity meant that two-way travel between city and outskirts was a daily or weekly occurrence for many.

From the mid-eighteenth century, the population of the City began to fall, as both the wealthy and the poor moved further afield, albeit to different destinations. The City increasingly became a space for work alone, including the 'silent warehouses and wharves' of a Sunday in Dickens' novel *Little Dorrit* (1855–7), rather than of work and life. The suburbs grew.

The use of leases aided developments, with estate owners retaining the freehold, but the developers taking the costs and profit. This process was important to London's expansion to the west. Much of the former church land surrounding London had come into secular hands at the Reformation and, whereas that which remained in church hands was characterised by slack management until the mid-nineteenth century, the management by secular owners was far more active. This management included the creation of the town squares that are such a distinctive feature of much of London from this period, underlining the extent to which London is a planned city. By the 1801 census, Westminster had more inhabitants than the City. The estates there gave their names to the streets, as with Harley and Oxford Streets which were part of the estates of the Harley family, who were earls of Oxford.

Shoreditch

Maps of newly settled areas recorded the spread of London. That of 1745 by Peter Chassereau showed both the expansion of Shoreditch – which had really begun in the 1680s – and the extent to which the parish continued largely to be farmland with the settlement concentrated in its southern parts. Market gardens and, beyond them, pastures for fattening animals, took up most of the parish including sections of its southern part. Much, however, was soon built on, the population rising from 10,000 in 1750 to 35,000 by 1801.

CULTURE

Meanwhile, across the arts, London provided venues, performers and audiences, as well as entrepreneurs seeking to produce multiple links between them. Having worked at Canons, composing anthems for James, 1st Duke of Chandos' choir, George Frederick Handel moved to the public market, transforming himself from a servant of the rich who composed Italian operas, into the nationalistic author of English language oratorios. Changes in any of the artistic factors of production could alter the cultural world. For example, the enlargement of Covent Garden in 1792 and of Drury Lane in 1794 led to theatres that were less intimate and, instead, more suited to the drama of spectacle. These changes in the London theatres interacted with that in national taste, as they proved especially conducive to the taste for Gothic drama in the 1790s, as well as to the increase in payments to playwrights and in the profits of theatre owners and lessees.

Profit and public also came together in the pleasure gardens, especially Ranelagh and Vauxhall. Their popularity reflected the density of London's population and the resulting proximity of suburban facilities. These were not only places to see and be seen, eat and meet, set and spot fashions and find spouses or whores, but also provided showpieces for all kinds of art and were major sites of entertainment, especially of music. In the season, Vauxhall, which was reopened in 1732 by Jonathan Tyers, had two programmes of music each evening, featuring music by leading composers. Johann Christian Bach wrote songs for Vauxhall in the 1760s and 1770s.

On the model of these pleasure gardens came others – such as Marylebone; a total of sixty-four pleasure gardens are known in London. At the same time, there was the variety to which the combination of London's diversity and the entrepreneurial search for profitable opportunity gave rise. In the case of pleasure gardens, there was an attempt to match services to the varied pockets of consumers, as entrepreneurs such as Daniel Gough at Marylebone sought to mesh emulation with distinctiveness. Gough, also a tavern keeper, himself reflected the range of the service industries devoted to catering for public tastes. Assembly rooms provided an enclosed equivalent to pleasure gardens, most obviously in James Wyatt's Pantheon in Oxford Street, a grand assembly room completed in 1772, although it was to fall victim to fire.

In addition to the pleasure gardens, there were parks such as St James's. The last change came around 1770 when 'Capability' Brown replaced the rectilinear 'canal' and walks with the natural look, the 'canal' becoming what is now St James's Park Lake. The development of a vista culminating in Buckingham House was also part of the park's transformation. Separately, by the 1770s, 'monument mania' meant that people flocked to Westminster Abbey for tours of the tombs.

The pull of London attracted talent not only from abroad – for example Mozart and Haydn – but also from the provinces. Alongside the famous came a host of others who were instrumental in making changes in their particular fields. London offered opportunity for opportunities and, as throughout its history, some of the talented it attracted rose to the top. For example, the great surgeon William Hunter (1718–83), educated at Glasgow and Edinburgh, went to London in 1741 and became a noted anatomical lecturer and, in 1768, the first Professor of Anatomy to the Royal Academy. His younger brother, John, rose to be head of the surgical profession in London. Anna Maria Garthwaite (1690–1763), the well-educated daughter of a Lincolnshire parson who came to London in about 1730, was one of the leading silk designers, producing and selling an average of eighty designs a year. Born in Whickham, County Durham, the son of a music-master, William Shield (1748–1829) was a key figure in Northern musical life, the leader of the Durham theatre orchestra and the conductor of the Newcastle concerts but, in 1771, he moved to become a violin player in London. He began to lead an active metropolitan musical life, including being composer at Covent Garden which, in turn, was to lead to him becoming Master of the King's Music in 1817 and to burial at Westminster Abbey in 1829. As an instance of the degree of inflow, fewer than a third of the clergy in the London diocese came from the area and, instead, many came from Wales, the West Country and Yorkshire.

Those from abroad who visited but did not stay, such as Montesquieu and Voltaire, were also impressed by London, commenting on its cosmopolitan character which they traced to religious tolerance. For Georg Christoph Lichtenberg, the London of the 1770s was an exciting centre of civilisation, where he could meet Joseph Priestley and see David Garrick on the stage. In turn,

London was influenced by the Continent. Cultural, stylistic, intellectual and religious fashions and impulses crossed the Channel and were taken up in London. They included Italian opera and French cooking and card games. The morning *levée* and toilet was introduced into London from France, as was the umbrella. A large number of French artists also practised in London, as did Italian painters and Swiss Italian *stuccatori*.

Culture, indeed, was a sphere of competition, a field of patronage and a commodity of vital importance to London's craftsmen, much of whose production was destined for the domestic luxury market. Foreign craftsmen were seen as rivals. Ten tailors, three gilders, three embroiderers and one dancing master were among those on the list of thirty-six French Catholics living in Westminster which the French chargé d'affaires handed the British government in June 1722. There was much hostility to cosmopolitanism and, in this, London acted as a metropolitan forcing house of political, social and cultural tensions, a role that has been significant over the centuries. In the shape of John Gay's English-language ballad-operas, especially *The Beggar's Opera* (1728), London was the scene for the development of an indigenous reply to Handel, then a composer of Italian operas. There were also riots against French actors, in 1738, 1739, 1743, 1749 and 1755. At the Haymarket Theatre in 1738, the audience 'interrupted with hissing, catcalling, ringing small bells, knocking out of candles, pelting etc.', leading the actors to quit the stage.

London, indeed, was the centre of cultural competition with France. The Anti-Gallican Association was founded there in 1745 'to oppose the insidious arts of the French Nation' and 'to promote British manufactures ... discourage the introduction of French modes and oppose the importation of French commodities'. Attempts were made to encourage British production of good quality bone-lace to counter French imports and the French invention of *papier maché* for decorative work – a threat to the livelihood of carvers – was condemned. In London, the same period saw Hogarth's vigorous espousal of the cause of British art.

From the 1760s, organised cultural anti-Gallicanism abated somewhat because of the ebbing of the Rococo style and the less obvious influence of French culture in the age of Sir Joshua Reynolds. Greater national self-confidence after victories in the Seven Years' War (1756–63) and the direction of metropolitan artisanal political interest towards domestic politics were also important. Attacks on French cultural influence remained frequent. In 1779, Robert Henley Ongley, a very wealthy London merchant, told the House of Commons that 'the French had contributed not a little to the increase of divorces, by the introduction of their *petit-maîtres*, fiddlers and dancing masters, who had been allowed to teach our wives and misses to allemande and to twist and turn them about at their pleasure.' The world of music, however, remained closely linked to the Continent. Mozart visited in 1764 and Carl Friedrich Abel and Johann Christian Bach launched a successful annual concert series in 1775.

London's development greatly influenced that of other British and colonial cities, not least because of the importance of image. In the *St James's Chronicle* of 6 August 1761, George Colman argued that the improvement in transport had pushed the example of London to the fore, a situation that was subsequently to be replicated with rail, steamships, motor transport and aircraft:

'Stage-coaches, machines, flys and post-chaises are ready to transport passengers to and fro between the metropolis and the most distant parts of the kingdom ... the manners, fashions, amusements, vices and follies of the metropolis, now make their way to the remotest corners of the land ... The effects of this easy communication have almost daily grown more and more visible. The several great cities, and we might add many poor country towns, seem to be universally inspired with an ambition of becoming the little Londons of the part of the kingdom wherein they are situated: the notions of splendour, luxury, and amusement, that prevail in town, are eagerly adopted; the various changes of fashion exactly copied; and the whole manner of life studiously imitated ... every male and female wishes to think and speak, to eat and drink and dress and live, after the manner of people of quality in London.'

Facilities for, and patterns of, social activity responded to the example of London, which was presented as the benchmark for conditions elsewhere. Taste and emulation focused on London. The Royal Academy of Arts helped to develop a national style that the provinces and colonies sought to emulate. Moreover, London craftsmen were in demand across the country. The Rococo silver basket in the dining room at Wallington in Northumberland was made by the London silversmith John Jacobs in 1750, while Thomas Bromwich (d. 1787), a noted metropolitan cabinet and paper-hangings maker, was commissioned to produce a *trompe d'oeil* wallpaper scheme for changes to the Long Gallery at Wentworth Woodhouse country house in Yorkshire.

London's publications spread designs. In about 1790, Thomas Sheraton (1751–1806) from Stockton, County Durham, established himself in London and began publication of a series of furniture design manuals. Thanks to such books, fixtures, fittings and furniture became more standardised and London fashions gained a national scope. The literary equivalent included works such as Charles Vyse's *New London Spelling Book* (1776). The norms of the language were set in London, as in John Walker's *Pronouncing Dictionary of English* which was published in the city. It provided 'rules to be observed by the natives of Scotland, Ireland and London for avoiding their respective peculiarities'.

London Eating

'Times are changed ... Here stood the large, plump juicy buttocks of English roast beef, and there smiled the frothy tankards of English beer ... Now ... our tables groan with the luxuries of France and India. Here a lean fricassee rises in the room of our majestic ribs.'

London Magazine, January 1773

Influence, however, only operated up to a point. For example, provincial silversmiths, such as those in Exeter, were influenced by London designs, but also produced work with unique features. It would be a mistake to ignore the capacity in the provinces both to preserve local practices and to take initiatives. Moreover, in part, London's impact was itself a product of its openness to influences from outside, both within Britain and from further afield.

The price of culture was higher than in most of Britain. For example, the cost of portraits in London and Bath was not matched elsewhere. Nevertheless, many aspects of London's culture were copied in provincial and colonial towns, with its squares imitated in cities such as Bristol, as well as in Rittenhouse Square in Philadelphia. A young Samuel Johnson (not the great Dr Johnson), described a modest subscription assembly at Islington that he visited and danced at in 1775:

'This assembly is quite a sociable meeting where the greatest part of the company is known to each other, and very like ours, a dancing room and a cold room, tea about ten, and breaking up about twelve, two or three fiddles, a tabor and pipe, and I believe a hautboy, and a horn, admittances five shilling, twelve or fourteen couples, but generally I believe nearer to twenty, minuets and country dances, two or three handsome ladies, one very handsome, one very good natured man (Captain Shirley) to unite the company together, and this I think a recipe for an agreeable assembly. All kinds of liquors such as punch are included.'

Gentility and equality were thus fused. The assurance of the former made it possible in theory for the company to set aside status and to act as equals, sidelining the concerns about social fluidity that played such a corrosive role in mixing. Indeed, London helped promote the interaction of bourgeois/ middle-class and aristocratic thinking and values, and did so more successfully than in the seventeenth century, in part because religious and political tensions were less prominent. The virtues and values summarised as sensibility were frequently contrasted with the commercialism and crassness of new money.

Lord's Cricket Ground

Thomas Lord opened a cricket ground at Marylebone in 1787 on what is now Dorset Square. In 1811, driven out by a rise in rent, Lord relaid the turf, only to be moved on once more, having occupied land on the route for Regent's Canal. His third ground, where play started in 1814, is now the most famous site in cricket and, thanks to a major building of stands in the late twentieth century, can now hold 28,000 spectators.

At the same time, the extent to which London offered different prospects to those of landed society was captured by George Lillo in his play *The London Merchant* (1731), which deliberately focused on ordinary people. 'A London apprentice ruined is our theme,' declared the prologue. In the dedicatory preface to the printed version, Lillo claimed that tragedy did not lose 'its dignity, by being accommodated to the circumstances of the generality of mankind . . . Plays founded on moral tales in private life may be of admirable use.' A London in which there was much social differentiation was the context for this remark: in Joseph van Aken's painting of *Covent Garden Market* (c. 1726–30), distinctions were reflected in clothes and in positioning, notably with the drabness of a maid with a shopping-basket standing behind a lady buying vegetables, the maid shadowed by her mistress. In his pamphlet *Thoughts on the Late Transactions Respecting Falkland's Islands* (1771), Dr Samuel Johnson, another Tory, was to refer to the 'sudden glories of paymasters and agents, contractors and commissaries, whose equipages shine like meteors and whose palaces rise like exhalations'.

Women

More generally, the variety of London society was captured in the very diverse roles of women. They could be prominent, dominating the lottery held by Thomas Coram's Foundling Hospital for nominating to places and also playing an important role in the debating societies that developed from the late 1770s. There was also involvement in less genteel activities, as with the criminal group centred on Moll Harvey in the 1730s. On 5 September 1759, *Lloyd's Evening Post* reported:

'On Monday night was fought at Stoke Newington, one of the most obstinate and bloody battles between four noted bruisers [boxers], two of each sex; the odds before the battle began were two to one on the male side; but they fought with such courage and obstinacy, that at length the battle was decided in favour of the female.'

Prostitution was the fate of many women. The *Middlesex Journal* of 21 October 1783, complaining about the number of prostitutes on the streets of London and their shocking obscenities, proposed that they be taxed and restricted to certain streets. No such restrictions were proposed for their clients. Decorated tiles – probably from a brothel or gentleman's club – showing explicit sexual positions were discovered following a fire at the Cheshire Cheese pub in 1962. One depicts a woman lying on the ground holding a rope that passes over a pulley and controls a wickerwork cradle in which a seated man is apparently being lowered onto his consort's waiting dildo. An important homosexual 'subculture' also existed in London, with its own vocabulary, dress codes, rituals and geography.

By European standards, social conventions were not rigid. The Comte de Gisors was surprised, when visiting the city in the 1750s, to find young women of quality paying visits alone without loss of reputation, but the French ambassador told him that it was the English habit to trust daughters to do this. In 1763, a later French ambassador was described as not being long enough in post 'to learn that the ladies here had much rather trudge up and down the stairs by themselves, than be escorted by anybody'. A degree of freedom had consequences in terms of relations with men. Prior to the mid-century, the majority of actions for divorce brought in the London Consistory Court were brought by women against their husbands for cruelty but, thereafter, the notion of romantic marriage and domestic harmony came to prevail among the prosperous and the practice of divorce for incompatibility grew.

Moral misdemeanours also attracted attention, Robert Trevor writing in 1729 about a notorious adulteress, 'Private persons have not escaped the notice and censures of our licentious press; nor can even the grave bury poor Lady Abergavenny's shame, every syllable of whose name, and every particular of whose life are hawked about the streets as articulately as old clothes etc.'

The discovery of an admiral's wife in a Charing Cross brothel in 1771 also provided good copy.

A Changing Cityscape

The social world that fostered the demand for new buildings and spaces was matched by the wealth of a growing economy, and by entrepreneurial activity, providing many opportunities for artistic skill. Aesthetically and practically, the transfer of Classical ideas to houses, churches and public buildings was not easy, as the prototypes were mostly ancient temples and baths, and it proved necessary to create a new architectural grammar for design and ornamentation. This need encouraged a recourse to books of designs. Yet, anglicised Classical ideas transformed architectural style.

The image of London also changed. Taking forward the impact of the Great Fire of 1666, timber and thatch were seen as dated, unattractive, non-utilitarian and, increasingly, indeed, non-urban, as were long-established twisting street patterns and ferries rather than bridges. Yet, these changes in urban image and practice were also an instance of the social polarisation that stemmed from urban improvement, as the new image was very much that propagated by and for the urban elite and their rural visitors.

The resulting cityscape was one in which those who lacked gentility seemed out of place. As a consequence, alongside issues of different access to cultural facilities, came those of social acceptability. Improvement was political in its broadest definition, reflecting a concern with the urban environment, a confidence that it could be improved and a determination to act. London, indeed, appeared to be one of the principal products of human activity, the section of the environment most amenable to action and the place where society was open to regulation. This view and practice reflected interacting functional, moral and aesthetic criteria and requirements that were aspects of the cultural activism of the period.

Alongside official edifices, the new stone and brick buildings offered definitions of urban function with an emphasis on leisure and retail and, more generally, on private space open to those who could pay (shops, subscription rooms), rather than spaces and places open to all, such as marketplaces and churches. The buildings themselves were seen more brightly as the night was more thoroughly lit with the introduction of street lighting. Nevertheless, until gas lighting and, later, electricity, transformed the situation, the change between day and night was far more abrupt than is the case today. As Hogarth's *Night* indicated, night-time offered different sensations, experiences and dangers and, as a result, the role of moonlight was much more important than today. In 1716, the City's shops were instructed to hang a lamp outside their premises from six to eleven o'clock in the evening.

Established in 1723, the Chelsea Waterworks Company used a tidal watermill to pump up water from the Thames near Pimlico, with linked reservoirs in Hyde Park and St James's Park. The system was later enhanced with pumping engines and an iron water main. The resulting supply helped in the expansion of the West End but was challenged by pollution, so that in the nineteenth century it became acceptable only to take water from above Teddington Lock.

Hospitals as Neighbours

'As the spot he has chosen to build on is situated close to St George's Hospital, and the inhabitants ... of this new building, will every morning, at breakfast-time, be saluted with those sweet smelling effluvias which are continually arising from disease and putrefaction.'

Morning Post, 17 March 1786, on building plans of the Duke of Rutland

---

The public buildings of the period greatly contributed to the fabric of society and also reflected it, as with the new British Museum when it was opened in 1750. Similarly, for example, four voluntary hospitals were opened between 1720 and 1780, but the purposes of medical and other charitable foundations revealed the poor state of social welfare, the failure of family networks to care for all the destitute and the grim nature of much of life. Broken families were a major cause of poverty, but families with two parents were also vulnerable, and vulnerability was increased by the burden of children. Charitable donors sought to provide adequate care for lying-in women and their babies, to rescue the all-too-numerous orphaned and abandoned children and to rehabilitate those driven into prostitution by poverty. The term hospital was also used for institutions concerned with the destitute, such as the Magdalen Hospital for the Reception of Penitent Prostitutes which was established in 1758.

Thomas Coram's Foundling Hospital, established in 1739 and in full occupation by 1753, was a testimony to the harshness of life, as many of the foundlings given up to care were not illegitimate but the children of couples who could not cope with sustained poverty and the impact of savage crises. The hospital thus testified as much to the problems of the poor as to illegitimacy and, during the Seven Years' War (1756–63), as many as 60 per cent of the children were legitimate. In contrast, from 1801 the hospital accepted only illegitimate children. Other problems of life also emerge from the study of the hospital. Death rates could be as high as 80 per cent but, as a reminder of the need to use sources carefully, they could also be low for the age, in part due to a care for foundling health and diet which included the dispatch of the children to nursing women outside London, where chances of survival were held to be higher. This was an important link between London and the provinces: the foundlings were sent to rural wet nurses for the first five years of their lives, before being returned to London for education and for placement in apprenticeships.

A far less benign situation was captured by Hogarth in the last painting in *The Rake's Progress* (1733–4), when he showed the insane inmates at Bedlam being visited by fashionable women. Moreover, the Lock Hospital founded in 1746 for sufferers from venereal disease put an emphasis on moral reform and excluded repeat cases.

The First Bypass

The growth of London made travel more difficult, encouraging the search for improvement. To make access to the City easier, while avoiding the congestion of Holborn, the 'New Road' and City Road were built from 1756 and 1761 to link Paddington and Shoreditch. The New Road, now the Marylebone, Euston and Pentonville Roads, was paid for by tolls.

COMMERCE

Changes within London were not only aspects of the shaping of the city by its interaction with the wider world, but were also played out in the full attention of a nation that saw London either as synonymous with the country or as a hindrance to it. Thus, alongside complaints from other trading cities – especially Bristol – about London's position, the reiterated stress on the city's commercial importance ensured that its trade was generally seen as synonymous with that of the country. Its merchants were able to press the government on policy, not least through Parliament, and also discussed matters with foreign envoys. The capital they could deploy helped shape the Atlantic world, while their entrepreneurship ensured that London did not follow Amsterdam into relative decay. The protection of their interests included the dispatch of pirates at Execution Dock in Wapping.

London's commercial and maritime role was celebrated in the triumphal works produced in the capital. John Bacon's statue of George III in the courtyard of Somerset House depicted him in a Roman costume, holding the rudder of a ship attended by a majestic lion and above a colossal figure of Father Thames. In James Barry's paintings in the Society for the Encouragement of Arts, Commerce and Manufactures, executed between 1777 and 1783, the figure of Father Thames was presented as a reborn Neptune. In the third edition of his influential *Universal Dictionary of Trade and Commerce* (1766), a work that first appeared in 1751, Malachy Postlethwayt, an active writer on economic issues, added a dedication to George Nelson, the Mayor, and to the aldermen and councillors of the City, that included the passages:

'London tradesmen appear to constitute the very active soul of the commerce of the whole British state; and they are an essential medium between the merchant, the country shopkeeper, and the consumers . . . The country-men shear their sheep, sell their wool, and carry it from place to place; the manufacturer sets it to work, to combing, spinning, winding, twisting, dyeing, weaving, fulling, dressing and thus they furnish their numberless manufactures in the whole woollen branch. But what must they do with them, if London did not take them first off their hands, and the London tradesmen, warehousemen, factors and wholesale dealers, did not vend and circulate them amongst the London merchants, as well as to all the remoter parts of the nation? London is the grand central mart.'

The city was also the forcing house for new developments. Thus, the insurance industry focused on London where companies included the Sun Fire Office, Royal Exchange Assurance and

Phoenix Assurance, founded in 1708, 1719 and 1782 respectively. Moreover, in 1773, a group of brokers subscribed towards the acquisition of a building which became known as the Stock Exchange.

Increasingly, successful provincial newspapers carried advertisements inserted by London firms, which represented an attempt by London businessmen to penetrate provincial markets paralleled by the spread of London newspapers noted in the *Observer* which, launched on 4 December 1791, promised that advertisers could rely on its being 'dispersed to the remotest parts of the three kingdoms'. Other forms of printing, such as engravings, also spread London's influence.

London's commercial importance was seen in the economic news carried in the press. Shipping and grain were the early staples. The *Supplement to the Weekly Journal* promised readers in 1716 that it would provide them with information of ships arriving at and leaving London, a service common to many newspapers. Reports on grain prices were also found in most newspapers. The prices invariably mentioned were those at Bear Key, the Bear Quay, where grain was landed and where a major corn market had been established. These prices, and the value of the leading London stocks, were also carried by many of the newsletters used by early provincial papers as a major source of information. By the 1790s, London papers which in no way specialised in economic news, such as the *Express* and the *Telegraph*, were providing in every issue nearly a column of information (a formidable amount when, for tax reasons, papers were only four pages long) on London markets ranging from the price of butter and hides to that of tallow and sugar. Its economic importance was displayed in the columns of the provincial press. By 1774, the *Kentish Gazette* was regularly providing half a column on the prices in the London markets. The *Newcastle Chronicle* in 1787 provided a description of the condition of the London markets as opposed to a mere list of prices. The 'Market

Herald', carried in the *Chelmsford Chronicle* in 1792, gave the London prices of grain, flour, seed, leather, raw hide, meat, tallow, coal, hay, straw and hops. *Woolmen's Exeter and Plymouth Gazette* in 1809 provided London grain, meat and leather prices and the *Sherborne Mercury* in 1837 reported on Smithfield as well as the local cattle market.

These prices were of interest not only because goods needed to be purchased from London, but also because it was by far the largest market for producers elsewhere; indeed, the market that set the tone and prices for other markets across Britain. The dependence of London on supplies from outside was captured in a painting by Robert Dodd (1748–1816) of a collier brig discharging her cargo of coal into lighters near Limehouse.

While linking in with crucial international markets, London helped to mould a national economic space, although it is clear that specialisation for the London market was accompanied by the persistence of more local economic patterns. Most of the food for London's growing population came from within Britain. Welsh cattle were driven to Kent to be fattened for the London market, while cows were also driven south from Yorkshire. Alongside saltwater fish landed in London, freshwater fish was brought from the Fens by wagon, the water in the butts changed nightly. In turn, London markets affected agriculture elsewhere. Thus, in Cleveland, enclosure of both open-field arable land and commons owed much to the increase in pastoral farming for the London market. After 1769, when the Tees was bridged at Stockton, large quantities of Cleveland wheat were shipped to London. Good-quality butter was also moved to London by sea; for example, from Malton via Scarborough, Whitby and Hull.

A less attractive aspect of London's economy was the danger posed by industrial processes, both to the workers and to others. For example, dressing and tanning leather polluted water supplies and, as a result, was located on the banks of the River Wandle south of the Thames, and away from the city. London remained very important as a manufacturing centre, not least in brewing and flour milling, each aspect of food processing reflecting the size of the city's population. When Thomas Jefferson, the future American president, came to London in 1785, he visited the Albion Flour Mill, a steam-powered mill at the southern end of Blackfriars Bridge that made a considerable impression on him. This showcase for steam power, however, was burned down in 1791, to public rejoicing by 'the mob'.

Greater energy efficiency, as a result of the work of James Watt, made steam engines less expensive to run in London than hitherto, and therefore more viable as there was no local coal. Nevertheless, opportunities in London in commerce and the service sector ensured that manufacturing did not dominate its economy, even though some plant – such as the major breweries – were substantial. Moreover, some industries were affected by serious industrial disputes, although this did not prevent their location in London. After the violent silk-weaving strike of 1768–9, peace was restored only once the Spitalfields Act of 1773 brought an unusual degree of outside regulation of wages.

The human and environmental cost of urban and industrial development became increasingly clear. In 1714, the French envoy complained repeatedly about the effect on his breathing of the coal smoke that enveloped London. An essay, 'Observations on the method of burying the parish poor in London, and on the manner in which some of the capital buildings in it are constructed and kept, as two great sources of the extraordinary sickliness and mortality, by putrid fevers, so sensibly felt in that capital; with hints for the correction of these evils', originally in the *Gentleman's Magazine*, and re-published in the *Annual Register* for 1776, criticised the dangerous stench from corpses that were buried in shallow graves, the hazards of crowded hospitals and public buildings and the general lack of pure air: 'In this city, where coal fires are principally used, with the inflammable, mephitic, and other matters thrown out, probably an acid is decomposed, and exhaled from the sulphur in the coal.' Despite such warnings, relatively little was done to improve the situation. It would be a mistake to think that there was no care and were no improvements prior to the mid-nineteenth-century movement for reform, but the existing urban structures proved unable to cope satisfactorily with the rapid growth of the period.

The Place to Eat

'The fortuned voluptuary may indulge his appetite, not only with all the natural dainties of every season, but with delicacies produced by means of preternatural ingenuity.'

John Roach, *Roach's London Pocket Pilot: or, Stranger's Guide Through the Metropolis* (1796), about London taverns

---

A focus on London can lead to a lack of attention to the city's wider significance within Britain. This significance was becoming more complex and intense; for example, in finance. Banking houses, single-unit partnerships with unlimited liability for their losses, developed in London and the provinces, especially in the second half of the century. Moreover, an inter-regional credit structure based on London was established, ensuring that local economies were very much linked to the situation in London and to each other via London. The foundation of a bank clearing house in Lombard Street in 1775 led to a great improvement as institutions were allowed to balance credits and withdrawals by a ticket system.

London also continued to play the key role in Britain's overseas trade and, with the shift of centrality in European commerce from the Netherlands to Britain, this trade was more significant than hitherto. London's role in foreign trade was practical and cultural, entrepreneurial and institutional, and these roles interacted with the situation within Britain. London helped secure the influence of commercial considerations upon national policy, at the same time as it served as a key centre for the military system. Thus, Deptford was not only a dockyard but also, from the 1740s, the headquarters of the Navy's Victualling Board. As such, it was a crucial support for naval and amphibious operations, one that drew on the bakehouse, brewery and slaughterhouses run by the board and the related stores. Other parts of the military infrastructure included the powder magazine of the Board of Ordnance, which was at Greenwich until 1768, being replaced by Purfleet. Guns were cast at Woolwich, the site of the Royal Arsenal which served as a factory until 1967 and as a Ministry of Defence facility until 1994.

There was a very bleak side, however, to this prominence. For example, in 1750–79, London had the second largest number of slave-trade sailings: 869, compared to 1,909 from Liverpool and 624 from Bristol. Moreover, the shipping of slaves was part of a complex trans-Atlantic trade, including colonial products coming to Britain, and this trade depended on credit. The role of finance, especially on the sugar commission business, ensured that London, where it was centred, was as heavily involved in the slave trade as Liverpool.

More generally, the growth in the numbers, assets, skills and functions of London's business community was important to Britain's successful participation in the Atlantic economy. Key individuals spanned the worlds of commerce and government, lending a London focus to policy. William Baker (1705–70) was a prime example of the London merchant-politician. The eldest son of a London draper, he was very active in trading with North America, not least with New York, and was also a major entrepreneur, buying land in Georgia and South Carolina. A director of the East India Company, with short gaps, from 1741 to 1753, he was its chairman in 1749–50 and 1752–3, as well as Deputy Governor of the Hudson's Bay Company from 1750 to 1760 and its Governor from then to his death. An alderman of London from 1739 and an MP from 1747 to 1768, he bought a country estate in 1757 and was knighted in 1760. Baker also played a role as a government contractor, victualling and paying troops in Nova Scotia from 1746. Baker was regularly consulted by ministers on colonial matters and was considered as a possible head of the Board of Trade in 1765.

Such personal links and the extent to which they reinforced each other – a lasting feature with the city's elite – helped make London central to national policymaking, at a time when London was the capital of the world's strongest empire, and reflected and sustained a situation in which Londoners played a disproportionate role. For example, the weakness of the short-lived ministry of William, Earl of Bath and John, Earl Granville in 1746 was indicated when the City withdrew a loan offered to the previous Pelham ministry. The major financial interests had close links with the Pelhams and during the War of the Austrian Succession there was a desperate governmental need to keep loans flowing to the government. Thus, partly due to the City, George II was forced to yield over government policy to Henry Pelham and his brother, Thomas, Duke of Newcastle, who had resigned in order to force his hand. They returned to office.

Interest in the outside world was, as ever, reflected not only in the careers of Londoners but also of those who came to London. Dean Mahomet (1759–1851), an India quartermaster with the Bengal army of the East India Company, came to Britain in 1784, married an Irish woman, became an assistant to Sir Basil Cochrane at his vapour bath in London, established the Hindoostane Coffee House in the capital in 1810 and subsequently opened Mahomet's Baths, which was patronised by such leading figures as Sir Robert Peel.

'The Grand Mart of the World'

'Walking in the streets of London is the true orthodox tread upon fairy ground – you have the spells of
pickpockets, the enchantments of beauty, the incan-
tations of pleasure and the lures of vice, around you.
You may have intoxication in a tavern – love in an
alley – music in the marketplace – coffee in every
street – and ox-cheek and oysters in every cellar . . .
London is the grand mart of the world . . . It is more
religious and more profligate – more rich and more
admired than all the cities of the world for its modern
excellencies . . . A man who has money, may have at
once every delicate, every dainty and every ornamen-
tal beauty of the four quarters of the world.'

*The Macaroni Jester, and Pantheon
of Wit* (London, 1773?)

POLITICS

'The eyes of the whole nation are constantly fixed on the
conduct and proceedings of this city, as the Primum Mobile
of Great Britain.'

Craftsman, 1727

With Parliament an annual event and elections on regular occasions, London became as much a political city as a place of government. Political developments and divisions excited more attention, especially when the city was affected by disturbances and
riots, as with – in a far from exhaustive list – the Sacheverell Riots
in 1710, the Excise Riots in 1733, unrest over the Gin Act in 1736,
the Wilkesite troubles in the 1760s, and the dramatic Gordon
Riots of 1780.

Political and religious radicalism were particularly associated with London. In 1742, Thomas Hay, noting the expression of discontent in Edinburgh, remarked, 'We have sometimes little poetical satires or comical and satirical pamphlets ... from London.' In 1762, Elizabeth Montagu was shocked by the extent of its critical sentiment:

'All mankind are philosophers and pride themselves in having a contempt for rank and order and imagine they show themselves wise in ridiculing whatever gives distinction and dignity to kings and other magistrates, not considering that the chains of opinion are less galling than those of law, and that the great beast the multitude must be bound by something. Alexander the Great was treated with contempt by a certain philosopher in a tub [Diogenes], but in this enlightened age the man who made the tub would use him with the same scorn.'

Troops were deployed to deal with riots in 1736, 1768 and 1780. These deployments reflected the strength of dissidence in London. In the 1760s, popular radicalism combined with the consequences of economic strain. The unwillingness of the House of Commons to accept the bitter attacks of John Wilkes was a key issue. Expelled from Parliament in 1764, he was elected for Middlesex in 1768, only to be imprisoned for blasphemy and libel and expelled from the Commons. Three times re-elected by Middlesex in 1769, Wilkes was declared incapable of being re-elected by Parliament and his opponent was declared elected, a thwarting of the views of the electors that aroused anger. Wilkes was the focus of more widespread popular opposition to the government and a measure of radicalism that led in 1768 to riots in London. Elizabeth Grenville was concerned about her husband's safety amidst 'the tumults and disorders in the city . . . God grant you safety in the midst of a wild, tumultuous and daring mob'. Already in 1763, there had been resistance in London to the burning of Wilkes's seditious paper *The North Briton*: 'Mr Harley, the Sheriff, no sooner appeared with the paper to give it up to the all devouring flames, than the mob among themselves immediately with the faggots already laid for the conflagration, drove Mr Harley back into his chariot [carriage] with the loss of some blood on his part.'

Politicisation in London owed much to the Wilkesite controversy, and this politicisation led to a different social politics, prefiguring the situation with the rise of Labour in the early twentieth century. Thus, in Surrey, there was the rise of Joseph Mawbey, a Vauxhall vinegar distiller, who became MP for Southwark (1761–74), a baronet (1765) and eventually, despite opposition to him as a parvenu, MP for Surrey (1775–90). Mawbey benefited electorally from the willingness of freeholders to ignore the county's 'natural' leaders. In London, a group of radicals, including John Horne Tooke and John Sawbridge, established in 1769 the Society of the Supporters of the Bill of Rights. This Society supported not only Wilkes but also political reform, specifically shorter parliaments and a redistribution of seats.

In turn, the American War of Independence (1775–83) divided opinion, with much initial support for the American cause, but also considerable anger and opposition to it, opposition that increased when the Americans turned to France. There was also periodic pressure from Londoners for radical political changes. The Westminster Association pressed in 1780 for universal male suffrage, annual elections, the secret ballot and equal constituencies and this programme was endorsed by the Society for Constitutional Information established in London that year by a group of Rational Dissenters, including John Cartwright and Thomas Brand Hollis. This society printed a mass of material, much of it free, in favour of parliamentary reform, at least 88,000 copies of thirty-three different publications in 1780–3.

The year 1780 was also the time of the Gordon Riots, with pressure from the Protestant Association for the repeal of the

1778 Catholic Relief Act leading to a challenge to order in the centre of empire. Already, in 1773, fear of accusations of crypto-Catholicism had led the Archbishop of Canterbury and the Bishop of London to block attempts by the Dean of St Paul's to commission religious paintings for the interior of the cathedral. On 2 June 1780, about fifty thousand members of the Association marched on Parliament to present the petition for repeal. The Justices of the Peace had only about seventy-six constables to control the crowds, but Parliament refused to be intimidated into repeal. The angry demonstrators initially turned to attack Catholic chapels and schools in Westminster and London, before threatening establishment targets such as the houses of prominent ministers and politicians thought to be pro-Catholic, and of magistrates who sought to act against the rioters. The prisons were stormed in order to release imprisoned rioters, while distilleries and breweries were pillaged and the Bank of England threatened. The riots reflected a popular Protestantism that was deeply suspicious of tolerant tendencies on the part of the elite. In the end, George III, who was unimpressed by the City authorities' response and 'convinced till the magistrates have ordered some military execution on the rioters this town will not be restored to order', summoned the Privy Council which empowered the army to employ force without the prior permission of a magistrate. George then sent in troops to end the riots. They did so and, following trials, twenty-six people were hanged.

These riots, in which 210 people were killed in the streets and seventy-five subsequently died from their wounds, were to leave a lasting impact in Charles Dickens' novel *Barnaby Rudge* (1841). The riots occur halfway through the story and The Warrens, the house of Geoffrey Haredale, a central figure, is burned to the ground, while his daughter Emma – the heroine – is kidnapped. A hostile Dickens wrote of the rioters becoming 'wilder and more cruel', changing 'their earthly nature for the qualities that give delight in hell'.

Very differently, St Paul's was to serve as the dramatic setting for the celebrations of George's recovery in 1789 from what appeared to be madness. The thanksgiving service on 23 April contrasted with the drama that was to unfold soon after for Louis XVI in Paris. Henry, 2nd Viscount Palmerston recorded, 'The entering into the church was very magnificent, an avenue all through it being formed by Guards and Beefeaters in a double row and in the centre, under the dome, the astonishing mass of charity children piled up quite round. Their singing as the king came in and went out had a great effect.'

As with many London occasions, reports and engravings spread accounts of the service across the country, for which London acted as the ceremonial centre, a role that was to develop further with state occasions for funerals of such figures as Nelson and Wellington and victory celebrations, and the development of a memorial landscape that took on new depth with the Cenotaph built after World War One.

A pronounced division of opinion in London nevertheless arose as a result of the French Revolution, which broke out in 1789 and led, initially, in London to a marked upturn in radical-ism, so that the radical London Corresponding Society, founded in 1792, grew in size and prominence. Indeed, Edmund Burke's famous critique of radicalism was entitled *Reflections on the Revolution in France, and on the Proceedings in Certain Societies in London Relative to That Event* (1790).

Concerned about the possibility of insurrection, the govern-ment moved troops nearer to London in late 1792. A major effort was also made to mobilise Loyalist support. On 20 November, the Association for Preserving Liberty and Property against Republicans and Levellers was launched at a meeting at the Crown and Anchor Tavern. John Hatsell, the Clerk to the House of Commons, observed, 'This appears to me a better plan than trusting to the soldiery and brings the question to its true point – a contest between those who have property and those who have none.'

Loyalist newspapers were launched, while opposition publications were suppressed by legal action. In 1792, for example, the *Argus*, a radical London paper, was brought to an end: its printer, Sampson Perry, was outlawed when he fled to France to avoid trial for libel. The presses were then used for a Loyalist newspaper, the *True Briton*, launched in January 1793. When, that month, news of Louis XVI's execution reached London the play at the Haymarket came to an abrupt end when the audience shouted out, 'No farce, no farce,' and left. In 1794, plans for a national convention of radicals at London were disrupted by the arrest of the leaders of the reform societies and in 1794–5 legislation, including the Seditious Meetings Act of 1795, made reform agitation more difficult. Partly as a consequence, the membership of the London Corresponding Society (LCS) declined. The proposal in 1794 that the Society remonstrate to George III, outlining their grievances in the hope that he might dismiss the ministry, was naïve, as was the alleged plot by the society to shoot the king with a poisoned arrow from an airgun. George's carriage was attacked by a mob en route to the opening of Parliament in October 1795 but, thereafter, London's response to the government was more orderly.

In 1796, the general election was a triumph for the government in London where the radical platform failed. Britain had been at war with France since 1793, a conflict that continued for most of the period until 1815. On the home front, this conflict led to a lack of tolerance for radicalism and to a rallying around the Crown. Despite anti-war demonstrations in 1795, London, instead, frequently became a stage depicting loyalism, as when George III reviewed volunteers in Hyde Park on his birthday in 1799 and 1800, or at Nelson's funeral at St Paul's in 1806, an occasion preceded by the body being taken up the Thames from Greenwich to Whitehall and then through the streets in a funeral vehicle modelled on the *Victory*.

Nevertheless, as a reminder of the central position of London in the nation's politics, the naval mutiny at the anchorage of the

Nore in 1797 was made more dangerous by the vulnerability of London to blockade, while in 1802 Edward Despard, a former army officer and disappointed petitioner, plotted to seize the Tower and the Bank of England and to kill George on his way to open Parliament. Betrayed by informants, the conspirators were arrested, tried and hanged. George, however, was sufficiently wary of London to urge the Home Secretary that Despard's trial be held in Surrey to avoid the independence of 'a Middlesex Jury'.

CRIME

In part, the use of troops to preserve public order – as in 1780 in response to the Gordon Riots – reflected the absence of an effective police force. In 1785, a Bill was introduced in Parliament to create a single, centrally controlled police force for London, in place of the existing local ward and vestry constables and watchmen. However, this Bill and a similar one in 1814, were defeated, due to fears about the consequences for liberty and opposition from local interests. Instead, local initiatives in policing owed much to entrepreneurship, as prominent and dynamic individuals saw opportunities and needs. For example, in West Ham, watchmen and constables earned reasonable sums from the reward system. The use of thief-takers, however, was rife and abuse was common, as in 1745–54 when they fabricated crimes in order to collect rewards.

Crime in London seems to have risen after wars ended, because men accustomed to fight were demobilised without adequate provision and found themselves in a metropolitan labour market in which unemployment and under-employment were chronic, poverty widespread and real wages shot through with insecurity. More generally, crime in part reflected desperation and, as in other periods, London's economic growth and importance was matched by hardship and despair. Yet, there were also periodic upsurges in social problems and crime. After the

War of the Austrian Succession, there was believed to be a crime wave in the early 1750s; the long-serving Austrian agent reported that, due to the rise in thefts and murders, London was unsafe both on the streets at night and even in peoples' houses, and that policing was negligent. Post-war demobilisation led to another reported crime wave in 1783–84.

In the face of periodic panics about crime waves, there were searches for new solutions and it would be mistaken to argue that policing was in a dire state prior to the establishment of the Metropolitan Police in 1829. For example, John Fielding, an active JP (Justice of the Peace) despite his blindness – and a half-brother of the novelist, and fellow JP, Henry – organised mounted police patrols by his Bow Street Runners in and around London in the 1750s. This initiative was funded by the government. Efforts were also made to deal with the problem of bringing prosecutions for, instead of having a system of public prosecution, it was usually up to the victims to decide to prosecute. They often did not do so for reasons of expense, which led in London in the late 1750s to the foundation of a prosecution association in which subscribers agreed to fund prosecutions. The 1792 Middlesex Justices Act extended the model of Bow Street, a court under stipendiary (paid) magistrates deploying a group of professional police officers to other parts of London. The Thames Police was founded in 1798 to prevent the theft of cargoes on and near the river. John Colquhoun, a key figure who was one of the new stipendiary magistrates from 1792, argued in his *Treatise on the Police of the Metropolis* (1796), that 'acts of delinquency and the corruption of manners, have uniformly kept pace with the increase of the riches of the capital' and estimated that London contained 115,000 criminals. The population by this time numbered a million, meaning that more than 10 per cent of citizens were not law-abiding.

Those convicted faced the possibility of capital punishment, but increasing reliance upon the transportation of convicts to the colonies, North America (until the War of American Independence) and, from 1788, Australia, ensured there was less need for the 'bloody code'. The Penitentiary Act of 1779 led to a further diminution by encouraging a tendency to imprisonment. In London, the forcing house of change in the system of punishment, there was a declining dependence on crude terror. The number of those hanged in the capital was far lower in the late eighteenth century than in the early seventeenth century. The percentage of those sentenced to death in London and Middlesex who were actually executed fell from 72 per cent in 1753 to less than a third in the 1780s.

Crime in London reflected the spread of the money economy and the extent to which it centred there. In 1784, Charles Price, nicknamed Old Patch, using high-quality paper and inks, was able to circulate £200,000 (approximately £25 million in contemporary currency) in forged notes and maintained three houses (and wives) to escape detection. Moreover, much smuggling served the London market and, indeed, it was insured there, which was a reflection of the role of London merchant capital in financing the country. The game trade, which flourished in the second half of the century, in part through the developing network of coach services, also focused on London, which benefited from poaching as well as the legal trade.

Profit was also made from the struggle against crime, not only by thief-takers but also thanks to the letting out to operators of sites near the gallows at Tyburn. Until the abolition of processions and public hangings there after 1783, the gallows was one of the major public shows in London. In 1746, Thomas Harris, a London lawyer, noted:

'This has been one of the most entertaining weeks for the mob ... yesterday (which was the top of all) Matthew Henderson was hanged, at whose execution all the world (I speak of the lowlife division) were got together; and he died to the great satisfaction of the beholders, that is he

was dressed and in white with black ribbons, held a prayer
book in his hand and, I believe, a nosegay.'

In practice, the social elite joined in finding such occasions of
great interest. From 1783, executions were held directly outside
Newgate Prison until 1868 when public executions ended, thereafter being within the prison.

It was the unemployed, the unconnected, the newly arrived
migrant and young single women who were generally the most
badly treated by the judicial system; they were most likely to be
suspected of crimes and brought before JPs without legal representation and the right to present their case to a jury; defendants
were at the mercy of the JP. The notebook of Henry Norris, a
Hackney JP in the 1730s, reveals that he was honest, but had little
sympathy with the plight of the poor and was rarely lenient, even
when they were obviously in want. Over two-thirds of the offences
brought before him involved some form of assault, while allega-
tions of theft or damage to property formed the second-largest
category.

Looking to the New Century

The second half of the eighteenth century saw London enjoying
both the wealth that made significant changes possible and also
the wish to do so. Thus, the major changes of the following
century – notably the arrival of rail and the development of a
sewer system and of the embankments – were pushed through in
a context of long-term change, rather than against a static background of pre-steam stasis. Under George III (r. 1760–1820),
Blackfriars Bridge was built, London Bridge widened (and houses
on it removed), the Fleet Ditch covered, part of the wall and its
gates demolished, and major routes opened up, notably Cornhill,
Houndsditch, Lombard Street and Threadneedle Street. Urban
'improvement', a contemporary goal, was seen with a range of

measures including improved street lighting and paving, fewer street and pavement obstacles and the numbering of houses. The City remained a significant centre for shopping which, in part, was an aspect of its wider commercial significance. Alongside markets, there were increasingly shops. Development reflected a qualitative change in the building industry, notably with a greater standardisation of construction methods and the organisation of building firms. Expansion and rebuilding were designed not only to provide housing and benefits for the affluent, but also for the bulk of the population with small, often wooden, houses replaced with brick terraces.

London was increasingly a cosmopolitan city, due to the reconceptualisation of Britain, a process registered by the Acts of Union with Scotland and Ireland. The Scots indeed arrived in London in considerable numbers. There were expressions of prejudice, but they lacked the tensions arising from the arrival of Irish migrants, many of whom were Catholic. A large number of the Irish migrants were also poor and congregated in the poorer end of town, notably in the St Giles 'rookery'. There were also more distinctive immigrant communities that contributed to the sense of London as 'foreign'. The location of these communities reflected the availability of property and work and the desire of immigrants to flock together and benefit from community networks: Huguenots focused in Spitalfields and Jews in Whitechapel. This situation added a new level of variety and complexity to the social differentiation of the city.

Alongside the grand buildings, this was London. It was a city where much of the modern world was already in evidence, not least the scale of life, with numbers, crowds, congestion and noise, as well as the attempt to define and implement civility, rationality, and order, as a way to cope with change and improve on it. Public museums, notably the British Museum, and a free press were part of the culture. Anonymous markets were crucial, not least in commerce and the arts, but participatory politics, social mobility and a specialisation in activity that centred for many on London, also moved in that direction.

After the crisis of the 1745–6 Jacobite rebellion, subsequent defeats for Britain did not threaten London in the same way and, alongside anxieties and difficulties, there was generally confident growth. Across the social spectrum, this engagement with change was a key aspect of the London experience, both in daily life and more generally. Being a Londoner required a particular type of resilience but also looked to the civic pride that was to become even stronger under the Victorians.

6

The Nineteenth Century: City of Power

....

'That phantom world which we see gibbering in the gaslight; flittering in the shadows of Westminster Abbey and among the trees of the Queen's Park; cowering in the bays of the bridges; brawling with tipsy revellers; shrieking in the stillness of the night; falling into fits on the pavement; struggling with the police; lurking on the bridges; hovering at corners; creeping by taverns.'

Charles Dickens, *Household Words*, October 1854

Until the Carnaby Street of the 1960s, and alongside images and experiences provided by war and royal occasions, key images of London were frequently Victorian. Charles Dickens and Jack the Ripper helped provide accounts of squalor and danger. These were both in practice partial views of London, but that was of limited consequence beside the ability of the world of print to disseminate such impressions. So also with the Sherlock Holmes stories. Moreover, these accounts circulated not only within the Anglosphere but also in the world as a whole. That helped make London more significant. It was not only the capital of the largest empire but also the centre of many spheres of informal influence. Alongside the physical communications structure, notably of docks and stations, came the post and telegraphy that moved ideas and literature.

By the early nineteenth century, new pressures and changes included an industrial world different to the manufacturing of a century earlier and with transport links to match. This was a world of new docks, and of iron railways, although not yet steam locomotives.

Yet, the central London that dominates the eye for travellers today, especially if looking above the shopfront level, is very much Victorian. Much of it is absolutely splendid, and notably so if recently freshened, such as the Waterhouse brick building on the north of Holborn or the St Pancras hotel. Other buildings are tired; for example, the hotel above Charing Cross Station, but it all contributes to the sense of a working city of depth, rather than a museum plaza of old buildings. The nineteenth century is most visible from Big Ben to Tower Bridge, and most important from sewers to tube lines. Indeed, the engineering of London is largely Victorian, one exemplified by the bridges and rail stations. And the twentieth century has built around this structure rather than suppressed it, and notably so in the central areas. Heathrow, the great twentieth-century addition, is off-stage.

Dramatically so with the Great Exhibition of 1851, London became the world city in the nineteenth century, thanks both to the growth of the Empire and that of the metropolis and its political, commercial and cultural centre. This was further marked by the commemoration in London of the splendour of triumph, with monuments to warriors – notably in Trafalgar Square – but also across central London. National greatness was also on display with new street names.

London, however, was no simple consumption centre of imperial greatness. It was also a place of enormous activity, one that was energised by the development of the docks and the creation of railways. Innovation was seen in all aspects, including the design of prisons. Yet, there was also terrible poverty.

Social Issues

The serial killings in Whitechapel in 1888 were only the most dramatic instance of a more general concern about London as a

Concern about the Poor

The Society for Bettering the Condition of the Poor noted of London in 1805:

'That many of the inhabitants of the more crowded parts of the metropolis suffer very severely under infectious fever ... that in many parts the habitations of the poor are never free from the febrile infection; there being not only courts and alleys, but some public buildings, in which it has continued for upwards of thirty years past; and that, by means of the constant and unavoidable communication which exists between the different classes of the inhabitants of the metropolis, and between the metropolis and other parts of the kingdom, this dreadful disease has frequently been communicated from the London poor to country places and to some of the more opulent families in the metropolis.

'... the parents [of Westminster] ... many of them are ignorant, and extremely ill-educated, while not a few are ... immoral and profligate ... [for London and its environs:] at least fifty thousand children are reared, and rearing up, every year, in the grossest ignorance and profligacy ... the morals of the inferior classes of society, particularly in the metropolis, are rapidly declining.'

Patrick Colquhoun JP,
*A New and Appropriate System of
Education for the Labouring Poor* (1806)

troubled world of misery and disorder. The flipside of its imperial greatness, this concern was frequently voiced in the press and was also the repeated subject of commentators. It overlapped with explicitly fictional accounts of the city, from Dickens to Doyle, most of which contributed to the same impression. In effect, London became the subject of social exploration, as by Henry Mayhew in a series of articles about the slums published in the *Morning Chronicle* in 1849 and then used in his *London Labour and the London Poor*. There were also visual accounts, notably by Gustave Doré. The Jack the Ripper killings of 1888 then proved an apparent culmination of a menace already seen in other episodes such as the garrotting scare of 1862. The resulting sense of menace was mocked in *Punch*'s cartoon 'Going Out to Tea in The Suburbs. A Pretty State of Things for 1862', which showed three young women escorted by six armed men.

The Song of the Garotter

'So meet me by moonlight alone,
Kind stranger, I beg and entreat,
And I'll make all your money my own,
And leave you half dead in the street.'

Punch 1862

There were obvious problems with the sources, not least the extent to which they depicted middle-class perceptions, and in a moralised fashion. Moreover, the argument that there was a criminal class separate to the working poor has been queried by those suggesting that much crime was a matter of necessity by the latter. Yet this approach has probably been taken too far, as there was not only criminality but also criminals. Violence, theft, abuse and alcoholism were all major problems while, alongside criminal networks, there was the often violent chaos of the street. Crime – which, in the case of the rich, included fraud and jerry-building – was not the sole challenge across society. Disease was another challenge due in part to the ease of infection, while poor relief served to link concerns about provision and cost, and notably so in periods of economic crisis such as the late 1810s.

The Great Stink

The heatwave of 1858 tipped the already noxious Thames – filled with sewage and animal carcases – into an even more overripe state, leading to the temporary abandonment of Parliament and to a major programme of sewerage. In 2021, marine archaeologists found a compacted layer of Victorian waste in the Thames near Tate Modern; the anaerobic environment of sewage, baked at the riverside in hot, dry weather had preserved the smell. A member of the Institute for Digital Archaeology referred to 'a very distinctive odour of putrefaction, human waste and sulphur . . . it's like a body blow when you smell it. It just stops you in your tracks.' The mud included the remains of leather shoes, pottery and clay pipes.

Downstream, the Victoria Embankment was built in 1862–70 as part of the transformation associated with Joseph Bazalgette, one that removed the broad tidal range as well as creating new road links along the river shores. On the opposite bank, the Battersea Marshes had been drained with the encouragement of Prince Albert and in accordance with legislation of 1846. Battersea Park opened in 1858, the same year as Chelsea Bridge. This brought a marginal area into regulation.

MIGRATION

The population grew rapidly, such that the percentage of that of England and Wales living in the capital rose from 12 per cent in 1801 to 15 per cent in 1891. Much of this growth was due to migration within the British Isles, including, from the late 1840s, Ireland. These people found particular problems from a Poor Law that provided a legal entitlement to individuals seeking relief from their parish, but not to non-settled applicants who could be removed to their home parishes. By the end of the century, London provided places for nearly a quarter of those on indoor relief (workhouses) in England and Wales, although negotiating skills were required to help applicants get the relief to which they were entitled.

At the same time, the costs of the Poor Law posed great pressure on many of the Poor Law unions, notably in the East End, where there were relatively low revenues but much need, in part due to the decline of shipbuilding on the Thames. This led, after much controversy, to redistribution by means of the creation – under the Metropolitan Poor Law Act of 1867 – of the Metropolitan Common Poor Fund, as well as the establishment of the Metropolitan Asylums.

Foreign trade and cosmopolitanism had been such facts of life for so long in London that, alongside prejudice, there was also tolerance and 'rubbing along'. Thus, after the War of American Independence, black Loyalists discharged in England settled in the East End, where a significant number took white wives and there was a good public response to the appeal for money to help poor blacks. In 1787, a settlement based on London's blacks was established at Freetown, Sierra Leone. The great majority of relevant London newspaper items were sympathetic in tone which suggests that racial hostility may have been less common than generally assumed. From the 1850s, a small African and Asian middle-class established itself, while Indian sailors settled in Dockland.

There was also immigration from elsewhere in Europe. Thus, large numbers of Russian and Polish Jews immigrated from the 1880s, until the Aliens Act of 1905 limited the flow. By the end of the nineteenth century, the number of Jewish immigrants in London had risen to equal that of the Irish but, by then, the latter appeared less alien, not least because they spoke English. Nevertheless, in court, Irish and Jewish people were likely to be suspected of criminality. Jewish communities focused on the East End, where the network of contacts and institutions established by recent Jewish immigrants encouraged fresh settlement. There was also Chinese immigration, especially to Dockland.

In part, notably with the Irish, London's growth was to some degree a matter of the imperial centre partly being taken over by immigrant groups from the Empire, as was more generally to be the case from the 1950s. Yet, immigrants also played a role in the developing energy of the Empire. Thus, in the 1880s and 1890s, Jewish immigrants used London as a base for benefiting from the production of gold and diamonds in South Africa. Alongside often complex cross-currents and interaction, there were common features of power and influence that were open to being penetrated by outside groups. This pattern has persisted into contemporary London, not least with the extensive role of the 'non-doms': non-domiciled foreign residents. Foreign influence took many forms, but was stronger in London than elsewhere in Britain. Thus, for food, London had French, Italian, German, Swiss-Italian, Indian and Chinese restaurants.

ECONOMY

London was a centre of technological development, not least in manufacturing. Aside from the New Albion Mill, steam also transformed newspaper production; in 1814 *The Times* announced, 'the greatest improvement connected with printing since the discovery of the art itself', as it switched to a steam-powered press, allowing the production of a thousand impressions an hour, as opposed to the 250 hourly from an unmechanised hand-press. Prefiguring the move of *The Times* to new production facilities in Wapping in 1986, the machinery used in 1814 was secretly prepared to prevent the opposition of workers, who had already mounted a strike in 1810.

Manufacturing continued to be important throughout the century, providing employment and profit that, in turn, fostered demand elsewhere in the economy. The concentration of activity proved beneficial for both the industrial and service sectors, and contributed to the presence of specialised industrial districts. Adaptability included the response late in the century to advances in retailing by means of the production of branded goods, which proved a way to provide scale in consumer-led industries.

London was also a centre of innovation in transportation, from the development of large-scale passenger train and omnibus services to that of the underground. Steam power made the headlines, but London's market was already the cause and beneficiary of major improvements, both in shipping services and in those on roads. Thus, the productivity of road freight rose with the cutting of journey times through night-running, which became more significant in the early nineteenth century, a period also of continuing road improvements.

The docks, where the foreign immigrants arrived, were a dramatic demonstration of London's global sway, and one that became steadily more impressive during the century, with no other place in the world matching London's capability. It was also a major centre of employment as, more generally, was the commercial world. Thus, in the early nineteenth century, the largest warehouse labour force in London was that of the East India Company, with over three thousand permanent labourers at its peak. As a whole, dock labour, in contrast, was casual, which increased the strains of income and life. Unskilled labour suffered particularly hard. There was also perpetual tension over discipline and pilfering. Dockland was very different to Whitehall or the City as an area of London as an imperial centre, but it was equally important. It was also more multicultural than any other part of London.

Turmoil in the Docks

'On Wednesday, Mr Yardley, the magistrate at the Thames police court, was engaged for several hours in the investigation of charges of assaulting, wounding and using threatening language, preferred against dock labourers, connected with the late strike for an increase of wages. The persons charged were, with one exception, Irishmen; and some of the assaults proved to have been committed by them were of the most savage description.'

Bell's Weekly Messenger, 13 August 1853

The Thames, however, was less important than hitherto for its shipbuilding centred on Poplar and Deptford. The switch from timber was important as Britain had major competitive advantages for ships built of iron and powered by coal but, although iron shipbuilding at Millwall and Blackwall flourished in mid-century, this development led to a new geography of shipbuilding, with the focus on the Clyde, the Tyne and the Wear, each near centres of iron-working. Warships were, however, still being built in London in the 1870s, including for the Brazilian and Ottoman navies. The city's shipbuilding was also hit by the higher costs of industry in London, including wages and overheads. This decline was of wider significance for London's economy as it meant that it would not benefit from a heavy industry in which Britain led the world into the next century. The knock-on impact was also significant. Shipyards employed large numbers of people, as did ancillary concerns, such as engine-makers and steelworks. Thus, London's downriver was not to be a centre of heavy industry. Had it done so, then the political complexion of the city might have been very different, with a much stronger hard-left component.

Returning to the Thames, a cosmopolitan maritime population – Chinese, Lascars (Indians), Americans, Europeans – crowded the dock front, embarking on, or disembarking from, vessels. This was very much an environment moulded by man. In 1913, Arthur Sarsfield, a London crime reporter who, under the pseudonym Sax Rohmer, published the successful novel *The Mystery of Fu Manchu*, about a sinister Chinese master-criminal based in Limehouse, described a journey down the Thames, the 'oily glitter of the tide' and 'on the Surrey shore a blue light ... flicked translucent tongue against the night's curtain ... a gasworks'. The pollution noted by Sax Rohmer had ended the fishing industry on the Thames in the 1820s.

Alongside its significance for commerce, and for raising funds for overseas enterprises, notably railways, the responsibility of the London service sector for the wider character and subsequent problems of the British economy has been much debated. Management failure has been linked to mistaken investment strategies and it has been argued that the institutional providers of investment in the City, especially the banks, shared in a culture of complacency and gentlemanly amateurism. This problem has been traced to a series of interrelated cultural norms and practices, such as a suspicion of expertise and technical skills that inhibited efficiency and encouraged mistaken patterns of investment. London, indeed, was the prime site of what has been called 'gentlemanly investment', but these criticisms are difficult to prove or quantify.

More specifically, it has been suggested that there was a preference for investing in well-established companies rather than in developing sectors. Risk or venture capital was thus insufficient and too expensive: interest rates were too high. Furthermore, aside from this pattern of industrial investment, there was also a preference for non-industrial investment, both on the 'money markets', for example in British and foreign government bonds, and in housing. Even when there was investment in industry – old or new – much of it was poorly directed because of an absence of sufficient professionalism in information flows within the capital market. Moreover, much investment was short-term, responding to institutional shareholders unwilling to commit sufficiently to long-term investments. Similar charges were to be made about the City in the late twentieth century and early twenty-first. In contrast, it has been suggested that American and German capital markets were more effective in providing large flows of investment income for technologically advanced industries before World War One, such as cars, chemicals and electrical engineering.

More positively, the combination of London's money and capital markets and the international links of British banks were unmatched. So it was also with the diversity and functional specialisation of London's financial sector, a situation that helped provide a basis for positive responses to change. Banking clearing associations – notably the Committee of London Clearing Banks – ensured orderly payments, stability and a measure of regulation. Policies over deposit and lending rates were cautious and competition limited, which helped ensure stability.

An emphasis on employment in industry, finance and trade runs the risk of failing to note the scale and range of jobs in the service economy, notably domestic servants, but also occupations ranging from doctors to milliners. Some of these jobs sustained London's high average wages and others serviced the consequences, while the variety of the service economy also reflected the availability of casual and inexpensive labour. The combination of this service sector with manufacturing provided London with a greater economic resilience than that of economic zones heavily dependent on only one particular sector. In 1899, London County Council (LCC) observers reported that about 10 per cent of commuters on the early-morning workmen's trains were women.

Railway Stations

Although London was the key centre of England's new rail network, it suffered, like Paris, from the lack of through-routes or a central station. This lack can be seen as a failure of planning akin to that after the Great Fire of 1666, but massive disruption would have been caused by such construction and schemes such as that of 1851 by Charles Pearson, Solicitor to the City Corporation, for a hundred–foot-wide tunnel with eight sets of tracks were not viable. As it was, there was massive demolition in the construction of London's stations, culminating with Marylebone, the last of the termini, which led to the destruction of Blandford Square. Shifts and expedients were significant with battles between English and Irish workmen at London Bridge where expenditure on the line itself meant that station buildings came later.

As part of the process by which the Victorian building of London continued, some termini did not last. Opened in 1858, Pimlico was a temporary, wooden structure made redundant when the Victoria Railway Bridge, the first dedicated railway bridge across the Thames, instead made more central Victoria possible. The twelve termini that remain today were opened between 1836 and 1899. They are a legacy of Victoriana, like so much else in 'modern' Britain. Some were truly impressive. At St Pancras, M. H. Barlow used what was, at nearly 250 feet wide, then the largest single-span structure in the world to cover the station's platforms, with a basement underneath with 800 cast-iron columns both supporting the station floor and storing beer from Burton-on-Trent.

Very differently, railway viaducts ensured that Londoners became used to operating 'under the arches', for example in Borough market.

ENVIRONMENT

The massive increase in the population, from one million in 1801 to 2.4 million in 1851 and six million in 1901, led to the extensive physical expansion satirically captured in the bombardment of the countryside in George Cruickshank's caricature *The March of Bricks and Mortar* (1829) and one that was to be taken forward far faster as a result of the coming of commuting by train. In *Trial by Jury* (1875), the description of Peckham as an 'Arcadian vale' got a laugh from the audience.

In addition to the energy of the secular owners of land ripe for development, the Church Commissioners, from the 1850s, in collaboration with private developers pursued a shrewd development policy – for instance in Hornsey and Finchley to ensure good-quality housing, and therefore a high rental income. In Crouch End, development was delayed to the same end. This rental strategy remained in place until the late twentieth century when the freeholds were sold off.

One response to the expansion of the built-up area was the open spaces movement from the 1840s. This had many aspects, notably the creation of Victoria Park, continuing with Hampstead Heath, the Commons south of the Thames, the saving of the City graveyards as open spaces, Epping Forest and municipal parks, and culminating in the saving of Kenwood from development in the 1920s. There were often far from altruistic politics behind these superficially grand generous gestures.

Growth was accompanied by a specialisation of usage that led the City to become a financial area, *Building News* declaring in 1857: 'Except for business purposes, the City may be said to be now uninhabited.' Indeed, the City of London Poor Law Union was the richest and least populated of all the metropolitan Poor Law districts. The 1851 census showed only 127,000 inhabitants of the City, many small tradesmen or junior clerks. The situation was bridged by large-scale commuting from Greater London. In contrast to that, no inland town in the South-East had a population of more than 50,000 in 1901.

The Railway Brings Development

Comprised of villages on the old Roman road of Ermine Street, Tottenham was largely farmland and marshland until the railway came in 1840 with stations at Tottenham Hale and Marsh Lane. In 1872, a different line with a station at Bruce Grove brought cheap workmen's fares and Tottenham grew rapidly, helped by the Cheap Trains Act of 1883. Commuters could go to Dockland or central London.

For both the expanded city and for the existing cityscape, there was acute pressure across the full range of economic and social provision and on living standards. Housing was a particularly acute problem, but so also were sanitation, education and law and order. Sanitation fed back into the very dynamics of population growth, and not least because of exposure to disease from elsewhere in the world. Other major problems included the lack of clean water, as well as air pollution – notably in forms of smoke and fog. The water question, which was in part one of sewage, was addressed head on due to its linkage with disease. In contrast, fog and smoke were not really addressed until the mid-twentieth century. Respiratory deaths in the winter reflected the impact of air pollution from coal fires. Furthermore, diarrhoeal infant mortality in the summer was an aspect of the continuing problems with clean water. Poverty and overcrowding both remained serious problems.

Sanitation was also an issue with the large numbers of horses required to move people and goods, such that by the 1890s, about a thousand tons of dung was being deposited daily, as well as

---

Fog

In 1888, Henry James, an American settler, praised the 'magnificent mystifications' of London's fog, which 'flatters and superfuses, makes everything brown, rich, dim, vague, magnifies distances and minimises details, confirms the inference of vastness by suggesting that, as the great city makes everything, it makes it own optical laws'.

The 1880s saw the most acute fogs, but the growth in population and fuel consumption had led to air pollution becoming more acute from the early century and in 1853 the Smoke Nuisance Abatement Act was aimed at a phenomenon vividly described that year in Dickens' *Bleak House*. Inspection and enforcement made regulation difficult, but legislation anyway excluded the households where inefficient coal-fed open fires produced what was to be called smog from 1904. Londoners preferred the term fog and saw it as part of their identity. Brilliantly captured by painters such as Claude Monet, fog provided opportunities for crime, causes of accidents and helped prostitutes by both providing cover from the police and making cautious clients readier to make an approach.

---

much urine. As a result, London smelled and was extremely messy and crossing-sweepers were necessary. The internal combustion engine ended this menace.

The bridges owed much to the talent of John Rennie, whose career reflected the ability of London to attract able individuals, as well as the extent to which it was a centre of national and international enterprise. Scottish-born and educated, Rennie (1761–1821) came to London in 1784 to take charge of the works at the Albion Flour Mill, where he designed the steam machinery. Rennie then founded an engineering firm at Holland Street, Blackfriars, the base for work in London and elsewhere on docks, canals and bridges, including the London, East and West India docks and Waterloo, London and Southwark bridges. He was buried in St Paul's. His eldest and second sons, George (1791–1866) and John (1794–1874), took over the business and their many works included the construction of London Bridge, for which John was knighted. Opened in 1831, the new London Bridge had fewer arches, which speeded up the Thames. This ensured that it did not freeze up, as it had done from the 1550s with major frost fairs – that of 1715–16 lasted nearly three months.

Politics

Yet, at the same time, there were serious uncertainties both about how to manage a city unprecedented in extent, population, wealth and growth and concerning the very consequences of this growth. In practice, a turn to violence on the part of radicals was far less common than the attempt to press for change while observing the constraints of the political system. This attempt was also one seen with governmental moves which, again, in large part reflected existing structures. Thus, the foundation of the Metropolitan Police in 1829 provided a key level of cohesion in policy, although, at the same time, this primarily represented rationalisation, standardisation, nationalisation and centralisation, as most London parishes already had professional police, in large part due to concern about property crime.

John Nash

Much of the shaping of inner London moved to pre-railway completion thanks to the work of John Nash (1752–1835), especially Regent's Street and the construction of Regent's Park. The names Regent's Street and Regent's Park reflected the patronage of George, Prince of Wales,

---

Prince Regent from 1811 to 1820, later George IV, although the key element in patronage increasingly was the support of a wide tranche of society. George's support for Nash's work of town building, notably the 'Royal Way' to join the new Regent's Park to the new palace at Carlton Terrace, had a significant impact on Londoners and one that remains to this day, notably with the sweep of Regent Street and the Nash terraces in Regent's Park. The extent to which earlier property rights alongside the extent of Crown land still had to be heeded is demonstrated by All Souls, Langham Place, built in 1822–4, a product of the impact on Nash's plans of his inability to continue the northward sweep of Regent Street as he wished. Nevertheless, it proved easier in the West End to achieve vistas than those planned but not realised in the rebuilding of the City after the Great Fire of 1666. Moreover, the new works were made attractive by extensive street lighting, with the earliest gas lamps installed in 1807. George's death in 1830 led to Nash taking the blame for the cost of building Buckingham Palace and he was sacked. William IV chose not to live in the palace and preferred, instead, to reside in Clarence House, which was more modest. Indeed, he proposed to the Duke of Wellington that the palace be converted into a barracks. Nash's design was not suitable for a populist monarchy which required a central, visible balcony and this was provided by Sir Edward Blore under Queen Victoria. In 1847, he designed the facade facing the Mall.

Nash's town-building captured the exuberance of the world city of the age, the capital of the leading empire and the setting for an energetic and questing society. It opened up areas for the expansion and redefinition of London, as with the foundation of the Zoo in Regent's Park in 1828.

The policing of London took many forms. The older moral dimension offered by the church had gone, being further weakened in the 1820s as Catholic and Nonconformist legal constraints were removed. Instead, the state extended controls in an episodic fashion. Concern over radicalism led to upsurges in particular periods, notably the 1790s and late 1810s, but often, it was the repeated nature of injunctions that captured their weakness or, rather, being part of a range of controls that rarely led to systematic action. This was the case, for example, with attempts to control the unlicensed theatres (and their democratic tone) which, in practice, increased greatly in number, as well as the 1824 Vagrancy Act which was designed to limit street performers.

The pressure for electoral reform that culminated in the Great or First Reform Act, passed in 1832 by the Whigs, did not lead in London to the violence seen in Bristol, Derby and Nottingham. In the 1831 general election, all the four MPs elected from the City were keen supporters of the reform legislation. The 1832 Act fixed a uniform right to vote in the boroughs – all men occupying property, either by owning or renting, worth ten pounds per annum – which brought the franchise to the 'middle class','as a result of which London had a large electorate. There were also five new constituencies: Tower Hamlets, Finsbury, Marylebone, Southwark and Lambeth, which ensured that London was less underrepresented than it had been prior to 1832, although it still had too few MPs for both its population and its electorate.

This reform did not alter the way in which London was covered. Indeed, for some years the pace of the city's development was scarcely matched by that of governmental mechanisms. The City Corporation and Livery Companies saw scant change and, indeed, both became somewhat divorced from business. Thus, of the 337 members of the Haberdashers' Company whose trade can be identified in 1837, only five described themselves as haberdashers. The City was untouched by the Municipal Corporations Act of 1835 and attempts to establish a London-wide elected authority failed.

Change only really came with the establishment in 1855 of the Metropolitan Board of Works (MBW) – a nominated, London-wide body designed to provide infrastructure – which took over the responsibilities of the Metropolitan Buildings Office established in 1845, and the Metropolitan Commission of Sewers which followed in 1848. The engineer with the latter from 1852, Joseph Bazalgette, was a key figure in the new body; indeed, he was Chief Engineer of the MBW until it was replaced by the LCC in 1889 and he transformed the sewerage system, ending cholera and cutting typhus and typhoid.

Meanwhile, London had not been a centre of turmoil compared to that of European cities, especially during the Year of Revolutions, 1848. There was a mass demonstration, but Chartism in London was non-violent. Thereafter, moreover, there was a generally peaceful London. Officially opened in 1852, the new Houses of Parliament were seen as a stabilising force.

Control in the capital was a matter not of violent contests for political control, but of law and order, with policing a major government tool in the attempt to maintain it. Urban planning was another: this involved opening up the city in order to clear away what was seen as the dirt of the past and, instead, permit the circulation of people and goods and the dissemination of progress. Building Charing Cross Road and Shaftesbury Avenue involved major disruption and the displacement of many people.

With Kingsway, the driving-through of the road was deliberately intended to destroy a neighbourhood judged criminal, degenerate and out of control: twenty-eight acres were cleared in 1900–5 to make way for that road and the Aldwych; it was a hugely expensive scheme. The LCC (London County Council), established in 1889, played a major role in the Kingsway project, not least as its powers were necessary to accomplish it. Slum clearance was not only undertaken for the sake of new roads, with the LCC building the Boundary Street Estate in what had been a slum section of Bethnal Green, as well as the Millbank Estate on the site of the Millbank Penitentiary. The LCC provided a degree of authority, cohesion and finance lacking from the Metropolitan Board of Works. It was part of the major 'churn' of London in the years before World War One.

Alongside housing estates such as Latchmere in Battersea, the LCC also sought to develop estates outside the congested areas of London, both in order to tackle overcrowding and to improve health. This was an attempt at regulation: parks but not pubs or cookshops were planned in what was intended as a means to pass middle-class values to the working class. From the 1900s, estates were accordingly developed in Wandsworth, Norbury and Tottenham, although most working-class housing was provided by private landlords.

Housing remained a prime area of social and spatial differentiation and became more so as a result of suburbanisation and the many differences this reflected and gave rise to. Transport was another key element in both social and spatial identity and differentiation with the various classes of tickets carrying specific costs and also being linked to a measure of separation. William Birt, the General Manager of the Great Eastern Railway, explained the timing of the cheaper workmen's trains with reference to the concerns of middle-class female shoppers about workers who 'smoke a good deal, and in smoking they are apt to spit, and the platforms get in a very filthy state'.

RELIGION

The reform of ecclesiastical provision was driven forward by anxiety about godlessness. Indeed, in 1828, when Charles Blomfield became Bishop of London at a time of marked challenge from Catholicism and Nonconformity, he pressed for the building of fifty churches, funded by the government in order to deal with the growth of London and concerns about the lack of religious

---

Walking for Purpose

'The different appearance of the streets of London and Paris is the first thing to strike a stranger. In the gayest and most crowded streets of London the people move steadily and rapidly along, with a grave collected air, as if all had some business in view.'

Anna Jameson, *The Diary of an Ennuyée* (1826)

The human response was seen as a key element in improving the environment. Moreover, in responding, individuals displayed their moral qualities. Thus, the stride which became increasingly significant from the mid-1820s was seen as more purposeful, healthy and safe than the then fashionable lounge, as well as making possible following a 'straight and narrow path of godly self-control'.

---

commitment, apparent commitment or – at least – godly living of much of its population. Separately, the Charlotte Street Chapel in Bloomsbury was built in the 1770s as an Anglican proprietary chapel funded by ticket sales from sermons, and many Methodist chapels were built on such ticket sales.

Quantity appeared a key desideratum in facing the challenge of change. Already there had been some provision of new churches, as with Sir John Soane's St Peter's, Walworth (1823–4). The 1818 Church Building Act, which granted public money to a new Church Building Commission, led to an increase in the pace of building, but one that was opposed by Dissenters as well as by ratepayers concerned about their contribution. Indeed, the cost of the new church at St Pancras led to particular bitterness. Church building, however, continued. In the 1830s, Pennethorne designed churches in Albany Street and Gray's Inn Road. Later in the century, social missions to the East End were an aspect of religious provision, as with Oxford House from which Sunday afternoon lectures were given in Victoria Park, Bethnal Green.

The Ecclesiastical Commissioners took over the management of the Bishop of London's estates in the mid-1850s, as land developers and house builders as well as church builders. Many London roads were named after Earl Stanhope, an early First Church Commissioner.

ARCHITECTURE

The most dramatic building of the period can only be glimpsed through illustrations. Visited by six million, the hugely bold Crystal Palace that housed the Great Exhibition in Hyde Park in 1851 was, with its standardised and prefabricated sections of glass and iron, a trailblazer of industrial design. Rebuilt in Sydenham in 1853-4, albeit far bigger than the original, it was accompanied by impressive gardens, including life-size models of dinosaurs. A popular destination for Londoners with, for example, a brass band festival in 1900, the palace burned down in 1936.

In the twentieth century, especially during the post-1945 Modernist vogue, Victorian architecture was much castigated and many buildings were destroyed, neglected or left stranded amid a new world of concrete and cars. Those demolished included the Coal Exchange and the Entrance Arch at Euston Station, while the Midland Hotel at St Pancras was left to rot, until restored in the twenty-first century as a giant apartment complex and hotel. Nevertheless, a large amount of Victorian architecture survives in Central London and these buildings remain an aspect of the culture that can be readily appreciated.

The early decades of the nineteenth century witnessed a variety of styles. Neoclassicism was particularly important. The Neoclassicism of the late eighteenth century drew heavily on Roman models, but that of the early nineteenth was dominated by Greek Revival; for example, the Doric and Ionic Orders.

Architects such as William Wilkins, Robert Smirke, C. R. Cockerell and H. W. Inswood all made lengthy trips to Greece.

Neo-Gothic was also highly influential, especially in ecclesiastical architecture, while the case was pushed hard by Augustus Pugin (1812–52), an architect who saw Gothic as the quintessentially Christian style. His arguments and designs hit home at the right moment as, after a long period in which relatively few new churches had been constructed, there was a period of massive church-building. This church building owed much to London's geographical expansion and, as an instance of a more general pressure for urban renewal, to a determination to resist what many at the time saw as 'Godless London'. Meanwhile, Catholic Emancipation in 1829 was followed by the building of many Catholic churches. Influential architects in the Gothic Revival included George Gilbert Scott, William Butterfield, G. E. Street, Norman Shaw and Alfred Waterhouse. They were active in building and 'restoring' churches. Butterfield's work includes All Saints, Margaret Street (1859). There was also much secular building in the Gothic style, especially from the 1850s as it replaced Greek Revival. Thus, Scott's work included the massive Midland Hotel at St Pancras Station (1865–71) and the Albert Memorial (1863), while other prominent buildings included G. E. Street's Law Courts (1874–82) and Waterhouse's Holborn headquarters for the Prudential Assurance Company (1895–1905). A form of Gothic was seen in the rebuilding of Borough Market in 1851–64.

Yet Gothic Revival did not enjoy an unchallenged ascendancy. Displaying the eclecticism that was a feature of the period, Sir Charles Barry (1795–1860) worked in both Gothic (Houses of Parliament, finished in 1860) and Greek Revival styles, but also developed a neo-Renaissance style, using Italian *palazzi* as models. This neo-Renaissance style was also employed by other architects, such as Gilbert Scott in his Foreign Office building. These grand buildings were central to the competition between the leading European cities as, in the full glare of publicity, they vied to hold the best exhibitions, build the most glorious monuments, develop the most impressive infrastructure and so on.

Architecture and construction also entailed functionalism; railways and other examples of new industrial technology brought a requirement for buildings – and in new forms. Railway stations and, more generally, iron-fronted commercial and industrial premises also recorded and helped popularise new styles. Thus, the east and west buildings of Smithfield Market were finished in 1868 at a cost of nearly £1 million. Functionalism took many forms. Large numbers of buildings were built for cultural ends, including museums, libraries and theatres. Indeed, by 1914 there were about five hundred theatres with a potential nightly audience of 400,000–500,000. In turn, this accentuated London's regional influence, as many customers arrived by rail. The Central Criminal Court – known as the Old Bailey after the street in which it was built – contains not only eighteen courtrooms, but also Dead Man's Walk, the route to the gallows, which was designed with arches becoming progressively smaller in order to stop the prisoners looking back. To glimpse different lives, or at least the processes of the law, it is interesting today to visit the courtrooms during trials. Demolished in 1904, Newgate Prison provided space for expansion.

The Old Bailey is an aspect of the institutional legacy of this period that remains important to London today. So also with the annual Proms series of classical music concerts which, thanks to the conductor Henry Wood and the impresario Robert Newman, began life at Queen's Hall in Langham Place in 1895. Opened in 1901, Whitechapel has an art gallery which has received less attention than Jack the Ripper and his 1888 attacks. The institutional legacy is also seen in education. Thus, the London School of Economics was founded in 1905, in part thanks to help from the LCC while, three years earlier, the LCC and the University of London founded the London Day Training College to provide elementary teachers, which became the Institute of Education.

Building for Leisure

Much of the built legacy of the Victorian period arises from the entrepreneurial response to the possibilities of greater leisure and more purchasing power. A wide range of sports was catered for. Alongside the obvious – notably football grounds – this included the London County Grounds, the track of the London County Cycling and Athletic Club in Herne Hill, opened in 1891 and now the Herne Hill Velodrome. It enjoyed rapid popularity. Founded in 1868, 'The All England Croquet Club' played lawn tennis from 1876 and an inaugural Wimbledon Championship the following year. In 1884, a ladies singles competition was added. The club moved to its present site in Church Road in 1922.

TRANSFORMATION

The legacies of sewerage and transport systems which made London's rising population easier to service are key elements of continuation from the Victorians. At the same time, the changes were scarcely problem-free. Aside from the disruption of construction, there were disputes over costs; for example, for water. Indeed, due to the ambitious nature of public policy, spending levels in London were higher than elsewhere, at about £232 per one hundred inhabitants in 1897–8, which was 50 per cent greater than in the county boroughs. In particular, London expenditure on roads and police was higher, due largely to the volume of services provided. London's much higher rateable values, however, ensured that the resulting rates per head were lower. The complaints that focused on the Royal Commission on the Duties of the Metropolitan Police of 1906–8 revealed, nevertheless, that low-level corruption, not least demanding money from prostitutes, was an aspect of this policing.

Transport developed rapidly to provide for the unprecedented numbers, not least as this was no longer a city that could be readily crossed on foot. Initially steam-powered when it opened in 1863, providing a link between Paddington and Farringdon, the underground rail system changed to electricity. It also received the royal imprimatur. In 1900, the Central London Railway from Shepherd's Bush via the West End to the Bank of England was opened by Edward, Prince of Wales who, in 1901, as Edward VII, went on to drive by car from London to Windsor. Horse-drawn trams and buses were switching over to new power sources. The Lots Road power station in Chelsea was built to provide the electricity for the tube lines.

Government was a major provider of facilities, but many other services emerged from developments in the private sector, both to serve the market of a far larger population and also to adapt to its differentiation and changing requirements. Thus, the fish and chip industry developed in London with the sale of fried fish from the 1830s. Yet, the result was gruelling work.

Praising the Tube

Robert Lowe, a Liberal politician, spoke at the lunch served on Farringdon station on 9 January 1863 to mark the opening of tube services:

'The traffic of London has long been a reproach of the most civilised nation of the world and the opprobrium of the age. Dr Johnson used to say that if you wanted to see the full tide of human life, you must go to Charing Cross, but Dr Johnson would have to raise his estimation of the full tide, or rather of the close jam of the full tide of human life, many hundred per cent before he could arrive at the state which the traffic of London has now reached . . . Through gas-pipes and water-pipes and sewers . . . and . . . the Fleet Ditch . . . The line has had to worm its way through a complicated and intricate labyrinth under difficulties almost insuperable.'

London Childhoods

Arthur Morrison's *A Child of the Jago* (1896) was a bestselling novel about children growing up in the Old Nichol slum behind Shoreditch High Street in the East End. It showed it as a dog-eat-dog world, full of parental neglect and police corruption, with crime, poverty, poor health and murders. Morrison was insistent that the book was entirely based on fact. The protagonist, Dicky Perrott, is corrupted by his upbringing and fatally injured during a gang brawl, as the real-life Charles Clayton, who inspired the incident, was in 1892.

Jipping Street (1928) by Kathleen Woodward (1896–1961) covers her early years in South London. Born into a very poor family, the story is of a child obliged to begin factory work at twelve and then to leave home at thirteen for another factory job north of the river.

In part due to a real fear of revolution, the state of the working class was a matter of continuing concern, not least also as Social Darwinism made an apparent threat to health, morality and order appear a challenge to the city as a whole and thus to the country. The Royal Commission of 1884–5 concluded, that despite improvements, 'the evils of overcrowding, especially in London' continued to be 'a public scandal'. There was still much for reformers to address. This, indeed, was a goal for both the rival groups in the LCC – the Progressives, who were in control between 1898 and 1907 and the Moderates, later called the Municipal Reformers. In addition, even Conservative vestries and boroughs, such as Hornsey, created council housing estates from the 1890s, some built in Arts and Crafts style. In large part, the reforming drive reflected concern about social problems and allegedly related political and moral consequences. It also entailed an emulation of the civic culture that had enjoyed stronger municipal coherence over recent decades in Manchester, Leeds and Birmingham. At the same time, the presence of Westminster and of high society meant that the politics of the LCC did not set a civic culture comparable to those cities. London remained highly distinctive in very many respects.

'The Battle of Edmonton', 1899

'Half a loaf, half a ham,
Sandwich-men onward!
Into the railway yard
Edmonton thundered;
Up by the workmen's train
More than six hundred!'

'Star', in the *Enfield Chronicle* of 17 February 1899, riffed on Tennyson's 'Charge of the Light Brigade' in describing disturbances in Edmonton and Liverpool Street stations over the failure of the Great Eastern Railway to provide sufficient tickets for the last workmen's morning train, a cheaper early-morning service. Food was thrown at the police. By 1914, legislation passed, against the wishes of the railway companies, had ensured that a thousand cut-price trains daily were taking workers into London.

7

From Edwardian Triumph to Giant Bombsite

....

'[Inspector] French, thinking of his recent job at Whitechapel . . .
the dreadful, sordid streets of London's slums.'

Freeman Wills Crofts, *The Hog's Back Mystery* (1933)

'The general spectre of destitution that spoils a man's
pleasure so often in a London scene was absent.'

Anne Meredith, *Portrait of a Murderer* (1933)

The massive expansion of suburbia was the most obvious
impact of these years on the London area. This was far more so
indeed than the bombing which caused such destruction,
notably in the part of London built prior to the 1880s, during
World War Two (1939–45) and which was responsible for some
of the iconic images of the city, notably that of flames surrounding St Paul's.

Conditions of Fitness

The design standards and operating conditions for London
taxis were laid out in 1906 by the Public Carriage Office,
then part of the Metropolitan Police. The first horseless cab
had appeared in 1897 but the last horse-drawn cab was not
removed from service until 1947. Compulsory in 1907, the
taximeter gave rise to the name taxi.

WORLD WAR ONE

Bombing was already a factor in World War One (1914–18), when German Zeppelin airships and, later, aircraft raids concentrated on London. The impact on society, especially with the blackouts used to make German night-time targeting harder, helped underline the 'total' character of the war, in the shape of its direct consequences for civilian life, as opposed to the losses to families and communities experienced at the Front. John Monash, an Australian army commander, wrote back to his wife in 1916:

'You can hardly imagine what the place is like. The Zeppelin scare is just like as if the whole place was in imminent fear of an earthquake. At night, the whole of London is in *absolute darkness* . . . Nothing is going on – in the shops, in the streets, anywhere – that has not a direct bearing on the war.'

Following up the Zeppelins, the Germans launched aircraft attacks in 1917 because they wrongly believed – possibly due to reports by Dutch intelligence – that the British public were on the edge of rebellion. The first (and deadliest) raid was in daylight on 13 June 1917, in which fourteen planes killed 162 people and injured 432, not least as a result of a direct hit on a school that killed sixteen children. This raid led to a public outcry as well as much talk of London being in the front line and was met by the speedy development of a defensive system involving high-altitude fighters, based on airfields linked by telephone to observers. This response led to heavy casualties among the German Gotha bombers, and to the abandonment of daylight raids.

More seriously, the rationale of the German air campaign was misplaced because, far from sapping British morale, the bombing led to a resolute popular response. This position remained the case even in the winter of 1917–18, when the Germans unleashed four-engine Zeppelin-Staaken R-series bombers. The alarm raised in sections of civil society by air

attacks, nevertheless, encouraged post-war theorists to empha-
sise the potential of air power, which led to fear about the consequences for London of any future war. This led to the mass
evacuation of children in 1939, as well as the preparation of a
large number of coffins.

Londoners had been more seriously, if indirectly, threatened
in World War One by the German submarine (U-boat) assault on
Britain's maritime supply routes. They shared this challenge with
the rest of the United Kingdom, but were also particularly affected
due to London's role in maritime trade and total dependence on
food grown elsewhere.

The shape and activity of the city was affected by the war,
notably with the growth of munitions production and military
hospitals on the edge of the city, for example in Enfield. Each
tended to be concentrated on new sites, although Woolwich
Arsenal grew to employ 75,000 by the end of the war and cover
1,285 acres. As a more general impact, the pace of pre-war residential development and of the improvement of the transport
infrastructure both slowed greatly or stopped during the war.
Subsequently, the legacy of the war included the many memor-
ials that added to London's commemorative landscape, notably
the Cenotaph erected in Whitehall. As with much in London that
had local significance, it was also national and imperial in its
origins, role and resonance.

Pie and Mash Shops

Across Britain, savoury pies were a key form of working-
class food. In London, pie and mash was an important
dish, the pie commonly filled with mutton or beef within a
pastry crust. Originally sold from carts or braziers, shops
were used from the 1840s. Stewed eels were also frequently
sold.

EXPANSION

World War One did not have an impact on London comparable to that which stemmed from the expansion of suburbia. In his *England and the Octopus* (1928), the architect Clough Williams-Ellis berated builders and planners for their destruction of the country-side and what he called 'the common background of beauty'. In the case of London, unprecedented expansion amounted to a vast new city in its spreading suburbia, a city that was far greater in scale than the 'garden cities', such as Letchworth, built in the country-side. Helped by lax planning regulations, as well as the break-up of aristocratic estates – in part due to death duties (which also led to the sale of London properties) – the low price of land and the post-war agricultural depression which encouraged farmers to sell land in order to survive, London became Greater London. Indeed, in the inter-war years (1918–39), Greater London housed, and thus provided for, more than one third of the population increase of the whole of England and Wales.

Between 1921 and 1937, on the other hand, despite immigra-tion – for example, by Greek Cypriots, a newly prominent group – the population of inner London fell by nearly half a million. There were particularly steep falls – of over 16 per cent – in the City (the largest percentage fall), Stepney, Poplar, Bethnal Green, Shoreditch, Finsbury, Holborn, Southwark, Bermondsey and Camberwell. The housing in much of this area was old, lacking in what were by then considered basic amenities – notably running water and electricity – and, frequently, relied on shared cooking and washing facilities. In turn, the growth of municipal housing outside this inner area, combined with changing labour markets, was important in these falls, which interacted with a transform-ation in the culture of working-class communities, not least as those who were successful moved to suburbia. Within the LCC area, only Hampstead, Wandsworth, Lewisham and Woolwich had an increase in population.

In contrast, the population of Greater London, the area covered by the Metropolitan Police District, grew from about 7.25 million in 1911 to about 8.7 million in 1939, forming about a fifth of the nation's population. Although a continuance of the pre-1914 trend, this was a greater percentage than that in earlier ages, although it is important to note that the Metropolitan Police District was larger than what became Greater London after 1965 with the formation of the Greater London Council, as the district includes substantial areas of what are still Surrey, Hertfordshire and other neighbouring counties. London's relative importance in the inter-war years owed something to the economic decline that hit much of Britain in the 1930s. Thus, many people moved from South Wales to the London area. Particularly marked inter-war rises occurred in Harrow, Hornchurch, Romford, Hendon, Epsom, Ewell, Chislehurst, Sidcup and Bexley. The influence of London between the wars was felt further afield, as people commuted long distances. Population growth was no less rapid in places such as Woking, Brentwood, Watford and Maidenhead, which lay well beyond any administrative definition of Greater London.

TRANSPORT

Physically, the city sprang forward a long way; for example, from Hampstead to Edgware. To support this spreading city, the underground railway system became a widespread overground to the west, north and east of London; and, to a limited extent, also to the south of the Thames. The surface lines (as opposed to the 'tube' – the bored tunnels) were already well into the country by 1914. The first post-war extension into greenfield areas was the Northern Line extension to Edgware in 1923–4, a project supported by Treasury money to help reduce unemployment. This was followed by the Metropolitan Line to Watford, Amersham and Uxbridge in 1925, the Metropolitan (later Bakerloo and then Jubilee) to Stanmore in 1932, the Piccadilly to Cockfosters in 1933 and another

Northern Line branch to Barnet in 1940, where the station was built on the site of Barnet Fair. Each of these lines organised an important section of London's expansion, while also providing a local pattern of housing, shopping and, in addition, areas that were to a degree bypassed by not having Underground lines and/or stations. In this, the pattern of train services was repeated. South of the Thames, the Northern Line reached Morden in 1926. The seventeen-mile tunnel between East Finchley (on the High Barnet branch) and Morden was, at the time of its construction, the longest continuous tunnel in the world.

The Underground was also responsible for the transformation of London's image with the 1931 map of the system by Henry ('Harry') Beck, an electrical draftsman who worked for the Underground; the map depicted the various tube lines diagrammatically and as straight. Prior to Beck's innovative and arresting work, maps presented by London Underground were designed to be accurate in terms of distance and direction. In turn, using a topological structure, and abandoning scale, Beck, imagining that he was employing a convex mirror, expanded the central stations for the sake of clarity. He also shrank the apparent distance between suburbs and the inner city, implying that peripheral destinations, such as Morden and Edgware, were within easy travelling distance of central London. Thus, moving outwards did not appear to be a case of leaving London. Instead, the ease of travel into the centre was emphasised, a visual effect that was encouraged by the use of straight lines on the map for the individual tube services. Describing his task as turning 'vermicelli into a diagram', Beck produced updated versions until 1959, establishing the iconic view of the city, but the copyright was held by the London Passenger Transport Board and he was embittered by the limited returns he enjoyed.

Different fare tariffs on the Underground played a role in the development of the linked housing system, for the 'tube' was consciously presented as integrating housing, transport and work. Fare tariffs helped, for example, to ensure that Edgware grew more rapidly than Stanmore, from where the fare to the city centre was higher in the 1930s.

> **'All London is within immediate reach of . . .'**
> 'Herga Court, Harrow-on-the-Hill . . . from Baker Street, Harrow-on-the-Hill station is twenty minutes on the Met . . . a safe paradise.'
> Advertisement in *Daily Telegraph*,
> 11 December 1936

A new governmental structure was established for transport, one that created a common experience for London, although the area covered was far larger than the London County Council (LCC) area. The London Passenger Transport Board (or London Transport) was formed in 1933 as a result of the London Transport Act, bringing together underground lines, tramways and buses. It was run from 55 Broadway, a proto-skyscraper near St James's Park, built in 1927–9 for the London Electric Railway Company with attractive step-backs and external sculptures. The latter included *Day* and *Night* by Jacob Epstein and the *Four Winds* by artists including Henry Moore.

South of the Thames, Southern Railways (created by amalgamation in 1923), the only rail company that electrified on a large scale, served London's massive expansion and remained outside London Transport. This encouraged a sense of 'South of the River' as being different. When I was growing up in North-West London in the 1960s, the 'tube' – both the Northern and the Bakerloo lines – took me 'into town' but, partly because it did not go much into South London, I rarely went there. The excision of South London from public attention was also seen in the version of the popular boardgame Monopoly that was produced for

London. Based on a trip to London in 1935 by the managing director of the Leeds firm of John Waddington, this game named four railway stations, none south of the Thames, as well as excluding any road there, bar the Old Kent Road. Many taxi drivers did not like to go 'south of the river'.

Not least due to the new art deco-style stations and to the attractive advertising, the new Underground system encouraged a sense of pride. Charles Holden's underground booking hall for Piccadilly Circus (1925–8) was followed by his work on a number of new stations, particularly on the Piccadilly Line, such as Chiswick Park and Turnpike Lane (both 1932). Serving the new suburbs, the underground system was much used and, by 1934, the city's public transport system was attracting 416 million passengers annually.

Road construction in commuting was also important. Buses competed actively with trams. In 1930, the LCC introduced 'Felthams' – comfortable, quick trams – but the greater flexibility of buses ensured that London was soon planning to close its tram routes by 1941. Meanwhile, in part as a measure to help tackle unemployment, arterial roads were constructed in the 1920s and 1930s; for example, the Great West Road from Gunnersbury to Hanwell and the Eastern Avenue from Wanstead to Romford. However, many of the advantages of the new arterial roads were very rapidly lost because weak planning powers, especially before the 1935 Ribbon Development Act, meant that the new highways were almost immediately edged by housing and cluttered with innumerable junctions and other impedimenta, which slowed traffic and created new congestion.

As in earlier periods, bolder schemes were on offer; the greater powers of government as well as the heady flight of technology appeared to make them more of a prospect. Sir Charles Bressey, the Ministry of Transport engineer who investigated traffic problems in central London in 1936, proposed a programme of massive road building, including large roundabouts and big flyovers. In the late 1930s, more fantastically, the Modern

Architectural Research Group envisaged huge, raised arteries – more than 200 feet broad – crossing London at rooftop level, carrying trains and buses, while the streets below were to be handed over to private cars. In turn, Patrick Abercrombie's *County of London Plan* of 1943 proposed a large number of new roads, including three orbital routes as well as radial roads, to join these rings and to provide routes from the centre to the major trunk routes in South-East England. His *Greater London Plan* of the following year proposed six ring roads, including E Ring, much of which is now followed by the M25, as well as ten radial roads, six airports and a dozen new towns. Abercrombie argued that fast through-traffic must be separated from local traffic because London, he claimed, was composed of cellular communities which should be carefully nurtured and, to that end, sealed from the main roads round them. These plans foreshadowed the GLC's commitment in the 1960s and 1970s to a motorway box for London.

Cars and roads, meanwhile, had led to new smells, as well as 'the sound of horns and motors' of *The Waste Land* (1922) by T. S. Eliot, one of many foreigners (in his case an American) living in London. The visual context of life was affected because the impact of motor vehicles on pedestrian behaviour had to be controlled by the development of safety measures such as signs, lamp-posts and traffic lights, a need earlier seen with horse-drawn trams, and one that ensured a new level of policing in London. The first traffic roundabout in London was constructed at Parliament Square in 1926, five years after the last horse-drawn fire engine was withdrawn from service. Roads led to new boundaries and commands, to zebra crossings and to the flashing safety lamps called 'Belisha beacons' after the Minister of Transport.

As a mark of the impact of cars and building on earlier maps, the *A–Z Atlas and Guide to London and Suburbs* appeared in 1936, the work of Phyllis Pearsall, who had walked some of the streets of London. Street-fighting gangs that guarded their 'turf' did not need these maps. Cars also affected crime, as well as the image of

London which, in film, was frequently used as the setting for crime stories. This situation remains true of television schedules today. The spread in the 1930s of large numbers of affordable cars with reliable self-starter motors, so that it was not necessary to crank up the motor by hand, led to a wave of 'smash-and-grab' raids, while greater mobility changed the pattern of crime. In response, the Metropolitan Police experimented with mounting ship radios in cars, and developed a fleet of Wolseley cars thus equipped with which to launch an effective response.

ECONOMY

Industry continued to move out of the centre of London. Initially, this was a continuation of the pre-war movement to the east (West Ham) and to the Lea Valley in North-East London, but, in the 1930s, there was a new geographical focus, one that marked a major change in the spatial distribution of employment in the London area. This focus was also an aspect of the prosperity and growth of the decade, both of which are forgotten with the emphasis instead on the Depression. Yet, the Great West Road became the site of a series of spacious factories that, with their use of electricity, were very distant from the smoke-shrouded world of dockland manufacturing and from the workshops of inner London. Aside from large-scale factories, such as those manufacturing Smith's Crisps, Gillette razors and Curry's cycles, and the Hoover factory, built in 1932–3 (all consumer industries), there was a host of small manufacturing works on the Park Royal estate, built on the former showground of the Royal Agricultural Society; and comparable development along the North Circular Road at Colindale and Cricklewood. In East London, Ford's car factory at Dagenham was also a major site. After 1918, most Irish immigrants landing at Liverpool went straight on to London and did not think about staying in Lancashire, their traditional destination.

'The river sweats
Oil and tar
The barges drift
With the turning tide'

noted Eliot in *The Waste Land* and the docks, which remained a centre of London's activity, were still the most important in the world. Moreover, the manufacturing in and near Dockland, notably the processing industries, continued to be major employers. Yet, London's industrial base was increasingly characterised by light industry using electrical power. This development of factory employment and factory districts meant the decline of workshops and thus of the working-class nature of the inner city. The factory districts were linked to the development of LCC housing estates, each an aspect of a form of development zoning that became a more apparent feature of London's spatial differentiation.

The financial position of London was hit hard by World War One, and New York benefited at its expense. Nevertheless, there was recovery and new developments including, in the 1920s, the swift emergence of a foreign exchange market.

SUBURBIA

Industry was generally kept at a distance from suburbia, the growth of which reflected the desire to live away from factory chimneys and inner-city crowds, a desire catered to in the posters advocating life in the new suburbs. Place and movement were particularly susceptible to change, as London altered and the motor-car spread in a symbiotic development: cars encouraged housing of a lower density, while the new suburbs were associated with road systems constructed for cars. The tightly packed terraces characteristic of Victorian London, for the middle as well as the working class, were supplemented by miles of 'semis':

semi-detached houses with mock-Tudor elevations, red-tiled roofs and walls of red brick or pebbledash, with a small front and a larger back garden, a small drive and a separate garage, which was often structurally linked to the house. This was a suburbia representing the application of pre-war ideas of garden-suburbs, notably with an emphasis on space, calm and the separateness expressed in individual gardens.

Suburbia had spread greatly in the late nineteenth century with the railways, absorbing previously separate villages, but development then had generally not moved far from the stations. In contrast, car transport permitted less intensive development although, in practice, this often meant more extensive estates that were otherwise as densely packed as the basic housing model permitted. In advertisements, such as those that pushed 'Metro-land' – a term devised in 1915, linked to the services of the Metropolitan Railway – cars were pictured against backdrops of mock-Tudor suburban houses. The Metropolitan Railway County Estates Limited developed railway-owned land into estates, notably at Wembley Park and Harrow Garden Village and in Pinner.

As with the car, the 'semi' expressed freedom: a freedom to escape the constraints of living in close proximity to others and, instead, to enjoy space, privacy and respectability. Semis were not the suburban villas of the wealthier members of the middle class, which continued to exist in what were now enclaves, but they captured the aspirations of millions, and offered them a decent living environment, including a garden. In *English Journey* (1934), J. B. Priestley wrote of the new England of suburbs and 'road houses' – pubs built along trunk roads, many of which were found in outer London.

In part, suburbia was a response to the cult of the outdoors, one mediated through, and in, the suburban garden and the many parks of the new suburbs. Thus, suburbia was linked to a ruralist image of England. Names of streets, estates and suburbs expressed the aspirations for new neighbourhoods, an appeal seen across the arts. The most influential of the tour guides, *In Search of England* (1927), by the Birmingham-born H. V. Morton, a work whose twenty-fourth edition appeared in 1937, presented a link to the national life of the countryside: 'Many a man has stood at his window above a London square in April hearing a message from the lanes of England.'

Suburbia, which came into use as a pejorative noun in the 1890s, also reflected sameness and national standardisation, but a predictability of product helped to make the new housing sell. The houses were mass-produced and had standardised parts. They also looked similar, as did their garages. A degree of individuality was provided by the gardens but they generally had similar plantings; for example, cherry trees. Writing in the satirical late twentieth century, Alan Coren was to quip, 'Were Edgware on a lake, would Venice stand a chance?'

At the same time, there were significant variations, which were understood and extrapolated by the residents of the new areas. Growing up in Edgware, listening to my elders and doing a paper round, I was well aware of differences not only in street layout and decoration (i.e. trees along roads or not) and house size, density and decoration – for example, tiling – but also in supposed characteristics of particular streets, whether exotic (alleged spouse-swapping, then called wife-swapping) or, far more commonly, the more mundane alignments and lineaments of class.

Much new building was done by private enterprise, often by speculative builders, such as John Laing (1879–1978) and Richard Rylandes Costain (1839–1902). They were largely responsible for the plentiful supply of inexpensive houses. Thus, originally Liverpool-based, Costain Group developed a large site in South Hornchurch in East London from 1934. By 1933, Costain had completed over four thousand houses in the London area. The ability to borrow at low rates of interest from building societies was also important. In the mid-1920s, houses cost between £400 and £1,000. This new housing was crucial to the process by which suburban culture, especially that in London, became increasingly defined and important, both politically and socially.

The suburbs had fairly standard mock-Tudor high streets and also enormous and lavishly decorated 'picture palaces' – cinemas – for example in Gants Hill, Becontree Heath, Hendon and Uxbridge. These cinemas represented the move of leisure to the suburbs. There, film studios were founded at Ealing in 1931. By the end of the decade, the biggest studios were at Denham, while Elstree became a key centre of film production from the 1920s.

HOUSING

Council-house building was also important, as well as providing a crucial link between housing and local politics. Treasury loans for local authority building had been available from 1866, but most local authorities had been reluctant to incur debts. From 1919, however, as a consequence of legislation, grants replaced loans, and council-house building expanded. This expansion was designed to give bricks and mortar to the Prime Minister David Lloyd George's promise of 'homes fit for heroes' for troops returning home at the end of World War One.

Following many of the recommendations about housing standards made in the Tudor Walters Report of 1918, the Housing and Town Planning Act of 1919 sought to provide lower-density housing for the working class. Minimum room sizes were decreed, as was the inclusion of internal bathrooms and kitchens. Indeed, the public housing of the period was generally of good quality and much of it is regarded as more desirable than much 1960s' public housing, not least because of the human scale of the former. The implementation of the Acts was hit by the financial crisis of 1921–2, but they still led to much construction, as did Neville Chamberlain's Housing Act of 1923 and the Wheatley Act of 1924, which was passed by the Labour government. As a prime instance of the scale of building, the LCC's Becontree estate, begun in 1921 and finished in 1932, occupied 277 acres and consisted of about 26,000 houses, housing 120,000 people. The LCC also built estates at St Helier near Morden, at Downham and at Watling, which between them housed about 89,000 people. Such estates were a sign of the LCC's power and ambitions, since elsewhere county councils were not, in normal circumstances, house-building authorities. Moreover, some of the boroughs built houses.

Following the 1915 Rent and Mortgage Interest Restrictions (War) Act, tenants' rights became more secure, private landlordship less profitable and renting from local authorities more important. Council houses increasingly came to the fore and there was therefore less private investment in the building of new properties for rent. Party politics played a role. The 1957 Rent Act, passed by a Conservative government, was a (botched) attempt to free up the private rental market. In contrast, the Labour government's Rent Act of 1965 established rent control on a secure legislative footing, a measure which hit the private rented sector hard.

In the inter-war years, there was also a rebuilding of some existing housing. The Greenwood Housing Act of 1930 gave local authorities powers to clear or improve slum (crowded and substandard housing) areas, in part as a realisation of longstanding beliefs that improved housing would enhance social mores. Passed by the Labour government of 1929–31, this Act provided the local authorities with subsidies related to the numbers rehoused and the cost of slum clearance and obliged them to produce five-year plans. The terms of the subsidies were renewed with an Act passed by the Conservative-dominated National Government in 1933, although Labour boroughs built more public housing than their Conservative counterparts. Much building was achieved thanks to the ready availability of labour, materials and low interest rates, while building standards were lowered in the 1930s to make houses more affordable.

Urban renewal took many forms. For example, cinemas such as the Ilford Hippodrome and the Rex at Stratford were converted theatres, part of the assault on music hall by film. Nevertheless, music halls remained part of the equation, now largely in a form of variety dominated by musicals. Dance halls were also important, their music and style part of the marked Americanisation of British leisure.

Poirot's Charterhouse

Charterhouse Square is best known today because one of its buildings, the Art Deco Florin Court, built of beige bricks in 1936, is used as the exterior of Hercule Poirot's residence, Whitehaven Mansions, in the David Suchet *Poirot* television series (1989–2013). The site earlier contained Georgian buildings that served as a vicarage and school and then, in 1872–1934, was an employees' hostel for workers in a Cheapside-based lace manufacturer and wholesaler.

Concern about housing was affected by its clear links with public health, which remained a serious problem, although far less so than in the Victorian age. There were still significant variations in public health across London. In Kensington, infant mortality was higher in the poor areas in the north of the borough than in the wealthier south. As well as poverty, the provision of medical services was also important: areas with comprehensive services, such as Stepney and Woolwich, had lower rates of infant mortality than Kensington where, alongside the lack of universal provision, there were deprived areas. In the 1930s, improved care from midwives and in hospitals was an important factor in the fall in infant mortality across London while, in the national context, London was relatively over-provided with hospitals and areas that had good access, such as Stepney, had low maternal mortality rates.

Under the Local Government Act of 1929, county borough health duties and powers greatly expanded, and it was possible to take over Poor Law institutions. The LCC ran both hospitals and schools and sought to establish effective healthcare and hospital provision without the stigma of the Poor Law. Under Labour – in control of the LCC from 1934, when it unexpectedly won 51 per cent of the vote – London was seen as a demonstration of the value of municipal socialism, one intended to appeal to those casting their votes in national elections, both in London and further afield. Indeed, by 1939, the LCC had nearly 60 per cent of all the municipal hospital beds in England while, in 1935, the LCC ended the ban on married women teachers, a key measure of gender discrimination. Herbert Morrison, the LCC leader from 1934 to 1940, constructed a coalition of support encompassing not only manual workers in deprived industrial districts, but also voters who were more prosperous. Clerks and teachers were among Labour's LCC candidates. Thus, Labour's electoral position in London did not match its opponents' claims that it was a sectarian party thriving on social antagonism, although Labour was helped by the movement of Conservative voters to suburbia outside the LCC. Labour retained its control of the LCC until its dissolution in 1965, and this long tenure very much helped to characterise the LCC.

Concern about the rate of the spread of suburbia and the threat to the environment – on the part of planners – combined with a growing willingness to accept government control, leading to the passage of relevant legislation, including in 1909 and 1932. The Greater London Planning Committee was established in 1927. The Restriction of Ribbon Development Act of 1935, which attempted to prevent unsightly and uncontrolled development along new or improved roads, such as those leading from London, was an admission of a serious problem.

Interest in planning increased in the late 1930s, prior to the devastation wrought by German air attack. Morrison pressed for a Green Belt that would put a limit on the city's advance at the same time as he was changing its electoral composition, which he allegedly sought to do by establishing big council estates in the suburbs in order to build the Tories out of London, a policy simi- lar to that of the Socialists in Vienna. In creating a Green Belt, Labour wished to preserve accessible open spaces for the city population while, also supporting the idea, the surrounding rural councils were opposed to the city's spread. The Green Belt (London and Home Counties) Act of 1938 was followed by the 1940 report of the Barlow Commission proposing more state control over development, especially in the London area.

Society and Culture

Change in London's material world was wide-ranging. In 1926, John Logie Baird gave the first public demonstration of television in London and, six years later, the BBC moved to new offices in Portland Place. Separately, Croydon became London's airport and, by the end of the 1920s, about twenty aircraft daily were leav- ing. Weekly flights from London began to Cape Town (1932), Brisbane (1934) and Hong Kong (1936).

Modernism, however, had relatively little impact in architec- ture, despite Giles Gilbert Scott's Battersea Power Station and the designs of Berthold Lubetkin, who worked in part for Finsbury Council and was responsible for the Highpoint block of flats in Highgate (1935), as well as the Penguin Pool at Regent's Park Zoo (1934). Charles Holden produced the design for the Senate House of the University of London, a vast Modernist lump begun in 1932. The university site in Bloomsbury had itself been acquired by the government from the estate of the Duke of Bedford in 1920. Liberty's in Regent Street, built in 1924 using Elizabethan timber, better expressed the widespread desire for a style suggesting continuity, rather than the new, while there was controversy over the destructive redevelopment of Nash's Regent Street. A poster for the British Empire Exhibition held at Wembley in 1924–5 showed Elizabeth I being rowed on the Thames towards a Tudor warship, with the caption 'Britain's Past and Present Beckon You to Wembley. British Empire Exhibition.'

There was also a political dimension to the tension between the challenge of the new and conservatism. Thus, in 1926, London was a centre both of the General Strike and of opposition to it. Volunteers, protected by police and troops, including tanks, drove buses from depots, as well as Underground trains, and kept many power stations in operation. The 114,000 volunteers also worked in the docks and distributed food. In turn, strikers attacked buses and lorries breaking the strike and battled the police in centres of the left, including Poplar, where the police mounted baton charges, and New Cross. Had the crisis lasted longer, it might have become a traumatic moment in the city's history – a secret map of 1926 identified military strongpoints in case the strike turned into rebellion. This is one of the many key episodes of London's history that could have worked out very differently.

Keeping the Meat Moving

Troops escorted lorries taking meat from the docks to Smithfield. *The Times* of 11 May 1926 announced:

'With the approval of the Board of Trade, the Smithfield Emergency Committee has undertaken the distribution of meat to and from Smithfield Market with the help of volunteer labour. Volunteers are called for, strong men to load and unload meat ... The Government undertakes to afford full protection to all volunteers.'

London was a focus of new ideas and practices and, yet, was also characterised by important continuities. Virginia Woolf argued, in *Street Haunting: A London Adventure*, an essay of 1927, that London threatened the established order by offering liberation and delight to women, who had formerly been marginalised. In practice, female workers continued to be mostly engaged in relatively low-skilled and low-wage work, despite London being one of the highest-wage global locations. As a separate point, many of the new female voters supported the Conservatives.

A fractured account was offered by T. S. Eliot, who lived in London from 1915, pursuing a number of careers including teaching, working for Lloyds Bank, editing a quarterly review and working in publishing. He gave a prominent role to London in *The Waste Land*, with commuters as spectral figures:

'Unreal City,
Under the brown fog of a winter dawn,
A crowd flowed over London Bridge, so many,
I had not thought death had undone so many.'

The Thames was polluted by human detritus and sexual activity and London was the latest in a series of doomed world cities, but the city also offered intimations of a prospect of salvation, with the theme centred on the Thames:

' "This music crept by me upon the waters"
And along the Strand, up Queen Victoria Street.
O City city, I can sometimes hear
Beside a public bar in Lower Thames Street,
The pleasant whining of a mandoline
And a clatter and a chatter from within
Where fishmen lounge at noon: where the walls
Of Magnus Martyr hold
Inexplicable splendour of Ionian white and gold.'

Meanwhile, films were spreading images of London to new audiences. Silent films often contained location shooting in London, while early documentaries included *London Life* (1929), which showed a stump orator in Hyde Park, hawkers on the steps of St Martin-in-the-Field and workmen in the Strand, which as usual is 'up', in other words having work done. Writers tackled the harsh realities of life, as in *London River* (1921) by the novelist and journalist Henry Major Tomlinson (1873–1958), who had been born in Dockland and had worked in a shipping office. Virginia Woolf wrote an essay on the docks, while George Orwell's *Down and Out in Paris and London* (1933) described the poorly paid life he had experienced in the late 1920s.

A cultural preference for continuity was notable in the 1930s. From 1931 the National Government presided over a pronounced conservatism. The rags-to-riches fantasy of the smash-hit musical *Me and My Girl* (1937), the source of the 'The Lambeth Walk', celebrated the 'Cockney Spirit', but was scarcely subversive. For the middle class, the cultural preferences of the 1930s were for an appearance of rural and natural life and values, both as part of an organic society. These preferences seemed fulfilled in suburbia.

At the same time, contributing to a profound shift in material culture, there was much change in the circumstances of life for many Londoners. In particular, household electricity supplies expanded greatly, replacing coal, gas, candles and human effort. This replacement had an impact on the consumption of power and the sales of electric cookers, fridges, irons, water heaters and vacuum cleaners. Such expenditure reflected, and helped to define, changing models of family life and class differences. Whereas radios, vacuum cleaners and electric irons were widely owned – in part thanks to the spread of hire purchase – electric fridges, cookers and washing machines were largely restricted to the middle class.

This difference in goods was linked to the major social divide between those who employed others and the employed although, as far as home help was concerned, the latter were increasingly the daily help rather than full-time, live-in, domestic servants. Whether defined in terms of income, occupation or culture, the middle class was proportionately more important in London and the South-East than in any other region, a situation that remains the case today. The new white goods required space and this need accentuated the relative deprivation of much inner-city housing as the kitchens there were too small for them.

POLITICS

The Conservative Party was very strong in outer London and the expansion of suburbia served its interests. There were also safe Conservative seats in inner London, although inner London was a key centre of the Labour Party, which controlled municipalities such as East Ham. Left-wing activity was more varied, with communists numerous in East London, not least playing a major role in opposing the fascists, notably blocking them in the 'Battle of Cable Street' in 1936, a police effort to clear the way for a fascist march under Oswald Mosley.

The Battle of Cable Street, 1936

'. . . One of my more lasting memories is of the pungent smell of that narrow thoroughfare for, in addition to having expropriated all the children's marbles to throw into the roadway and so prevent [police] horses venturing into the street, the inhabitants of all the houses had flung down from their upper windows every smashable glass bottle they could lay their hands on. The mingled odours of camphor, vinegar, vanilla essence, eucalyptus, kerosene, cough syrup, ammonia, brilliantine, lime juice, turpentine, alcohol and methylated spirit filled the air.'

Yvonne Kapp, witness seminar, 1991

Public displays of radical activity included the invasion of the Highbury pitch at half-time during a match between Arsenal and Charlton Athletic in January 1939, with unemployed demonstrators holding up a placard reading, 'Kick With Us For Work Or Bread'. In practice, the general prosperity of the London region lessened social tension.

Sport

Arsenal itself did particularly well in the 1930s, drawing large crowds like the other major London clubs. Football facilities had been expanded with the building of the stadium at Wembley Park, on which work was completed only four days before it was used for the first Football Association Cup Final between Bolton and West Ham in 1923; the Rugby League Cup Final was played there from 1929. The 1923 match saw a vast crowd, estimated at 250,000 – compared to the 100,000 who had been expected – many of whom invaded the pitch before the kick-off. Ten mounted policemen carefully edged the crowd back, notably George Scorey on his horse Billy, possibly the most famous individual animal in London's history, although many other animals have played a role, with the ravens in the Tower being particularly iconic.

World War Two, 1939–45

This world war brought much more disruption to London, although not, initially, the savage air assault anticipated at the outset of the war when there was widespread preparation for airborne gas attacks and large numbers of cardboard coffins were prepared. Already, during the Munich Crisis of 1938, trenches had been dug in Hyde Park. Under the apparent threat of air attack, 690,000 Londoners were evacuated by rail from London in September 1939 at the start of the war, while blackout regulations were implemented.

In the event, the attacks came the following autumn (by which time many of the evacuees had returned) and did not include gas attacks. From 7 September 1940 – 'Black Saturday' – the Germans bombed London heavily in what became known as 'the Blitz': 320 German bombers attacked when defences were taken by surprise: there were only ninety-two anti-aircraft guns ready and their fire-control system failed. The fighter squadrons proved inadequate. Four hundred and thirty people were killed in the East End, where the docks were hit hard. The fire officer at the Surrey Commercial Docks called the central dispatcher: 'Send all the bloody pumps you've got. The whole bloody world's on fire.' Another 412 were killed in a night raid on 8 September. It was only on 11 September that anti-aircraft fire was sufficiently effective to make the Germans bomb from a greater height.

From 7 September until mid-November 1940, the Germans bombed London every night bar one. There were also large-scale daylight attacks between 7 and 18 September, as well as hit-and-run attacks. The attack on the moonlit night of 15–16 October proved particularly serious, with four hundred bombers active, of which only one was shot down by the RAF's forty-one fighters. The railway stations were hard hit, as was Battersea Power Station and the BBC headquarters at Portland Place. By mid-November, when the attacks became less focused on London, over 13,000 tons of high-explosive bombs had been dropped on London as well as nearly one million incendiaries.

German aircraft losses were modest. Because of the absence of good aerial radar, it was difficult to hit German bombers after they switched to night attacks in September in response to their operating near the edge of their fighter escort range. From mid-November 1940 to the end of February 1941, eight major raids were mounted on London. In the attack of 29 December, 22,000 incendiaries and 400 high-explosive bombs were dropped, 10,000 of the incendiaries in the first half-hour. Fifteen hundred fires were started that night, three in the City graded as conflagrations, including that which destroyed much of the Barbican. Some 240 people died across London, among them twelve firemen (nearly four hundred fire fighters died in the war overall). Thereafter, the focus was on the ports until May 1941 when, after a devastating raid by 550 aircraft, on the night of 10–11 May, the bomber forces were moved to prepare for the invasion of the Soviet Union launched the following month, although air attacks on London were still mounted subsequently. The docks had been particularly heavily bombed. Even in the early 1960s, a river trip from Hungerford Bridge down to beyond Tower Bridge went past serried ranks of burned-out warehouses. Moreover, much of the dockland townscape was destroyed, especially the inter-connection of places of work and tightly packed terraced housing. By the late spring of 1941, the defence had become more effective, thanks to the use of radar-directed Beaufighter planes and better ground defences.

In bombing London in 1940–1, the Germans set out to destroy civilian morale, and the strain on the population was indeed heavy but, although there were occasional episodes of panic, on the whole morale remained fatalistic, with an emphasis on 'taking it'. Pre-war anticipation of a collapse of popular spirit proved totally inaccurate. Instead, there was an emphasis on forbearance and making do, notably at the docks, which continued operating. This helped ensure that Londoners were well fed. About half London's population sheltered at home, often using basements, a quarter used Anderson shelters in the garden and another quarter took to public shelters. All companies with more than thirty staff had to provide shelters.

Although initially banned from doing so, as the system was still a working one, Londoners sheltered in tube tunnels, providing images for artists such as Henry Moore. Most of their young children had already been evacuated, but many minors were in these tunnels. By late September 1940, about 177,000 Londoners were sleeping underground, although the vast majority did not.

There was a degree of social tension in the response to the bombing despite the government's theme of equality in suffering. Thus, Londoners from the much-bombed dockside district of Silvertown – where there was a lack of shelters – forced their way into the Savoy Hotel's impressive shelter and then had a whip-round to tip the porter.

Although other causes were also crucial, not least Britain's global position, film helped ensure that the Blitz was the episode of London's history that was most dramatised for a wide audience, far more so than traumatic events such as the Black Death, the Peasants' Revolt, the Plague, or the Great Fire. Photographs of St Paul's surrounded by flames and devastation, as that taken by Herbert Mason of the raid on 29 December 1940, acquired totemic force. Documentaries included *London Can Take It* (1940), shot during the Blitz and featuring iconic shots of St Paul's; *Christmas Under Fire* (1941), which included a tracking shot down an escalator to people sheltering on an Underground platform; and *Fires Were Started* (1943), which featured location shooting in the docks.

Moreover, the bombing had an impact on literature and poetry. The lasting impact was indicated by the number of novels in which characters were killed as a result or lost loved ones. Louis MacNeice, an Irish-born poet who worked in London for the BBC, wrote *Brother Fire* (1943), beginning:

'When our brother Fire was having his dog's day
Jumping the London streets with millions of tin cans
Clanking at his tail . . .
Night after night we watched him slaver and crunch away
The beams of human life, the tops of topless towers.'

This was very different to the popularity of 'A Nightingale Sang in Berkeley Square', a romantic song written in 1939 and made famous by Vera Lynn in 1940, when it was published.

In turn, from 13 June 1944, ground-to-ground V-1 flying bombs were launched, 2,419 hitting Greater London, with the highest casualties on 18 June when a V-1 hit the Guards' Chapel while a service was in progress, killing 121 people. This bombardment led to renewed large-scale evacuation of children in Operation Rivulet. V-2s travelled at up to 3,000 mph and could be fired from a considerable distance. These could not be destroyed by anti-aircraft fire as the V-1s could. Their explosive payload was small and they could not be aimed accurately, but that was scant consolation to those killed and maimed. A total of 517 V-2s hit London between 8 September 1944 and 27 March 1945, killing over 2,700 Londoners and injuring many more. Londoners could readily differentiate between the V-1s, whose buzzing engine could be heard overhead until it cut out, heralding the landing of the bomb, and the V-2, which made no sound and appeared without warning. The British gave false reports of V-1 and V-2 landing sites in order to persuade the Germans to redirect their targets to fall short of London. The V-1 bombardment of London resumed on 3 March 1945, when long-range V-1s were fired from the Netherlands. That month, 275 missiles were launched, indicating the extent to which the threat to London lasted until the close of war with resulting casualties, disruption and a challenge to morale.

If, throughout, the V-rocket assault was irrelevant to the course of the conflict, nevertheless, in total, during the war, 29,890 Londoners – including one of my uncles, a young fire-watcher – were killed by air and missile attack and 50,507 other citizens were seriously injured. Particular calamities included accidents such as the Bethnal Green disaster of 1 March 1943, when 173 people died mostly from suffocation as they fell due to an accident as they sought refuge in the underground tube station. Fifty thousand houses in the LCC area were destroyed, and another 66,000 in Greater London, while 288,000 required major repairs. One in six Londoners were left homeless while four-fifths of the houses in Poplar were destroyed. Aside from the savage devastation of residential areas, especially in Dockland, but also across much of the suburbia of South London, many of London's historic buildings were also severely damaged, including the Guildhall, the House of Commons, the Inner Temple and Gray's Inn. Livery Company halls and their records were also hit, as was Buckingham Palace. This was a destruction that was more insistent than any previous programme of 'urban renewal', as well as being mass-murderous in intent and effect.

Bombing, evacuation, rationing and single-parenting – all central conditions of London life during the war – brought much disruption and, notably homelessness, as well as the heavy demands of voluntary work in the midst of war. Evacuation was a formidable undertaking and strain, with large numbers of children moved, as well as some accompanying adults. There were problems, however, with homesickness and with parents missing children, and 'drift back' had to be resisted by providing parents with inexpensive train tickets so that they could see their children. There was also concern about the infectious diseases that would be spread by London's children. Evacuation certainly revealed the gap between the life experiences of the inner-city children and rural England, as well as capturing the tension between the hopes of regeneration through the evacuation of many children from urban squalor to rural health and the traditional social practices, such as the poor girls from London who were placed in domestic service elsewhere. Some wealthy families sent women and children overseas, mostly to North America, but this option was not available to most Londoners.

Social mores were greatly affected by the war. There was more freedom for women, because far more were employed, while there was a general absence of partners, as well as different attitudes. In June 1943, the Mass-Observation Survey, reporting on female behaviour in some pubs, found 'a free and easy atmosphere in which it was very easy and usual to pick up with a member of the opposite sex'. Aside from changes resulting directly from the war, such as the presence of large numbers of the military, aspects of life as diverse as crime and religion, work and the arts, were all greatly affected. Religious observance declined markedly, but the cinema remained very popular, including during the air raids. London was less closed down than it was to be during the (very different) Covid pandemic of 2020–2. The varied impact of the war included an attempt to disguise the city not only with the blackout but also, for example, with the security restrictions that affected the *A–Z Atlas and Guide.*

The extent to which the war led to a consensual society is unclear. There was certainly a language of inclusiveness and sharing and a stress on the 'Home Front' which made social distinctions seem unacceptable. Yet, there was also resistance to government policy, not least with the insistent 'black market' which proved to be a way to evade rationing and extended the makeshift economy to include much of society. Nevertheless, the overwhelming reality measured up to the public reputation: Londoners displayed tremendous fortitude and individual and collective self-reliance and mutual assistance, in the face of a sustained and deadly assault. It was a noble stance in a great cause.

8

Post-War Revival to . . . ?

In *The Long Good Friday* (1980), the protagonist, Harold Shand, a self-made 'boy from Putney', played by Bob Hoskins, a millionaire businessman with ambitions for Thames-side property development in his 'manor', spans crime and business. Criminal London is presented as awash with new money, but also under pressure from stronger, international forces. The film implied that London had both been laid open, and had laid itself open, to foreign influence – if not control – not only through the American investors, themselves linked to the Mafia, but also with the IRA. Barrie Keefe's script captured a sense of profound uneasiness already present at the outset of a decade that was to bring profound change – to the Docklands, the City, and much else of the physical and social fabric of London. Wooing American investors, Shand is attacked by a shadowy group who use extreme violence and turn out to be the IRA, inadvertently crossed by Shand's gang. They are able to wreck his favourite pub, a classic London image of locality and longevity that had replaced the parish church, and to capture Hoskins at the close. Much of it shot on location, the film also recorded the physical change of property development and social change, not least with Shand's new money, seen in his clothes, flat and Rolls-Royce (the victim of a car bomb) and his best friend, a homosexual stabbed to death when cruising at a swimming pool.

'Only a film,' this movie captured a sense of disorientation alongside the change optimistically presented by so many 1960s' films. Buffeted from 1939 by the impact of war and much else, London, more generally, was greatly affected by the decisions of national government, not least the decolonisation that ended its claim to being in practice the world capital; its change in status further helped to strengthen the relative significance of New York.

PLANNING

The shape of the city changed less in the post-war years than in the earlier period or – looked at another way – the city came to encompass much of the South-East of England, as the Outer Metropolitan Area expanded and commuting to London increased and spread. The key element in the shape of the more restricted (and conventional) understanding of London was the planning regime and, in particular, the determination by planners to control the extent of contiguous suburbia. Legislation took forward pre-war ideas about restricting London's development favouring, instead, a combination of a Green Belt with planning garden cities in the greater South-East. Under the post-war Labour governments of 1945–51, the New Towns Act of 1946 was followed by a new Town and Country Planning Act in 1947. New Towns were designed to complement Green Belts: London was to be contained, with a Green Belt, and New Towns were to be built outside the belt. The first, Stevenage, was chosen in November 1946. Within three years, another seven were designated for London overspill: Harlow, Hemel Hempstead, Crawley, Bracknell, Basildon, Hatfield and Welwyn Garden City.

With jobs and people pushed out of London, the New Towns became major centres of employment in their own right; but the growth of dormitory settlements which were not planned in that way led to an increase in long-distance commuting into the capital. Moreover, the growth of both the New Towns and dormitory settlements contributed to the large-scale shift in population from London to other parts of the South-East. Outside London – the population of which fell between the 1940s and the 1980s – the population of the South-East rose rapidly. That of Berkshire, for example, more than doubled between 1931 and 1971. Expansion there was concentrated in the east of the county, the part best suited for commuting to London. Thus, building of the New Town at Bracknell started in 1950 and, by 1981, the population there numbered 49,000. With time, especially from the 1970s, commuting from further afield became more common, notably from East Anglia, the Midlands and the West Country. Long-distance travel was encouraged by the practice of the weekly commute, which entailed living in London during the weekdays.

The London Green Belt was finally secured with an Act of 1959. Thanks to this, which has remained reasonably firm, despite development pressures, especially those linked to the M25, London did not leap forward from Edgware to Elstree and the Northern Line extension via Elstree to Watford – planned before the war – was not built, although preparatory work had been done. Nevertheless, as much urban development simply passed the Green Belt, it created new pressures further afield; for example, around Ipswich and Reading, while there was a major expansion in the population of Peterborough and Northampton. Thus, if London is seen in terms of a wider daily commuter belt – rather than the area currently covered by the Greater London Authority – then the shape of the city has changed greatly, indeed more significantly than ever before, and its frontier of settlement is now out past Peterborough. The situation would look even further-flung if weekly commuting were to be considered; indeed much of England would be included.

This issue raises the question of the scope of any study of London. In particular, if the City is seen as an inadequate basis for discussion of, say, London in the sixteenth century and, still more obviously, the nineteenth – or the LCC area for the 1930s – it is unclear why the recent or present situation should be defined in terms of the GLC and GLA. The basis for the study of London is therefore problematic – indeed, inherently unstable – and this point challenges the attempt to discuss the long-term history of London solely in terms of the particular resonances of its centre or central area.

Expansion did not only take place outside London. Within the Greater London area, council-house building was halted by World War Two. Thereafter, it revived, driven on by severe wartime damage to the housing stock which left many living in temporary accommodation or as part of extended families, as well as by expectations of a better life, and a post-war rise in the birth rate. Under legislation of 1944, councils had the right to purchase bombed sites.

The devastation of war pushed forward the planning process. In 1943, the Ministry of Housing and Local Government was created, providing a context for a national planning policy. Moreover, Professor Patrick Abercrombie, a leading town planner, was appointed to draw up plans for London and in 1944 his *Greater London Plan* looked at the wider regional situation as a key context for London, putting the LCC in a planner's framework. This plan suggested moving houses and jobs away from London to New Towns built beyond the Green Belt on greenfield sites around the capital. New industry was to be banned within inner London and 415,000 people were to be moved from that area to the New Towns. There was no sense of consultation and, examined today, the plan seems disturbingly naïve, not least in its assumptions about providing prosperity. Like most others, this plan took the zoning of urban space as the norm of planning analysis and policy.

The overriding drive was for a reconstruction that would not entail a return to the pre-war situation. This conviction characterised the governance of London in the late 1940s, especially by the Labour governments of 1945–51, but also by the LCC and the boroughs. Labour did well in London in the general election of 1945, winning such seats as Wimbledon. The Labour leader and new Prime Minister, Clement Attlee, was an experienced London politician and, in many respects, the Labour years of the late 1940s were London years, as other prominent Labour leaders such as Ernest Bevin, Herbert Morrison and Harold Laski were also London figures, although Bevin's origins were in the South-West. This situation was to recur in the late 2010s and early 2020s although, by then, it was a very different Labour Party and, indeed, its metropolitan character and sympathies (real or alleged) contributed to Labour's unpopularity across much of the country: alienation from London was matched by a perception of alienation by London in the sense of condescending metropolitan views.

HOUSING

Problems with the housing supply were an important aspect of a generally troubled city during the austerity years of the late 1940s. Rationing continued into the mid-1950s, there were serious shortages of coal – the basic source of energy and fuel – people were often cold, and much of inner London remained a wasteland of bombsites, which was captured in the films of the period, such as *Passport to Pimlico* (1949). Other films featuring location shots in London included *Hue and Cry* (1947) and *The Blue Lamp* (1950). Both were produced by Ealing Studios and offered a real sense of place, using the bombsites as locations, as well as White City Stadium in the latter. *The Lavender Hill Mob* (1951) continued this trend, as well as showing London's railways very clearly.

The political and trade union situation was unsettled. The government claimed that communist conspiracies were behind strikes, most prominently the London dock strike of 1949. The docks were particularly prone to unofficial strikes, in part because the dockers resented the discipline of the Dock Labour Scheme introduced in 1947. This brought a measure of job security, but curtailed worker freedoms enjoyed under the earlier, casual system.

There was a massive extension of the power of the state through a series of nationalisations. These included the Bank of England (1946), the hospitals (1948), railways (1948), the electricity supply (1948) and gas (1949). Far more Londoners were brought into state

employment, which underlined the possibilities for central planning, as did the shortage of resources in the private sector. The
creation of the National Health Service (NHS) in 1948 represented
an opportunity to improve medical services in London. The NHS
also marked a tremendous extension of state control and direction. Hospitals in the London region were in effect nationalised.
In the long term, it has been far from clear that health provision
benefited greatly from the new system of control but, at the time,
there was a strong sense of new beginnings and the provision of a
universal 'free' – only at the point of delivery – health service was
perceived as a reward for winning the war.

A severe shortage of resources in the post-war economy, as
well as the priority given to industrial reconstruction after wartime
disruption, ensured that the house building that took place was
insufficient. In the late 1940s, by necessity, many London families remained with their parents long after they wished to move.
The Temple Hill council estate in Dartford, opened by Attlee in
1947, was an example of the council-funded housing designed
both to move people from slum dwellings and to replace war-
damaged stock. The houses on this estate were concrete, with pre-
fabricated parts.

The Conservatives correctly saw the shortage of houses as an
electoral opportunity and, in the election of 1951 – which they won
under Churchill – made much of a promise to build more homes.
Helped by a higher allocation of government resources, co-
operation with the house-builders and a lowering of the building
standards for council houses, the Conservative government –
which remained in power until 1964 – achieved its target and this
success permitted extensive rehousing in the 1950s. Thus, large
numbers of East-Enders were rehoused in new council housing
estates which included those at Debden, Hainault and Harold
Hill.

The effects of this policy are a matter of controversy as it is
unclear how far problems readily apparent during the 1960s

existed during the 1950s when there was a greater desire simply for new housing. The buildings of the 1950s – many of which were low-rise and fairly generous with space; for example, the Lansbury Estate in Poplar – should be distinguished from the system-built tower blocks largely built in the 1960s. There is considerable evidence to suggest that the problems of poorly built estates were much more apparent in the 1960s, and that earlier developments were often better-built and more popular. Furthermore, the experience of poor Londoners greatly changed as a result of the building. Many of the new houses provided people with their first bathrooms and inside toilets. The dynamics of family space and the nature of privacy were transformed as a result. The 1950s was also a decade of low crime rates in London, certainly in comparison with what was to come, although *The Frightened City* (1961), a powerful film, depicted violent protection racketeers who are in the ascendant until they fall out.

A critical view about slum clearance and re-housing dominated subsequent discussion. Aside from the social disruption of the move to new locations, a disruption particularly felt by those who had never previously moved, many of the new neighbourhoods were poorly planned and also unpopular with their occupants. These new neighbourhoods tended to lack community amenities and means of identification, such as local shops and pubs. Moreover, the social fabric that had greatly helped Londoners cope with strain was sundered. Families were separated, affecting the support systems crucial for childcare and for looking after the elderly. On the new housing estates, there was a decline in the three-generation extended family and a move towards the nuclear family, which hit traditional communities and patterns of care, although the problems posed by these had also been considerable. Grandparents were more socially and geographically isolated as a result of these changes and many old people found the estates alien, if not frightening. These were no longer walkable communities or lives.

Furthermore, the inter-connection of work and tightly packed, terraced housing seen in many pre-war neighbourhoods was not replicated. Instead; for example, in dockland areas of such a focus or of utilitarian notions linked to harbour activities, there was an application of generalised notions of supposedly progressive town-planning, the dire consequences of which can still be seen. Whereas there had been a considerable degree of proximity between working-class and other housing in the Victorian period, there was now a more marked differentiation, which could be regarded almost as a segregation of the working class into housing estates.

More generally, concern about urban sprawl and the pressures arising from the 'baby boom', as well as a critique of suburbia, not least in Tom Nairn's 1955 attack on 'subutopia', encouraged higher-density housing than in the inter-war years or indeed immediately after World War Two. Alongside architectural and planning fashions and land prices – themselves greatly increased by Green Belt policies, all of which encouraged high-density housing – this concern about sprawl contributed to a high-rise development that matched that around many European cities. Pre-fabricated methods of construction ensured that high, multi-storey blocks of flats could be built rapidly and inexpensively and the LCC and some borough councils in the 1960s took pride in their number, size and visibility.

Extolled at the time and illustrated in guidebooks, municipal multi-storey flats were subsequently attacked correctly as of poor quality, ugly, out of keeping with the existing urban fabric and street-pattern, lacking in community feeling and serving as breeders of alienation and crime. Frequent heating and ventilation problems caused condensation, lifts often broke down, vandalism became a serious problem, and the morale of tenants unsurprisingly fell. Flat roofs let in water, while many public spaces – such as stairwells – were neglected and became sites of urination and crime. Moreover, in place of individual gardens, there were unfenced green spaces for which none of the residents had responsibility and which were apt to be desolate and sometimes became dumping grounds for rubbish.

For many Londoners, this – alongside poor schools and services – was the 1960s; not Carnaby Street and the new 'swinging London' of the pop scene that attracted so much attention. Moreover, the mid-1960s saw increased concern about poverty in London, although in practice, what were termed 'problem' families had already been an issue in the 1950s. Equally, the 1960s in London could be seen in terms of serious industrial decline, with consequences in terms of rising unemployment.

New estates were designed as entire communities, with elevated walkways called streets in the sky. Most estates, however, were failures – not only because they were poorly built, but also because they did not contribute to social cohesion, which was abundantly true, for example, of the LCC's Elgin Estate in Paddington. The deadly collapse, killing four, of part of the newly opened, twenty-two-storey Ronan Point tower block in Canning Town in Newham in 1968, after a gas explosion, was correctly seen as symptomatic of a more general failure of tower blocks and modern construction methods. It was a precursor to the later response to the deadly 2017 fire at the twenty-four-storey, 1974-completed Grenfell Tower in North Kensington.

Disenchantment has continued, so that the decision of English Heritage in 1998 to list five blocks on the Alton Estate in Roehampton as an architectural masterpiece was widely deplored by the tenants. Elsewhere, there were many demolitions by the 1990s, not only of high-rise estate buildings – including Ronan Point itself in 1986 – but also of low-rise, deck-access blocks, such as the Chalkhill area in Brent, demolished in 1998–9. On the other hand, high-density, low-rise council housing, like the Alexandra Estate in West Hampstead, the Brunswick Centre in Bloomsbury and Stoneleigh Terrace in Highgate New Town, though brutalist, have been very popular with residents, won numerous prizes and now, privatised in many cases, command higher and higher prices.

The legacy of decades of public building, as well as of the lack of much building of public housing from the 1970s on, included many dwellings in need of fresh investment, although that problem was also true of sections of the private rental market, especially in poor areas, where the quality of provision was anyway bad. A lack of affordable housing was correctly seen as a comment on the failure of public provision and this lack became a particular issue for those termed essential workers, such as teachers and nurses. Not only were too few new houses built but, in addition, the cost of rehabilitating existing housing stock made the process too expensive, which underlined the crisis in housing. The selling off of assets, for example, police houses, contributed to the crisis.

Housing Problems

'Standing in a corridor on the fifth floor of a tower block on the Aylesbury estate in South London is a miserable experience. The wind whips along unending concrete walls that are uniformly grey and permanently damp (though the occasional vomit stain provides a splash of colour). The stairwells reek of urine and cheap disinfectant and the smell of decaying rubbish wafts from the disposal chutes ... The estate is a grim monument to Britain's failed postwar experiment in social housing.'

The Economist, 1 October 2005

Affordable housing was a political issue (as it remains), but one that neither of the major political parties could address successfully, in part because of the inherent clash between the governmental wish to control and allocate and the exigencies of commercial value. These exigencies had played a role in the late 1950s and early 1960s in what was known as Rachmanism: the use of the 1957 Rent Act to push out low-paying tenants in order to raise rents or redevelop properties. The use of intimidation, which revealed a persistent undercurrent of violence in much of London, made the practice a scandal, but the same tendency played a role more generally.

On the other hand, rent controls – the response of the national Labour government elected in 1964 – hit landlord profits, led to the replacement of private landlords by owner-occupiers and resulted in a decline in the amount of property available for rent. This fall reduced the flexibility of the housing market and exacerbated the consequences of the decline in new public housing from the 1970s. The marked rise in London's population from 6.7 million in 1988 to 9.3 million in 2020 – as new jobs and immigration focused on the capital, a rise that more than compensated for the earlier fall from 1939 – in turn proved a major factor. The private rental market was to revive in the 2000s in large part due to the ease of obtaining buy-to-let mortgages, but that revival contributed greatly to an unsustainable rise in London property prices. In 1990, for London households headed by someone aged thirty-five to forty-four, the home ownership rate was 69 per cent but, by 2018, it was less than 50 per cent. Partly as a result, the number of families with children in private rented accommodation tripled between 2004 and 2018. Property prices continued to rise thereafter.

Successive governments encouraged 'brown-field' building on derelict ground within existing urban areas in London and pressed for greater housing density, but these wishes were at marked variance with public demands for space within and around their homes. Moreover, the move of many people out of London, and/or into the suburbs, as well as, on a smaller scale, to gated communities within London, represented a rejection not only of what appeared to be the hostile nature of crime-ridden townscapes, but also of government views of the desirability of high-density, socially mixed populations. The British Social Attitudes Survey in 1999, by the National Centre for Social Research, showed that those who lived in big cities were the group keenest to move and current polls indicate that many Londoners would prefer to leave. Anxieties about crime and about the quality of local schools were oft cited by those dissatisfied with metropolitan life. These anxieties affected both those living in affluent owner-occupation and in neighbouring public housing estates where social deprivation and alienation were pronounced. The Covid pandemic of 2020–2 interacted with this situation.

Yet, as far as the experience of living in London was concerned, the situation was complex, with marked differences in prosperity between parts of the city. One indication was the nature of tenure. Owner-occupied households were more common in the outer boroughs and rented households more likely to be found in inner London, a situation that remains the case to the present day.

The contrasts in population density within London remain very pronounced. For example, despite the post-war redevelopment of the bombed-out site of the Barbican, the City remained an area devoted to commerce rather than housing and many of the flats in the Barbican were not, as originally intended, used by clerical workers, but instead provided town bases for workers with primary residences elsewhere. At the weekends, City shops closed as so few people lived in the area. In 2021, in response to Covid-linked changes, the City planned to convert empty office blocks to housing.

ARCHITECTURE

Alongside much unattractive and poor-quality municipal housing in the 1960s, there was also a brutal rebuilding of municipal centres within London; for example. in Swiss Cottage and also in outer London, with the massive redevelopment of central Croydon as a major office centre. Professional planners played a significant role in this process, which sought both to cope with traffic congestion and to provide modern images for the centres. Modernism was to the fore. And much was torn down. In the 1960s, the Doric Arch, Great Hall and Shareholders' Room were needlessly destroyed when Euston Station was rebuilt.

'Away with Bloomsbury'

In practice, Bloomsbury became the focus of one of the earliest environmental protest groups and this forced major changes in planning, notably with the British Library, which was forced to move from its original planned location immediately south of the British Museum to St Pancras.

The progressive architectural style and planning ideas of the 1930s became an orthodoxy that was used for the widespread post-war rebuilding, for urban development and for the new construction made possible by the investment in hospitals, schools and New Towns. A centrepiece was the first major post-war public building, the Royal Festival Hall (1951), designed for the Festival of Britain's South Bank Exhibition, by Robert Matthew, the Chief Architect to the LCC. The Thames-side site, previously largely factories and wharfs, had been extensively bombed during the war. Whatever the success of the Royal Festival Hall, the ugliness of much subsequent Modernist building, such as the Chelsea Barracks of the 1960s, led to depressing, if not inhumane, vistas. Earlier, the *Daily Telegraph* on 21 April 1955 noted 'widespread criticism of the designs of new buildings in the City', particularly since the war.

Stamps

The London of new buildings was celebrated in stamps from the 1960s. The International Geographical Congress in London in 1964 was marked with a set including 'Flats near Richmond Park. Urban Development.' Another emphasis on novelty was the set produced for the opening of the Post Office Tower in 1965. This featured two stamps, the first with the Tower and Georgian buildings and the second with the Nash Terraces in Regent's Park. In each case, the emphasis was on the Tower and the other buildings were in the shade, both visually and in terms of the colour used. In 1975, the National Theatre was commemorated in the set for European Architectural Heritage Year and in 1983 the Thames Barrier in a set for engineering achievements. A Datapost motorcyclist against a London backdrop including new tower blocks appeared in the 1985 set for the 350th anniversary of the Royal Mail public postal service.

Yet, the dominant impression was very different for the overwhelming majority of images of London focused on its past. The 700th anniversary of Simon de Montfort's Parliament led to a stamp showing Hollar's 1647 engraving of Parliament's buildings (1965), an air-battle over St Paul's appeared in the set for the 25th anniversary of the Battle of Britain (1965), there were two stamps for the 900th anniversary of Westminster Abbey (1966), and St Paul's appeared in the 1969 set of cathedrals. St Paul's, Covent Garden followed as part of the Inigo Jones series (1973), and then two stamps of the Houses of Parliament for the Commonwealth Parliamentary Conference in 1973 and another for the Inter-Parliamentary Union Conference in 1975, four stamps linked to William Caxton for the 500th anniversary of British printing (1976) and the Tower and

Hampton Court for the historic building series in 1978. 'London 1980', the montage of buildings presented on a stamp for the International Stamp Exhibition, was largely an account of traditional scenes – the Tower, Tower Bridge, St Paul's, Big Ben, Nelson's Column, Westminster Abbey and Eros, with only the Post Office Tower to mark the new.

Similarly, the series called 'London Landmarks', designed by Sir Hugh Casson in 1980, provided stamps of Buckingham Palace, the Albert Memorial, the Royal Opera House, Hampton Court and Kensington Palace, with nothing more modern. Greenwich Observatory was featured in the 1984 set for the centenary of the Greenwich Meridian, the mails leaving London in 1828 for a 1984 series on mail coach runs and the Crystal Palace and the Albert Memorial for a 1987 series on Queen Victoria. Kew Gardens was celebrated with a series in 1990, Greenwich appeared anew that year and St Paul's with searchlights was shown in a Europa Peace and Freedom series in 1995. The role of the past was also demonstrated in the five-stamp series on the Lord Mayor's Show, produced in 1989 during a period of fundamental transformation in the City, and in the five-stamp series on Shakespearean theatres that appeared in 1995, which was a period of great activity on the modern London stage.

DOCKLANDS

Later in the twentieth century, new space was found for development on the riverbanks as a result of the closure of the East India Docks in 1967, the London Docks and Surrey Commercial Docks in 1970 and of the Royal Docks in 1981. These closures were matched by the failure of associated industries and a major rise in unemployment. Docklands had been thriving in the 1950s, handling a third of Britain's trade and directly employing 28,000 dockers and sustaining a range of businesses. However, it declined rapidly from the 1960s, notably due to containerisation, but also with the redrawing of global trade routes as imperial links ebbed.

These challenges were exacerbated by the failure to match competitors benefiting from post-war development, especially Rotterdam, such that there was a move of activity from London back to the Low Countries in at least one aspect of their long-standing rivalry and relationship. Within Britain, ports such as Felixstowe and Dover proved better able to respond to the challenges and opportunities of containerisation because they were less unionised, whereas the London docks faced serious and persistent labour problems. Militant trade unionism scarcely encouraged investment in London or indeed Liverpool. Aside from containerisation, there was a rise in roll-on, roll-off trade, with lorries driving directly onto ferries, which benefited Dover, Felixstowe and Harwich. By 1975, Ipswich, Felixstowe and Harwich, counted together, ranked second only to London in both the value and tonnage of non-fuel exports and, by 1994, Felixstowe handled nearly half the country's deep-sea container traffic. London, by then, had been hit by a vicious spiral of technological change, notably the acceleration of containerisation and its impact on a labour-intensive workforce prone to union militancy and disruption.

Because London's maritime trade was focused twenty-six miles downriver at Tilbury, the now derelict Docklands provided an unprecedented development opportunity near the centre of a major city. The development was politicised with the Conservative government of Margaret Thatcher (Prime Minister 1979–90) taking a close interest in directing the process. The creation of the London Docklands Development Corporation (LDDC) in 1981 led to the regeneration of much of East London, with the building of houses and offices and an improvement in the transport system. Some dock basins were filled in; for example, in the former Surrey Commercial Docks, Rotherhithe, and new roads and houses were constructed. New industries in Rotherhithe included the printing works of the *Daily Mail*.

The government regarded the local authorities, workers and unions as conspiring in a way that was destroying their communities and damaging the economy. The LDDC was a government body designed to circumvent the constraints of the Greater London Council and local boroughs, both of which were under Labour control and regarded as anti-entrepreneurial, while the Conservative government also abolished the South-East Economic Planning Council because its planners were seen as antipathetic to growth.

An enterprise zone was created on the Isle of Dogs in 1982 and the LDDC lasted until abolished by the Labour government in 1998. There was no comparable regional economic planning for London as a whole. The regeneration was heavily subsidised as the government bore all of the cost of clearing the site – including cleaning up contaminated land – and of infrastructure, especially transport, significant investment by a government that decried subsidies. This was to recur with the cost of preparing the 2012 Olympic Games.

The financial centre of Canary Wharf on the Isle of Dogs, on which work started in 1988, proved an abrupt contrast to earlier patterns of work within Dockland. By 2003, Canary Wharf contained 13.1 million square feet of office space and many City companies had moved their headquarters there, including newspapers from Fleet Street. The social context of employment in the Isle of Dogs, and London as a whole, was transformed although, from a different perspective, the contrast between Canary Wharf and the continued poverty of the borough of Tower Hamlets suggested, instead, a reshaping of traditional patterns of social differentiation. Indeed, there was criticism of the LDDC on the grounds that it brought few benefits to the local people, instead helping create jobs and houses that were inappropriate to them: they were unable to afford the new houses, while the new jobs required skilled workers who came from outside the region. Tower Hamlets had wanted to use the land for industrial development that would create blue-collar jobs. Conversely, there was an unfair comparison of the LDDC with the GLC's less-than-inspiring attempt to develop Thamesmead on the Erith and Plumstead Marshes as a new town within London itself: the GLC had fewer resources for the task and notably did not benefit from a comparable investment in infrastructure.

The office tower blocks of Canary Wharf were a symbol of the new economy and were seen in that light. The bombing of Canary Wharf by the IRA in 1996 was intended not only as a practical demonstration of their capacity to hit hard at Britain's economy, but also as a symbolic strike at the legacy of Thatcherism. This new economy was a system in which London and the South-East were clearly the focus of economic power, not least as there was a serious decline in traditional manufacturing regions, such as the North-East and South Wales, in the 1980s. The Conservatives, and the Establishment in general, became more focused on London, the South-East and their world of money and services, largely to the detriment of traditional interests that they had also represented. This process continued under Tony Blair, Labour Prime Minister from 1997 to 2007, with the South-East being responsible for a growing share of GDP.

Transport Links

Unlike the inter-war years, the post-war transport system in London changed not with the expansion of suburbia but with new capacity within the already built-up area. From the 1960s, the Underground expanded considerably. The Victoria Line, opened in 1968–9, the first automatic underground railway in the world, was followed by the Jubilee Line, completed in 1979, the Piccadilly extension to Heathrow, opened in 1977 and the Jubilee extension to Greenwich and Stratford in 1999. The Docklands Light Railway was opened in 1987 and its extension to London City airport ran from 2005 and to Lewisham from 2009. The expansion of the Underground from the 1960s helped, to a degree, to compensate for the earlier neglect of South London, although part of that neglect was due to the intractable sub-surface of South-East London. Although not part of the Underground, the Heathrow Express provided a rapid underground link to the airport, which assisted the growth of centralised national air travel from Heathrow. Later, the use of Oyster travelcards and debit cards to pay for tickets on trains increased the integration of the transport system, not least easing travel south of the Thames and the use of suburban railway lines.

At the same time, the significant role of London as an international transport hub was enhanced and underlined in 1992 when the Channel Tunnel was opened to rail travel. Initially, Waterloo – where the Eurostar terminal was completed in 1994 – was the London terminal, to be replaced, from 2007, by St Pancras as a glitzy cross between Victorian engineering and modern consumerism. In contrast, Broad Street station was closed and destroyed in 1986 as part of the development of the new Liverpool Street station, with much of what had been Broad Street station becoming the very ugly Broadgate Centre development.

A fighter airfield in the war and the site of one of the city's oldest prehistoric settlements, Heathrow airport opened in 1946 and was followed by Gatwick in 1958, the year in which Croydon airport closed. By 1999, Heathrow handled 62 million passengers, making it the fourth-busiest airport in the world and the busiest outside the USA. It was also a key centre of employment for West London and doubly important because of the collapse in alternative employment, especially with the decline of the engineering and electrical industries in Ealing and Hounslow from the

1960s. Gatwick, Stansted, Luton and London City (opened in Docklands in 1987) airports further contributed to London's role as a regional, national and international hub. By 2008, there were 480,000 flights over London a year, a formidable challenge to the city's environment and, due to the noise imprint, part of the local pattern of London's politics. The expansion of Heathrow became a persistently contentious issue.

On the roads, meanwhile, trams were finally totally phased out in favour of diesel-engined motor-buses. The last tram ran in 1952 and the last trolleybus in 1962. The cost of electricity and the maintenance costs of the wires hit trolleybuses, of which London had had a maximum fleet of 1,811 and the largest system in the world, while motor-buses benefited from greater manoeuvrability. The rise and fall of the trams and the trolleybuses is a reminder of the rapidity of change in communications. From the 1990s, there was a small-scale revival in Croydon of trams, now seen as a viable alternative to buses. More Londoners, however, came to travel by car, while commuting – much of it by train but, as the M25 shows every weekday, in large part by car – became more significant in the South-East. In 1981–91 alone, there was a 7 per cent increase in commuting into London. Bus use in London rose in 1998–2012, but production, while once a major industry, followed most of London's manufacturing into decline, with the bus works closing in 1976.

At the neighbourhood level, major road routes became obstacles, as their high-street sections were turned into busy through-routes; for example, at Hendon Central or along the South Circular. This problem encouraged the building of new through-routes unrelated to existing neighbourhoods, with the M4 being driven through the Osterley Park country estate in 1965 and the GLC proposing, in the Greater London Development Plan, an inner London motorway box. The plan also encompassed orbital motorways in London's suburbia, as well as motorways designed to link London to the national network. However, there was large-scale opposition and most of the plan was discarded, although the western and eastern parts of the inner box were built. In turn, roads such as the Westway caused destruction as they were built, and left blight in their aftermath, as noted by P. D. James in her novel *A Certain Justice* (1997).

The M25 around London, completed in 1986, became the busiest route in the country, as well as helping to define London's geographical identity and shape. The usage of the M25 indicated the need for an orbital route, not least due to the growing congestion caused by heavy traffic trundling through London. Much of this traffic was caused by the switch of Britain's trade towards the Continent and by London being athwart the route, although no longer able to take advantage of it economically, as it had historically done. Yet the usage of the M25 also showed the extent to which new roads led to new demand. This demand contributed to the pollution in London and also to a more general environmental degradation.

Those neighbourhoods that were not bisected by through-routes were still affected by the car. Side streets became 'rat runs', quick shortcuts linking busier roads and the sides of all roads filled up with parked cars. Parking space came to take a greater percentage of London's space and the problems of parking became a major topic of conversation. In response, the Congestion Charge was adopted in central London in 2002 to limit the movement of cars into the city centre and the Congestion Charge Zone was extended westwards in 2007 to Kensington, Chelsea and part of Westminster. Charging has remained a contentious issue to the present, one that brings into sharp conflict different views on public health, personal freedom, mobility, social equity and finance. So was also the case with the related issue of road closures which became more significant during the Covid-19 pandemic of 2020–2.

While often deplored by planners, commentators and many Londoners, cars were widely used. Greater mobility for most – but not all – of London's population, however, exacerbated contrasts between different parts of the city, emphasised social segregation and caused pollution. Thus, car ownership brought a sense – maybe an illusion – of freedom and an access to opportunities and options for many, but not all.

The division of the population into spatially distinct communities, defined by differing levels of wealth, expectations, opportunity and age, was scarcely new in London's history, but it became more pronounced during the twentieth century and an obvious aspect of what was termed the underclass was their relative lack of mobility. This lack of mobility was doubly important because of links between cars, status, independence and notions of virile masculinity. The theft of cars reflected their appeal. At the same time, buses, cycles and walking remained important as means of travel, the last mostly much underrated in accounts of London's transport system.

ENVIRONMENT

There was a transformation in London's air. The problems of air quality in part reflected London's location in a bowl created by surrounding hills, as well as the particular difficulty created by warm air trying to rise while trapped by high-pressure skies above. The trapped air, if polluted by smoke, provided obstacles to vision and breathing. The actor Patrick Cargill described how some London theatres had interiors that let in the smog and became quite foggy during plays. The very bad London smog of 1952, which killed more than four thousand people and, indeed, asphyxiated cattle at Smithfield Market, led to the designation of London as a smokeless zone in 1955 and to the Clean Air Act of 1956, which required the conversion of buildings from coal-use and made individual households responsible for the cost. This legislation was made possible by the fact that (as never before) the means for such conversions were now readily to hand as gas became the principal source of heating. However, as with clean water and the end of cholera a century earlier, improvement was not instantaneous. London had a further smog in 1957 and then lost another 750 people to a serious smog in 1962, which led to another Clean Air Act in 1968.

The decline of London's industrial base, which was especially pronounced in the late 1960s to early 1970s, also contributed to the change in the character of the capital's pollution. The conversion to smokeless fuel led to an atmosphere that was no longer acidic nor heavy with sooty smuts and helped ensure that London became cleaner and brighter. Yet, other particulates and chemicals became more significant in London's environment, in part as a consequence of more use of the car. In response to this pollution, there has been far greater concern about, and mapping of, levels of such substances as carbon monoxide, ozone, sulphur dioxide, hydrocarbons and nitrogen dioxide. The legacy of past pollution was also heavy. The Millennium Dome was built in Greenwich in 1997–9, on the site of what had been Europe's largest gasworks. It had made coal gas in a process that produced toxic waste, including arsenic, asbestos and cyanide. To clear the site, much of the waste was buried in rural dumps, while the site was sealed with crushed concrete, plastic and clay, and each building had to have a gas-tight membrane underneath.

The cleaning up of the Thames led to the return of fish, with the first salmon for a century caught in 1974. However, the water situation was a complex one. Under London, the water table rose as industrial extraction, for example, by breweries, declined. The resulting flooding of cellars and underground car-parks led to investment in pumping away water. An analysis of multiple radar images acquired by European satellites between 1992 and 2003 revealed an uplift in elevation in North-East London around Docklands as the factories that took water from boreholes closed. The rise in the water table led to one in land elevation. In contrast, there were areas of subsidence, notably from St James's Park to

London Bridge along the route of the Jubilee Line extension, and also south-west from Battersea Park where there was a tunnel for electricity cables. Moreover, the water table fell in South-West London due to increased extraction. Indeed, development in London and the South-East as a whole, not least the greater number of appliances – such as washing machines and dishwashers – strained water supplies and emphasised the problems stemming from the absence of a national water grid. As a result, the reuse of water is particularly high in London, with recycled water, on average, flowing through several people as a result of the system of treatment plants.

Bazalgette's great achievement, which had been so important to the ability of London to overcome disease and create a safer living environment, was supplemented in the late twentieth century by improvements to the water supply designed to deal with the problems posed by the corrosion of the cast-iron pipes through which water was supplied. Like Bazalgette's system, this involved another major work of engineering. The Thames Water Ring Main, constructed at a depth of about 135 feet (roughly twice that of the Underground system) from 1988 to 1993, linked the treatment works at Coppermills, Hampton, Kempton, Walton and Ashford Common to the pump-out supply shafts. The Ring Main is 51 miles long and by 2008 the system was supplying about 1,300 megalitres daily.

However, the growth in the volume of rubbish – much of it non-biodegradable – proved especially attractive to rats and foxes. Moreover, assumptions about appropriate attitudes towards animals ensured that the repertoire of means hitherto available for action against vermin was markedly restricted, with limitations on the poisons that could be used. Shifts in attitudes were complex. Thus, in 2007, seeing pigeons as a health and environmental hazard, their feeding in and near Trafalgar Square was banned. At the same time, there were also more benign developments, such as the growth in the number of herons, encouraged not just by the return of fish to the Thames but also by the increased popularity of ponds. The marked rise in the number of parakeets is also notable, adding very different sights and sounds.

ETHNICITY

Shifts in the location of ethnic groups affected the timbre of London. Playing a major role in construction work and the NHS, the Irish – like other migrant groups – were informed by family and friendship networks and went to places where they knew people, leading to a snowballing of communities such as Kilburn, which became the capital of the Irish in England after 1945. The London Irish both followed work and embarked on a process of suburbanisation, in time moving out along the axis of Kilburn, so that the Irish population of Kingsbury increased from the 1950s.

Other earlier immigrant groups also moved out of inner London and into suburbia. Jews moved from the East End into North-West London and, in turn, from Golders Green to Edgware and then, in the 2000s, into Hertfordshire – notably Radlett. Their movement out of the East End created spaces for Bangladeshis and other immigrants. Alongside the movement of Jews within the region, there was a decline in the Jewish community, in large part due to 'marrying out' with non-Jews. As a result, much Jewish community activity was increasingly that of the more orthodox, who congregated in particular areas, especially Stamford Hill.

New immigrant groups had varied trajectories. World War Two led to large numbers of refugees as well as a shortage of labour in London. The Poles – many of them former soldiers who did not welcome the prospect of living in their homeland under communist rule – were joined by Estonians, Latvians, Lithuanians and Ukrainians. Until Italian economic growth became more marked from the 1960s, the Italians were another important immigrant community.

Immigration from the Empire brought in Hong Kong Chinese and Cypriots, the latter focusing on Camden Town, with a renewed immigration from Hong Kong in the early 2020s. There was also immigration from Malta, with criminals taking over prostitution and pornography in Soho, developing links with the Vice Squad that affected the reputation of the Metropolitan Police as a whole in the 1960s and 1970s. From the 1950s, there was large-scale immigration from the New Commonwealth, although many of the immigrants intended only a limited stay. A temporary labour shortage in unattractive spheres of employment, such as transport – especially the buses – and nursing, led to an active sponsorship of immigration that accorded with Commonwealth idealism of the period.

Black people encountered severe discrimination in the housing market, as well as much personal hostility, a theme explored in the film *Pool of London* (1951), where a Jamaican merchant seaman is a key character. Many immigrants found landlords unwilling to accept them as tenants. The cooking smells of West Indians and Indians were criticised, while the former were condemned for loud parties and sexual immorality. Racism played a role in neighbourhoods and workplaces and 'White flight' came to be involved in the housing pattern. Notting Hill in 1958 witnessed a race riot with white thugs attacking recently settled blacks. In response, the Notting Hill Carnival was started the following year, while Oswald Mosley failed in his attempt to exploit the immigration issue during the 1959 electoral campaign. At the same time, the limited incorporation of West Indians into the community was shown in the 1959 election: of the seven thousand West Indians entitled to vote in North Kensington, only a thousand did so.

Much of the initial New Commonwealth immigration was from the West Indies, but South Asia subsequently became more important. Areas such as Southall came to seem 'Little Indias' to other Londoners and the railway station has Indian signs. Due to immigration, there were significant variations in settlement patterns across London. For example, whereas over ten per cent of the population of six boroughs – Hounslow, Ealing, Brent, Harrow, Redbridge and Newham – were of Indian background in 1991, thirteen boroughs had a figure smaller than 2.5 per cent. The concentration in the case of Bangladeshis was more pronounced, with over 10 per cent in Tower Hamlets (replacing the Jews who had moved out), over 5 per cent in Newham and Camden and fewer than 1 per cent in most of the boroughs. From the late 1990s, Tower Hamlets promoted the Brick Lane area as 'London's Curry Capital' and Banglatown, an idea originating in the late 1980s and reflecting the approximately 80,000 British citizens of Bangladeshi heritage living there. Brick Lane, which had a mosque from 1976, became the stereotypical cultural centre for successive waves of immigrants but, less benignly, Lutfur Rahman, the directly elected Mayor, was thrown out in 2015 for election fraud among charges of corruption.

Brick Lane Mosque

Opened in 1978, the building was first constructed in 1743 as the *Neuve Eglise* for the Huguenots of the area. In 1897, the building was acquired by orthodox Lithuanian Jews. The steel tubular structure it now includes is a minaret.

Additional immigrant flows included Vietnamese to Hackney in the 1980s and Iraqis to North-West London in the 1990s and 2000s. In an immigration that began in the 1970s, over ten thousand South Koreans live in the 'Koreatown' in New Malden, which includes restaurants, food markets and travel agencies. These are examples of the range of new Londoners, with their distinctive experiences. Those not born in Britain were 37 per cent of London's population in the 2011 census, in which 44.9 per cent of the city's population were 'white British', while about 5 per cent of London's population are illegal immigrants. Many flee hardship to find broken expectations.

London faced the major social burden of coping with half the net international immigration affecting the United Kingdom. Partly as a result of this immigration, the city's population – which had risen to about 8.7 million by 1938, before falling to 8.2 million in 1951 and 6.7 million in 1988, as large numbers moved to new housing in the Outer Metropolitan Area – rose to 9.3 million in 2020. These were very significant changes, in individual, aggregate and percentage terms, changes that helped contextualise – if not characterise – the experience of being a Londoner or a member of a London-linked network.

In response to changes in the ethnic composition of London, there were developments in religious provision. The first Hindu temple in London was opened as late as 1962 and in Neasden the largest Hindu temple outside India opened in 1997. For the construction of the latter, the many different woods and marbles were shipped from around the world to a region of Gujarat in India where specialised craftsmen carved the extraordinarily elaborate details and shipped the resulting vast 'kit' to London for assembly. The rise in the Muslim population had already led to the official opening in 1944 of the East London Mosque and in 1978 of the Central London Mosque in Regent's Park. The London Muslim Centre followed on Whitechapel Road in 2004.

In turn, the Church of England was not only ministering to a smaller percentage of London's population, but also faced serious problems. In *Honest to God* (1963), a widely read book, John Robinson, Anglican Bishop of Woolwich, sought to address the inability of the Church to reach out to many, especially in rundown urban areas, by pressing the need for a determination to respond that would include a new liturgy. The Church of England was not alone in facing problems. Thus, Catholic churches in London suffered a decline in congregations in

1989–98 of 19 per cent, although the Baptists reversed an earlier fall, instead seeing an 11 per cent increase. In turn, Polish immigration in the early and mid-2000s helped to increase the size of Catholic congregations, while black Pentacostal 'megachurches' developed in South London.

1950s

Alongside an understanding of change from a thematic perspective, it is instructive to adopt a chronological one, not least because this is a key way in which change is experienced. The 1950s provide a useful backdrop as this was a decade in which change largely occurred within established social, economic, political, cultural and religious patterns. The Conservatives, in power nationally from 1951 to 1964 (although Labour ran the LCC), did not support large-scale state intervention. The nationalisations of the 1945–51 Labour government were largely left in place, but there was no equivalent to the extension of state control comparable to the National Health Service. Instead, the rebuilding of London in the 1950s was mostly carried out by private developers. The Conservative government overturned previous planning controls, ensuring that tall buildings were constructed despite the protests of the LCC. Thus, in 1956, a Regency terrace looking onto Hyde Park was purchased by Charles Clore, who built the twenty-eight-storey London Hilton on the site. Much of the City was rebuilt, while large buildings further west included Bowater House in Knightsbridge.

Look Back in Anger (1956), by the London-born John Osborne, set in London and staged at the Royal Court Theatre (turned into a film in 1959), was pointed in its angry attack on Establishment values and hypocrisies, as was the highly influential art exhibition *This is Tomorrow*, staged in 1956 at the Whitechapel Art Gallery. However, the 1950s, especially the early part of the decade, were in many respects characterised by an attempt to return to 1930s'

London. Physically, there were many similarities, not least with coal fires and smog, while the attempt to keep the city as the imperial metropole appeared valid in the 'New Elizabethan Age' proclaimed to mark the coronation of Elizabeth II in 1953. Clothes were more similar to those of the 1930s than those of the 1970s and reflected hierarchies of class, gender and age.

In the late 1940s and 1950s, there was also a shift towards the Conservatives in general elections for seats in the LCC area. In the 1959 general election, Labour won twenty-four of the forty-two seats in the LCC area and the Conservatives the other eighteen. In Middlesex the results were eight and twenty-one respectively, in the Kent and Surrey suburban constituencies two and thirteen and in Essex nine and five; leading to a suburban total of nineteen Labour and thirty-nine Conservative seats and an aggregate LCC and suburban figure of forty-three Labour and fifty-seven Conservative.

1960s

The 1960s destroyed a cultural continuity that had lasted from the Victorian period. This destruction reflected the impact of social and ideological trends, including the rise of new forms and a new agenda moulded by shifts in the understanding of gender, youth, class, place and race, as well as by secularisation. London both moulded change and provided a stage for it: it was a stage in particular for the 'Swinging Sixties', the idea of new lifestyles and fashions that were presented to the world from a series of London settings, such as the clothes boutiques of Carnaby Street and the Abbey Road recording studios used in particular by The Beatles. Working-class talent provided a powerful infusion of energy in this world of show, a world in which pop stars, hairdressers and photographers were celebrities. The mid-1960s saw a cycle of 'Swinging London' films including *A Hard Day's Night* (1964), *Darling* (1965) and

Blow-Up (1965), which threw light on the morals and mores of the permissive society. British youth culture was reconfigured towards metropolitan interests, notably with the hippies and drugs of the 1960s. In turn, to reach a wider audience, punk in the late 1970s had to be taken up by London's record companies and television. Consumerism, meanwhile, was reconfiguring the metropolitan world. For Alfie – the eponymous protagonist played by Michael Caine in the 1966 film – women, clothes and cars were commodities that proved one could get on in the world without the privileges conferred through birth and education. Supermarkets provided new, anonymous shopping spaces.

Politically, there was change. In the 1966 general election, Labour surged forward at the expense of the Conservatives, taking thirty-six seats in the LCC area, thirty in the surrounding boroughs and 49.9 per cent of the popular vote, compared to, respectively, six seats, twenty-eight seats and 40.7 per cent.

Institutionally, London itself was transformed. The Herbert Commission on Greater London Government – a Royal Commission which met from 1957 to 1960 – proposed revisions in the two-tier system of the LCC, including creating fifty-two Metropolitan Boroughs, a separate City of London handling local government functions and a Greater London Council (GLC) to handle large-scale issues. In the event, under the London Government Act of 1963, the Conservative government's decision to abolish the LCC and Middlesex and to create the GLC (established in 1965) passed Parliament against much Labour opposition. However, helped by the government yielding to pressure from areas that wished to be excluded – including Staines, Sunbury, Esher, Walton, Banstead, Epsom and Caterham – the Conservatives were weaker in the GLC area than had been anticipated. In the first GLC elections, Labour won sixty-four of the hundred seats including nearly every marginal borough. The LCC area, 117 square miles, contained 3.2 million people in 1961, but the GLC covered 610 square miles with over seven million residents.

Within the new GLC area, the boroughs were totally reorganised into thirty-one new boroughs and the Cities of London and Westminster. Many of the earlier boroughs had been, in effect, single-party monopolies of power, with relative social homogeneity diminishing the chance for effective political pluralism. The consolidation of boroughs reduced this homogeneity by linking many disparate areas. St Pancras joined Holborn and Hampstead in the new borough of Camden, while Battersea joined Putney and Tooting in Wandsworth; Westminster absorbed Marylebone and Paddington and Chelsea merged with Kensington. The boroughs opposed amalgamation but, in doing so – and as an aspect of declining local democracy – they lacked the public support that had held up the process in the 1890s. This amalgamation appeared to lessen the need for the overarching authority of the GLC, not least because the independence of the boroughs meant that there was scant support for the idea of the GLC as a strategic metropolitan authority. Moreover, central government retained control of the police and took over transport from the GLC. Central government's rate support grant also lessened the role of the GLC as a redistributive agency between the boroughs.

New borough identities did not necessarily work or offer much beyond administrative convenience. Some boroughs followed lines of transport communication so that, for example, Hampstead residents were already familiar with Camden Town and Holborn. East–West boroughs found this harder because, for example, the residents of the western parts of Haringey had little motive to visit Tottenham and vice versa. The creation of numerous local history societies in the late 1960s and early 1970s was an aspect of a continuing interest in local identity.

The new boroughs did not engage public loyalty and residents were more likely to identify with parts of their neighbourhood that were often related to the former borough. As a result, with ties affected by geographical and social mobility, rehousing and a disengagement from bureaucratic local authorities, community localism was limited, certainly more so than in many other towns and, again, usually well below the borough level. The boroughs, indeed, acquired a stronger administrative role, while partly losing their representative one.

The political consequences of the formation of the GLC, bringing together the Labour LCC with Conservative suburbia and inner and outer London, were initially unclear. The Conservatives gained power in the 1967 GLC election and retained it in 1970, but lost it in 1973, as a result of a vociferous and popular campaign against the GLC's road-building plans, which owed much to Abercrombie's 1944 scheme. Labour took charge, bringing to a rapid close plans for the Ringways and the Motorway Box and for a redevelopment of Covent Garden that would also put an emphasis on through-roads.

The City also changed as a system of financial and mercantile power. Its role had been undermined with Britain's loss of empire and of the global function of sterling, but the City was reinvented as an international financial centre. In part, this was because the power of established practices and the City Establishment were challenged, leading to changes in the practice of corporate finance and also more effort to appeal to shareholders. A series of contentious takeovers registered the effort. In 1958, the successful contested takeover of British Aluminium saw S. G. Warburg – a banking house then outside the City Establishment – outmanoeuvre the latter, not least by writing to shareholders over the heads of their boards and by talking to the press. At the same time, takeovers extended London's influence. In 1969, Barclays and Martins merged. Martins was the last national English bank to have its headquarters outside London and, with the merger, Liverpool lost this status.

1970s

The confidence and optimistic energy of the 1960s had given way to a more troubled 1970s, with economic crises, falling employment in manufacturing, rampant inflation, serious labour disputes and political instability seen, for example, in the IRA bombing campaign. This situation led to a sense of cultural malaise as with the urban decay and the closed theatre in the spoof horror film *Theatre of Blood* (1973). These problems also led to the anger seen in the violence of the punk aesthetic, such as *London Calling* (1979) by the band The Clash, which considered unemployment, racial conflict, drug use and environmental issues. The album sold over five million copies worldwide and the titular single was adopted as a match-day anthem by Arsenal and Fulham, two of the leading London football teams.

Born to Struggle

Born to Struggle (1973) by May Hobbs in part recounts the transformation of Hoxton where she was born in 1938, and which is depicted in terms of a 'great sense of community' based on neighbourliness, as well as pie-and-mash shops. Hobbs finds life in London tough, as she changes places, jobs and partners and has serious problems with rent and harsh landlords. A night cleaner who found the union bureaucrats unhelpful, Hobbs established the Cleaners Action Group. Her book testifies to the nature of much working life: 'I was feeling really exhausted and irritable.'

A sense of malaise affected the perception of London, as well as the amount of effort that could be, and was, put into improving and preserving the urban environment. In his dyspeptic novel *Jake's Thing* (1978), Kingsley Amis described urban neglect in

Mornington Crescent: 'Weeds flourished in the crevices between the paving-stones . . . a heap of waterlogged and collapsed cardboard boxes and some large black plastic sheets spread about by the wind . . . along with after-shave cartons, sweet-wrappers, dog-food labels and soft-drink tins.'

In the winter of 1978–9, London was hit hard by the 'winter of discontent' with strikes by refuse collectors leading to mounds of rubbish. Ambulancemen and hospital ancillary workers were among the others who went on strike, and this disruption led to a rallying of support to the Conservatives under Margaret Thatcher in the 1979 election. She won power with a national swing that was especially strong in suburbia.

1980s

Other pressures contributed to the political mix and added different levels of action and anxiety. In the 1980s, racial issues played a major role in disturbances in London. In 1981, crowds rioted, looted and fought with the police in Brixton and Southall, as they also did outside London, most prominently in Liverpool. Relations between black youth and the police were a specific issue and became the focus of the report from the Scarman Inquiry that was set up after the Brixton riots. Lord Scarman blamed 'racial disadvantage' for the riots. The Broadwater Farm riots followed in Tottenham in 1985 with a policeman murdered during the rioting on a supposedly model estate that had rapidly became a classic instance of the social failure of these environments.

Authorities increasingly responded against racism, the *Chelsea News* of 22 October 1987 reporting the first occasion in which the council had threatened a tenant with eviction on the grounds of racial abuse. However, the role of the police continued to be contentious. In October 1994, the 28,000-strong Metropolitan Police Force contained only 679 ethnic-minority officers, while the failure to secure a conviction after the murder of Stephen

Lawrence, a young black man, by a white gang in Eltham in 1993 led to accusations of institutional racism on the part of the police, which was a finding of the official inquiry that reported in 1999.

Inner-city discontent was not simply a matter of racial issues but, in part, a consequence of the economic transformation caused by the decline of manufacturing. The results included the loss of unskilled and semi-skilled work and the development of an economy of shifts and expedients which led to an openness on the part of some to criminal behaviour such as drug-dealing.

London, meanwhile, proved a major centre of formal opposition to the Thatcher governments of 1979–90. This opposition focused on the GLC, which was led by Ken Livingstone, 'Red Ken', a vocal Labour militant, who had displaced his moderate colleagues in 1981 and deliberately challenged Thatcher. The 'Fare's Fair' policy – public subsidies to cut bus and tube fares – was a particular point of contention, angering outer London boroughs such as Bromley that did not benefit from the Underground and was ruled to be illegal.

In turn, in fulfilment of a pledge made by the Conservatives during the 1983 general election campaign, the GLC was abolished in 1986 by the Local Government Act, which ended all the metropolitan authorities and left London without an overarching authority. Once the GLC had gone, support for it fell. Power, instead, was exercised by the boroughs as well as residuary bodies and the national government. Thatcher, herself MP for the London constituency of Finchley, was in part driven by a suburban dislike both of inner London and of the controlling tendencies of a centralising London authority. County Hall, the Thameside headquarters of the LCC (and then GLC) from 1922 that stood opposite the Houses of Parliament, was sold off and much of it was converted into flats and a hotel from 1995. In 1990, the abolition of the Inner London Education Authority, seen as a centre for socialist control, fulfilled another of Thatcher's goals.

As with much of its political history, this process found London exemplifying national trends. At the same time as centralisation was intensified at the national level, there was also a driving back of public powers at the local level. The extension of compulsory competitive tendering for a wide range of local government services in 1988 was designed to challenge the role of council workers and their unions. It led to the entrance of private sector contractors into public service work; for example, refuse collection. Certain Conservative authorities – especially Wandsworth and Westminster – were flagships for this process, while Labour counterparts – such as Lambeth – were markedly opposed. Although part of a national process, the privatisation of London's utilities, such as water and gas, also ensured a loss of public control and patronage.

Ungovernability?

'NUPE [National Union of Public Employees] boiler workers broke their union's pledge of co-operation with Camden Council this week by calling an unofficial strike over travel expenses – leaving hundreds of households without heating or hot water.'

Hampstead & Highgate Express, 23 October 1987

The sale of council houses, a key Thatcherite policy, was also intended to help in shifting the electoral composition of London by lessening the vested interests behind Labour. The policy was defended as an assault on council fiefdoms and an empowerment of individuals, most of whom were expected to vote Conservative. The council houses were sold to their tenants at a heavy discount and many of the former tenants rewarded Thatcher by supporting her in the 1983 and 1987 general elections. In Westminster, council house sales were encouraged as a means of gerrymandering.

These sales contributed to growing spatial differentiation between socio-economic groups across London, a differentiation that has thwarted all efforts to prevent it. Moreover, this process was not restricted to the exclusion of the poor but, instead, operated all along the social scale, such that in Westminster, Kensington, Chelsea and Hampstead the middle classes have been extensively replaced by the seriously affluent.

In social terms, council house sales opened up a divide between skilled manual workers and welfare dependants who did not switch to the Conservatives but whose electoral turnout was low and falling. Whereas Britain swung to the Conservatives as a whole by only 0.3 per cent between 1979 and 1992, the swing in London was 1 per cent although, in turn, this was less than the swing in the South-East, which was 2.8 per cent. In the 1983 general election – when Thatcher's national position was greatly strengthened – the swing to the Conservatives was inversely related to unemployment. The inner zone, characterised by an unemployment level in the recession of 1981 of at least 8 per cent, delivered a swing lower than an outer zone where the unemployment rate had been lower. The Conservatives also benefited from division among the opposition in 1983, winning fifty-six seats on 44 per cent of the vote in Greater London to twenty-six (30 per cent) for Labour and two seats (25 per cent) for the Liberal/Social Democrat Alliance.

In the 1987 general election, the Conservative advance was greatest in Greater London and the Outer Metropolitan Area, the combination of which provided nearly a quarter of the British electorate. That year, Labour lost Thurrock, its sole seat in the Outer Metropolitan area, while the two seats across the country in which the Conservatives had the biggest increase in their share of the vote were Newham South and Ealing North. Yet, in the local elections of 1994, the Tories lost Barnet and Croydon and only held Bromley, Kensington, Wandsworth and Westminster.

ARCHITECTURE

Meanwhile, there was an aesthetic anxiety about the nature and intention of Modernist developments. Modernist functionalism had driven the pace of development with buildings such as Eric Bedford's BT Tower (completed as the GPO Tower in 1964), Richard Seifert's uncompromising slab-like Centre Point (1967), Basil Spence's contemporaneous, but uglier, Home Office, and Richard Rogers' Lloyd's building (1986). However, Modernism was increasingly criticised by conservation movements and on aesthetic grounds. Indeed, buildings such as Denys Lasdun's National Theatre (1965–76) and the Institute of Education (1970–8) were attacked as the 'New Brutalism', lacking a human scale and feel. This criticism was popularised by Prince Charles, Prince of Wales, in the 1980s and 1990s, not least with his description of the initial plans for the extension to the National Gallery as a 'monstrous carbuncle on the face of a much-loved and elegant friend'. He also condemned the plans for the new British Library as a 'dim collection of brick sheds and worse'. By the 1980s, Modernism was being challenged by a Neoclassical revival pioneered by Quinlan Terry.

Nevertheless, a determination to embrace modern shapes and materials and to focus on functionalism was seen in important works of the late 1990s and early 2000s, such as Nicholas Grimshaw's Eurostar rail terminal at Waterloo. Far from being seen as a redundant form, skyscrapers were increasingly built or projected in the 2000s and the 2010s, including 30 St Mary Axe, the Swiss Reinsurance Tower (2002–4) – generally known as the gherkin or the erotic gherkin – which was designed by Norman Foster on the site of the Baltic Exchange wrecked by an IRA bomb in 1992. Indeed, Mayor Livingstone, in part under pressure from developers, supported the idea of clusters of high-quality skyscrapers in order to retain London's financial pre-eminence, secure benefits from developers – including affordable housing – assert identity through impressive architecture and to maintain the sustainability of the city in the face of development pressures.

Much other work was far removed from Neoclassicism, including Richard Rogers' Millennium Dome (2000) and his Terminal 5 at Heathrow, Foster's Millennium Bridge and his egg-shaped (and inefficient) Greater London Assembly building (2002), Herzog and De Muron's Tate Modern (2000) and the award-winning Canary Wharf tube station. Tate Modern – like the Millennium Dome and Bridge, the GLA building and the London Eye – opened up a series of new vistas, notably to riverside scenes. The city looked very different in its central areas. Opened in 2013, Renzo Piano's Shard, near London Bridge, was part of the contrast that went into the revitalisation of that mixed area, one followed by the rebuilding of the station. The location of tall buildings in part reflected planning constraints, notably the views of local authorities, with Westminster Council particularly opposed, and restrictions to protect views of St Paul's Cathedral and the Palace of Westminster as seen from the larger parks.

There was also the reworking and refurbishment of existing buildings. The Great Court of the British Museum was successfully reinstated with a glass canopy designed by Foster, while Somerset House was transformed from 1997, as Inland Revenue offices were replaced by the Courtauld Gallery and other activities geared to visitors, including annual ice-skating. The process of refurbishment was also seen in entire areas, including Covent Garden (from the 1970s), Notting Hill and Shoreditch. Gentrification was also the case in Islington. Very differently, the new Shakespeare's Globe theatre, a reproduction of that burned down in 1613, was opened in 1995.

The nature of patronage was instructive, being largely for public or financial purposes. New buildings included the very expensive headquarters of the security services: Thames House for the Security Service (MI5) and Vauxhall Cross for the Secret Intelligence Service (MI6).

CULTURE

While London extended its already strong sway over the regions in the second half of the twentieth century through radio and television, and estuarine became the pervasive accent of the country, the cultural world of London was itself open to foreign influences. The USA proved particularly influential across London life and activity, most obviously through popular music and the ubiquitous television. In his novel *Money* (1984), Martin Amis described his part of London 'going up in the world. There used to be a third-generation Italian restaurant across the road . . . It's now a Burger Den. There is a Burger Shack too, and a Burger Bower.'

There were also important Continental influences. From World War Two, French plays, especially by Sartre and Anouilh, were frequently performed in translation. From the mid-1950s, Brecht had a significant impact and major productions of his work were staged in the National Theatre in the 1960s. The 'theatre of the absurd', a term applied in 1961 to non-realistic, modern drama, was centred in Paris but was followed in London, where works by Samuel Beckett and Eugene Ionesco were produced frequently. Beckett influenced the London playwright Harold Pinter. In London concert halls, the works of the Russian composer Dmitri Shostakovitch were frequently performed in the 1950s and 1960s, and in the 1960s and 1970s there were performances of those by Luciano Berio, Pierre Boulez and Witold Lutoslawski.

There was also a variety offered by the ethnic diversity of London's population. An acceptance of different cultural traditions was seen in 2002 when the celebration of the Queen's Golden Jubilee brought carnival dancers and gospel singers into the Mall. More edgy transitions were seen in popular music, with Asian influences playing a role in the musical forms known as grime and dubstep and also in the development of Asian-British films, which became a highly successful genre.

Changes in restaurant provision reflected a long-term shift in cuisine. In P. G. Wodehouse's *Ukridge* (1924), the 'ordinary' Price family of Clapham Common are imagined having 'cold beef, baked potatoes, pickles, salad, blancmange and some sort of cheese every Sunday night after Divine service'. A century later, the menu is very different, both in content and in variety. Londoners now face a range of products heavily mediated by the dominant supermarkets, but also enlivened by the choices available as a result of new fashions and of ethnic diversity. The gastronomic geography of the capital is richly varied. There has been a marked rise in vegetarianism while, as far as meat is concerned, chicken has become more popular, beef less so and mutton – let alone eel pies – have largely disappeared. Chinese and Indian restaurants have become very prominent – and not simply in areas with concentrations of immigrants – while their cuisines are also extensively stocked in supermarkets. The National Catering Inquiry published in 1966 indicated that 11 per cent of Londoners had visited an Indian restaurant at some point. The percentage subsequently increased sharply, with newly affluent young males playing a key role, while the cuisine was altered to suit British tastes. In contrast, Afro-Caribbean cuisine and restaurants have had less impact either on the white British diet or that of other ethnic groups, a marked contrast to the strong Afro-Caribbean impact on popular music. Other ethnic groups that have also failed to make a wider impact include Somalis. The contrasts in part reflect the availability of investment capital and of entrepreneurial networks in the restaurant trade.

Fiction provided a marked sense of transition in London, with the city offering an unsettling backdrop for Martin Amis's novels *Money* (1984), *London Fields* (1989) and *The Information* (1995). His was a depiction of a cityscape and society under strain and buckling under the pressure of change, a theme also seen in Margaret Drabble's *The Radiant Way* (1987). A troubled view of London, specifically the Docklands, could also be noted in Iain Sinclair's novel *Downriver; Or, The Vessels of Wraths* (1991), while the often sinister ambiguities of the city's past emerged from the novels of Peter Ackroyd; for example, *Hawksmoor* (1985), *The House of Doctor Dee* (1993) and *The Clerkenwell Tales* (2003), or, for the more recent past, Jake Arnott's *The Long Firm* (2000). A sense of a lack of fixity, of a flux in perception, was captured by Julian Barnes in his witty novel *Metroland* (1981): 'The value of Kilburn depended on not knowing particularities, because it changed to the eye and the brain according to yourself, your mood and the day.'

Film Images

Some of the films of the period, such as *Mona Lisa* (1986), showed London as patterned by crime, with class, sex and race suffused by themes of individualism that some critics linked to Thatcherism. Even in *Sliding Doors* (1998), a romantic film set in London, an attack by a mugger played an important role. In the Hanif Kureishi-scripted films *Sammy and Rosie Get Laid* (1987) and *London Kills Me* (1991), London emerged in an ambivalent fashion, reflecting the absence of cohesion.

In the powerful visual images offered on the screen, there was a continuing tension between historical London, as in *Shakespeare in Love* (1998); a quaint London, as in *Four Weddings and a Funeral* (1994) or *Love Actually* (2003), and more edgy accounts, such as *Lock, Stock and Two Smoking Barrels* (1998). The cinema image can also be divided between the 'heritage' or 'tourist' London packaged for American consumption that presents London as a romantic space – as in *Notting Hill* (1999) and *Sliding Doors* and a realist London, as represented in *Lock, Stock and Two Smoking Barrels*, which re-imagined the East End as a site of gangsterism. Moreover, there is a retro London on film.

Ethnic identities and issues of assimilation and difference emerged as key themes in a series of novels including Hanif Kureishi's *The Buddha of Suburbia* (1991), Zadie Smith's *White Teeth* (2000), Monica Ali's *Brick Lane* (2003) and Gautam Malkani's *Londonstani* (2006). British-born descendants of immigrants have contributed much to an understanding of the creation of new, multiple identities. Kureishi and Smith have been particularly successful in doing so for the benefit of readers who lack their background.

Another testimony to change was *House of Ghostly Memory*, the concrete cast of an East End terraced house that won Rachel Whiteread the Turner Prize in 1993, only for the council to demolish the house soon after. The art world in London in the 1990s was particularly vibrant – to its supporters – and disorientating and self-indulgent – to its critics. London was the focus for competition over cultural values, specifically the tension – if not 'culture war' – between the criteria and ranking set by the artistic Establishment that influenced and directed government funding and those that made sense in the vernacular culture of popular taste. *Freeze*, an exhibition masterminded by Damien Hirst and held in 1988 in a warehouse in Docklands, marked the origins of the Britart movement, which took much of its anger from the determination of artists living on the breadline to reveal the harshness they saw; in short, this art was a savage product of the harshness of much of 1980s' London. The success of the movement owed much to Charles Saatchi, a collector who had made a fortune in advertising and who from 1992 organised exhibitions under the title *Young British Art*.

Drawing on punk and pop culture, the works of Hirst, Chris Ofili, Marcus Harvey, Tracey Emin and others set out to shock, as did their lifestyle. The controversy reached a height with the *Sensation* show at the Royal Academy in 1997, which led to unprecedented media attention, much related to Harvey's large portrait of the sadistic murderess of children, Myra Hindley, a portrait painted with the template of a child's hand. The range of printed opinion over *Sensation* indicated the ability of the arts in London to focus attention. On the one hand, there was the clash between social convention and individualism, but other critics saw the show as part of the rhythm of cultural change, with the former rebels having stormed the London bastions of the artistic Establishment. This was an aspect of a long-term process in which genres that would not have been considered art became lauded classics.

The opening of the Tate Modern (1999), built in the disused Bankside Power Station originally designed by Giles Gilbert Scott, provided a showcase for modern art, but the debate over fashion was given an annual outing in the popular media with the award of prizes to works that did not strike many Londoners as art. This was particularly so with the Turner Prize, which was won in 2001 by a light installation. Meanwhile, the work of these artists helped direct fashionable attention to the areas in which they lived – Shoreditch, Hoxton and Whitechapel.

Rebellion had entered the mainstream, with Punk giving birth to new and positive music, such as 'two-tone', and affecting style in fashion and design. Vivienne Westwood, who first came to prominence because of her links with the Sex Pistols was, by the 1990s, one of the country's leading fashion designers. The 1990s were also the years of Britpop, in which the London band Blur took a leading role. Britart was readily purchased because London in the mid to late 1990s and early to mid-2000s was largely prosperous, in large part due to the strength of the service sector. A high rate of female participation in the workforce was also important to this prosperity, both to middle-class London and also to the economy of the working class. Margaret Calvert celebrated this in her roadsign-style exhibit *Woman at Work*, displayed at the Royal Academy in 2008.

PROBLEMS

The high rate of deindustrialisation in the 1970s nevertheless had led to a major rise in unemployment that was readily apparent in subsequent recessions, while there was also what, in the 1990s, was increasingly termed the underclass. Large numbers of beggars appeared on the streets of London. The closure of mental hospitals created serious problems, as the alternative policy of 'care in the community' proved inadequate. Cases of tuberculosis among the homeless rose. Parts of London, especially on the South Bank, became a 'cardboard city', as the number who slept rough increased, usually teenagers who had left home to look for work or to escape parental pressure. The number of rough sleepers in London, according to the GLA, rose from about three thousand in 2000 to nearly nine thousand in 2018, with a marked rise from 2010 – a period of falling housing benefit and resulting evictions from the private rented sector. In London, according to the charity Crisis, the broader problem of homelessness increased to about 170,000 households, most of whom lived in hostels. However it was defined, the so-called 'underclass' challenged confidence in urban living, but was not a new problem: there are parallels between ideas of the underclass and the late-nineteenth-century notions of the residuum.

More generally, contrasting health indices in London were dramatic, with the death rate for social class 5 males (casual workers, those on social security) far higher than for social class 1 males (higher managerial, professional). In place of a mid-twentieth-century stress on a (then) sexy form of consumption – alcohol, cigarettes and gambling, all made glamorous in films such as *Alfie* – came healthy eating and an emphasis on firm stomachs, gyms and personal trainers. This shift reflected a change from enjoying things that were supposed to be bad for one towards the vanities of trying to look good. In London, smoking (and not going to the gym), as a result, became very much part of a dwindling working-class culture. Fads, however, operated in different ways. For example, opposition from 2002 to the MMR (measles, mumps and rubella) vaccine given to children led, in parts of South London, to a fall in the vaccination rate and thus to increased risks of the diseases striking.

A sense of rising crime was also an issue in the late twentieth century and early twenty-first century and featured heavily in the election literature produced by the mayoral candidates in 2021. An increase in criminality, notably in contrast to the 1950s, was related to a widespread breakdown in the socialisation of the young, particularly of young males, the percentage of whom with criminal records rose. Crime hit most in run-down neighbourhoods, caus-ing further de-socialisation and encouraging outward movement by those who could afford it. Crime rose even though unemploy-ment rates were low and the standard of living of the poor rose: robberies rose by 105 per cent between 1991 and 2002, a period of falling unemployment. Knife crime became more prominent in the 2000s, in part because large numbers of young men began to carry knives to give themselves a sense of protection. The resulting killings ensured that the murder rate increased from the late 1990s and led to a change in the age profile of violent death among males. Crime was also strongly linked to competition over drug sales.

Alongside the rise in crime, life in London was more regu-lated for poor and wealthy alike and, with the massive spread of CCTV, daily existence was literally under supervision. In Timothy Mo's novel *Sour Sweet* (1983), the tax inspector upbraids the Chinese restaurateur in London, 'Do you realise you have a legal obligation to keep a record for sales tax and purchase tax?' *Only Fools and Horses* (1981–2003), a popular television series set in Peckham, depicted a world of semi-legal expedients as a residue of the entrepreneurial spirit and a way of life. *Minder* (1979–94), another popular series, did the same.

There was also more overt opposition to government. Although most Londoners paid the community charge or Poll Tax introduced by the Thatcher government, there was also a mass demonstration in Trafalgar Square on 31 March 1990. Two hundred thousand people took part and the demonstration culminated in a riot. Although only a small number were involved in the disruption, the resulting scenes suggested the precariousness of public order. Similarly, economic change did not generally lead to a violent response, but the move of newspaper production from Fleet Street was resisted in the case of News International: in 1986, Rupert Murdoch broke the restrictive practices of the print unions by moving to a new plant at Wapping. There was violent picketing, but it was thwarted by the police. At the same time, Murdoch was successful in part because he could turn to the Electrical, Electronic, Telecommunication and Plumbing Trade Union (EETPU) to provide an alternative labour force.

The move in newspaper production was part of a process in which manufacturing moved out of Central London. There was also an important decline in manufacturing jobs in Greater London, bringing to an end a period of growth in the 1950s and 1960s, one in which London's manufacturing assets had also become more important, thanks to the decline of manufacturing in the traditional heavy industrial areas such as the North-East. Small firms in inner London proved especially vulnerable as they lacked liquidity and space. Moreover, it was difficult for these firms to compete with larger concerns built on greenfield sites. By the 2000s, much of London had deindustrialised and industrial estates were frequently sites for warehouses and large retail units.

The decline of manufacturing industry ensured that service activities became proportionately more important. Retail was the most significant in employment, although financial services brought in more money. Moreover, tourism was seen as a job creator, a source of income and a possible tool in urban regeneration. Other service activities included what was termed the sex industry, one that involved the exploitation of many young women brought in from Eastern Europe.

Another aspect of spatial change was offered by hospitals, particularly with the movement of provision out of the centre and into outer London, notably Northwick Park, as well as into the South-East as a whole. In some cases, entire hospitals moved – St George's from Hyde Park Corner to Tooting – while other inner London hospitals merged, including St Bartholomew's with the London Hospital and St Mary's with Imperial College.

FINANCIAL SECTOR

Meanwhile, the financial services industry was transformed. Although London could not recover the interwar role of sterling, it was able to become the most important financial centre outside New York, in large part due to the origins in the City of the Euromarkets in the 1960s. Dealing in eurodollars and eurobonds focused in London because the British authorities – notably the Bank of England – favoured the entry of foreign banks and the development of foreign currency transactions and were willing to see British-owned merchant banks bought up. In contrast, American and French financial centres were more tightly regulated. In 1986, the City was further deregulated in the 'Big Bang', a key element in the 'bonfire of the regulations' under the Conservative governments of 1979–97 and one designed to retain British financial competitiveness, especially with Frankfurt. While the money supply was loosened, restrictions on the activities of financial concerns were removed or relaxed with, for example, the end of minimum commissions on the stock market. London benefited from its time-zone position which enabled it to do business while New York, Tokyo and Hong Kong were open. The hyperactive open trading floor became an image of the new London and the bonus culture a matter of public report.

At the same time, the profits and bonuses reflected a high level of activity, as well as an ability to respond to opportunities, developing trading in new financial instruments. Substantial fortunes were made, helping fuel the property market in London, while a speculative building boom changed the face of the City, not least with large Modernist buildings. The functionalism of large, open trading floors prevailed in skyscrapers such as the NatWest Tower. The Lloyd's building, opened in 1986, was followed by the Broadgate Centre in 1991.

The growth in the City's international role resulted in a large-scale arrival of overseas financiers who helped fuel the service sector, while the twenty-four-hour nature of City trading as a result of its role in global money markets led to pressure to live close to work. This pressure accentuated the drive to develop areas near the City, such as Spitalfields, for housing. Clerkenwell and Hoxton followed in the 1990s, while parts of Islington became very prosperous. Moreover, the practice of weekly commuting developed, with City flats and rural houses replacing the pull of suburbia for many workers in financial services. Rising property values encouraged the movement of other kinds of markets out of central London: Covent Garden Market to Nine Elms in 1974, Billingsgate Market to the Isle of Dogs in 1982 and Spitalfields Market to Stratford in 1991.

In London and the wider South-East, economic activity was transformed with management, research and development jobs increasingly separate from production tasks. The former concentrated not in traditional manufacturing regions, but in parts of the South-East, which was a key aspect of the degree to which the Establishment in general became more focused on London and the South-East, with the world of money and services more important than traditional industrial interests. No other part of the country saw office development to compare with that in Docklands in the 1980s. As London and the South-East had higher average weekly earnings than those elsewhere in the country, these regions also paid a disproportionately high percentage of taxation. As a result, Londoners benefited from the major cuts in taxation under the Thatcher government. Income tax, capital gains tax and corporate taxation were all cut: the standard rate of income tax fell from 33 per cent in 1979 to 25 per cent in 1988, while the higher rate was reduced to 40 per cent.

In turn, the greater purchasing power that resulted, as well as rising real earnings and easier credit, fed through into consumer demand that helped the service sector. Spending became a major expression of identity and, indeed, a significant leisure activity. The move to twenty-four-hour shopping and the abolition of restrictions on Sunday trading were symptomatic of this shift. Yet, as a reminder of the variety concealed within aggregate regional indices – a variety that was central to the very diverse experience of change – there was also much poverty in London and the South-East. Indeed, comfortable films such as *Notting Hill* (1999) were not even accurate for their particular area.

1990s

Electoral support for the Conservatives ebbed markedly in London in the 1990s. In the 1992 election, the swing to Labour was particularly strong in London and, in the following election of 1997, Labour won affluent London seats such as Putney. Moreover, the economic growth that followed the recovery from the recession of the early 1990s and the abandonment of the European Exchange Rate Mechanism benefited both London and the Labour government of Tony Blair that won power in 1997. Skyscraper offices that had seemed unviable filled up, and rents and profits rose, to the benefit both of the City and of a government that used its tax revenues to support its social programmes across the country. Indeed, the City served as an equivalent to North Sea oil and received a similar lightness of regulation and a favourable tax regime. Financiers and the architects they sponsored referred to London as Manhattan-on-Thames. This city provided the setting for Labour's somewhat complacent pursuit of an image of Cool Britannia, a concept focused on the plans for the Millennium Dome.

Moreover, the governmental structure of London changed as a result of Labour's victory. The Blair government set out to recreate an overall authority for London and, under the Greater London Authority Act of 1999, the GLC was in large part restored as the Greater London Authority. The GLA is responsible for the same area as the GLC. The new governmental system includes an elected Mayor as the head of the executive and the Mayor and Assembly together constitute the Greater London Authority. The Mayor's responsibilities include transport, police, fire and preparing a strategic plan for the city, although not education or social welfare. Mayoral powers are also affected by those of both central government and boroughs; for example, in the area of transport. Thus, the boroughs are responsible for most of the roads.

2000s

Ken Livingstone, who, in May 2000, became the first elected Mayor, a position created that year by a referendum, won as an independent rather than a Labour candidate, despite Blair's efforts to block him. By then, Cool Britannia was ebbing. A failure to control Islamic extremists had already resulted in French anti-terrorist police describing London as Londonistan and this term became more commonly used, not least because of the inability of the government to prevent radical preaching that stirred up hatred against the host society. Deadly suicide-bomb attacks on the London tube and bus system on 7 July 2005 lent fresh point to these concerns, which were exacerbated by the hunt for other would-be bombers. The febrile atmosphere of that July highlighted worries.

However, the racist inflection of the capital was also changing. Alongside terrible episodes, there was a greater acceptance of multiculturalism. Moreover, the presentation of everyday life became less bigoted. Thus, the television comedy *Till Death Us Do Part* (1965–80) offered a racist protagonist, unlike *EastEnders* (1985–).

London was also nicknamed Londongrad as a result of an influx of wealthy Russians who invested in property and, even more conspicuously, in ownership of Chelsea Football Club. This influx was simply the most obvious strand of an inflow of wealthy foreigners who, in part, reflected the strength of the financial services industry, as well as a favourable tax regime for 'non-doms', or non-domiciled foreigners. This inflow also reflected significant improvements in the city's appeal, notably in education, transport and policing. The broad-based nature of the city's economy also provided a range of jobs, both high- and low-income. In addition to financial services, the creative industries became more prominent, as did the tech sector.

Having been re-elected as Mayor in 2004, beating the Conservative candidate, Stephen Norris, Livingstone was defeated in 2008 by Conservative Boris Johnson. The bitterly fought election revealed the major divides of the city, with inner London largely supporting Livingstone, only to be outweighed by outer London.

2010–21

In a return match in 2012, Johnson again beat Livingstone with 51.5 per cent in the second-round vote. Livingstone had pressed for a cut in public transport fares but his tax affairs became a matter of contention. In the 2016 election, Sadiq Khan won for Labour with 56.8 per cent of the second-round vote, defeating the Conservatives' Zac Goldsmith. The cost of house purchase and renting were campaign issues, as were fares, hate crime and the extent to which either side was 'playing the race card'.

Also in 2016, London voted Remain heavily in the Brexit referendum: by 59.9 per cent, while only five of the thirty-three boroughs voted to leave – Barking, Bexley, Sutton, Bromley and Havering. The contrast with the national result produced a degree of anger in London, one articulated by the newly elected Mayor, and also accentuated a sense of difference between London and the remainder of the country, one already satirised by *Private Eye* in the 'It's Grim up North London' series. In the national elections of 2017 and 2019, Labour did disproportionately well in London, the constituency base of successive leaders from 2015.

Yet, as so often, tensions involving London both interacted with pressures within it, and crossed with other differences in the country; for example, between the North and the South of England. Alongside these differences came internal migration, with London being the destination of about a third of new graduates in 2021, a year in which, in addition, as part of a 'churn' linked to age-related movement, 3.1 per cent of London's population moved to other parts of Britain, mostly southern England. EU citizens in London separately sought to define their new position. In 2019–20, 1.6 million Londoners, about 17.7 per cent of London's population, made applications to the EU settlement scheme, becoming EU citizens with settled status rights. This equated to 40 per cent of those in the UK with such a status. Newham and Brent were the boroughs in which this was most pronounced. Long-established European communities, such as the Portuguese in Southwell and the French in Lambeth and Kensington, thus found another identity as Londoners.

The current state of London is a matter of speculation and contention to a degree greater than has been the case for at least several decades. Its ethnic composition has changed, with international migrants a key factor: between 2008 and 2018, 550,000 more Britons left London than moved to it. In part, this was a matter of seeking more affordable and larger properties from which to commute into the city and, linked to that, generational change. Yet, there was also a degree of 'white flight' or, more correctly, movement that in part reflected what was revealed by successive well-being assessments by the Office of National Statistics: many individuals found London too expensive and were worried about crime, while companies moved jobs to less expensive locations outside London.

The 2011 Riots

It is all too easy, when fighting the constraints of space, to leave out events that made a big stir at the time but were rapidly forgotten by most of those not directly affected. The first draft of this book did so with the last major riots to occur in London, but they were important for the light they shone on society.

The killing by police of Mark Duggan, a gangster, led first to a demonstration and then to serious rioting, including throwing petrol bombs at police and much looting. Hackney, Haringey and Croydon faced particular problems, with gangs such as the Pembury Boys in Hackney playing a role. Rioters from run-down estates, for example, West Ealing's Copley Court, attacked nearby prosperity. *The Times* of 13 August quoted one sympathetic bystander: 'We're caged like animals here while the rich get richer.' In contrast, on Tottenham High Road, the Pancerow family made homeless by the riots, 'had to take their four-year-old daughter by the hand and flee on to the streets'. Two people were killed in London.

THE IMAGE OF LONDON

There were soon other elements in the mix. At first, there was 'simply' the question of the impact of Brexit and of the linked period of politics that led to discussion of such issues as a change of emphasis within the United Kingdom related to moving away from a stress on London and the South-East. The discussion took a number of forms, but the common characteristic was an alleged need to redress the situation within Britain. The Covid-19 pandemic of 2020–2 also played a role by making London less attractive as a place to live, and by cutting commuting and revenues. There were increasing predictions of decline, *The Economist* on 23 May 2020 declaring, 'For three decades, London was in the ascendant. Now it may have gone into a Covid-accelerated decline.' Attacks on the city's role were incessant. Seen as London-centric, the BBC was a focus of criticism from across the political spectrum on 'metropolitan bias'. In May 2021, Andy Burnham, re-elected as the Mayor of Manchester, argued that Labour had to end its 'London-centric' focus.

Radio programmes from outside London frequently carried criticism of the city, as with the claims in BBC Radio 4's *Any Questions* on 29 May 2021, an episode from Bridlington, Yorkshire, about transport expenditure being lavished on London. At the same time, London 'brands' successfully spread into the provinces. By 2021, Winchester had a Hoxton Steam Bakery, while both Exeter and Winchester had Ivy restaurants. Meanwhile, in May 2021, in the mayoral election in London postponed due to Covid-19, Sadiq Khan was re-elected with 55.2 per cent of the vote in the second round, although the Conservative Shaun Bailey did far better than anticipated, not least in the outer boroughs. In the first round their percentages were 40 and 35.3.

Climate Change

Climate change accentuates the long-standing risk of the drowning of some or much of London and of its hinterland. While global warming is a key factor, there are also issues specific to a smaller region, notably long-term and continuing structural adjustments from the removal of ice cover during the latter stages of the Ice Age. As a consequence of these adjustments, at the same time that Scotland and northern England experience uplift, a downwarping is especially apparent in East Anglia and the South-East.

The resulting risk of flooding led to the construction of the Thames Flood Barrier at Woolwich (1982), a major feat of civil engineering, which bears comparison with Bazalgette's work in the nineteenth century on the sewage system and the Thames. Once seen as a white elephant, the Barrier has turned out to be very useful.

Climate change means a need for a new barrage, as well as raised banks for the Thames and its tributaries in order to cope with the risk that a higher North Sea will prevent the movement of river water downstream. Thus, alongside the general issue of rising sea levels and their consequences for river levels, these levels will also be related to tidal patterns in the North Sea, not least seasonal high tides and tides linked to winds in the shape of storm surges. Such flooding would be a major challenge, both to particular areas such as Richmond, and also to the operation of the entire tube system.

More generally, both the Covid pandemic and the rise of sea levels indicate the instability of the environment and the dependence of human history on physical factors over which human control is limited. Yet, the very ability of cities to create viable living environments also suggests that some such control is possible and, moreover, that the end result may be prosperous, safe and even pleasant. For example, the capacity to insure commercial property is an important limitation of risk, while the creation of the wide-ranging underground system reflects human capability to mould the environment.

In many respects, the challenge from climate change is far more serious than previous emergencies, such as the Great Fire or the Blitz, as they were time limited and did not prevent a rapid process of recovery. The difficulty with raised water levels, in contrast, is that of an environment that has changed and to an unprecedented extent in the history of the city. In competitive terms, moreover, London's position near the sea makes its future situation more serious than Frankfurt, Paris and Manchester. The investment requirements of new flood defences are considerable and it is unclear that the planning regime is capable of mounting a swift response. This point is equally pertinent at the national and regional level. Any new flood defence system will have to be handled at a level above that of the Greater London Authority.

Warming may lead to summer droughts, winter storms and the onset of diseases such as malaria, resulting in pressure for the drainage of surface water, as in the Lea Valley (and also garden ponds). Water availability will probably be a key issue. It is unclear that rationing by price will solve the problem. Combined with continuing demands on land for housing and a resulting commitment to smaller units, the issue of water availability will probably affect planning regulations with, for example, a move from baths to showers, which use less water. Harsher summers will also take the green sheen off London's parks and, in the face of hosepipe bans, will lead to pressure for different plantings in gardens. The impact of climate change on immigration is unclear, but likely to be important as desertification in, for example, North Africa and Spain will greatly encourage the northward movement of people. There may also be a large-scale return of expatriates.

Energy availability is another key issue, one that faces Britain as a whole, not least with the obsolescence of much of its generating plant. In the late 2000s, the London Array Project, a plan to build 341 wind turbines in the Thames estuary with the capacity to generate 1,000 megawatts of electricity, was supported by the Brown government, but hit major problems from its backers because it was uneconomic. The timescale of climate change is unclear, but it is certainly far more imminent than the geological changes arising from shifting tectonic plates that will finally doom the city and remould the region, probably after the end of the human species. Yet, the consequences of climate change do not always enter into discussion of London's future.

CHANGING TIMES

As far as demographic trends are concerned, predictions about London's future are closely intertwined with those for the country as a whole and also specific to the city. During the 1940s–1980s fall in population, there was discussion among politicians and city planners as to how best to maintain infrastructure as the population fell. Now again, a fall in population and/or persistent economic problems or a rise in interest rates would make it difficult to sustain London's building stock and, notably, many of the large infrastructure projects brought to completion in recent decades, let alone those that are unfinished. For example, the durability of skyscrapers is in part dependent on maintenance, although technological progress plays a role, notably with the replacement of the issues posed by metal window frames, especially fighting rust, as a result of the use of mainly plastic extrusions.

There are other issues involved in the ability to sustain resistance to hostile creatures such as cockroaches, rats and mice. A sense of challenge increased in the 2000s with the problems of the speed of infection and hospital cleanliness involved in 'super bugs', especially MRSA. Economic difficulties may well ensure that the resistance to these and related challenges diminishes, both because of a crisis in public finances and the reduced profitability of private concerns, such as the water companies. Indeed, the failure of the latter to maintain the sewers to earlier standards has been blamed not only for the leakage of water but also for the marked recent increase in the population of rats. This issue of hospital infections also raises a classic problem about the viability of cities, namely whether the concentration of people (and other life) they represent causes a particularly acute race between possibilities for human life and the threats to it, an issue revived with the Covid-19 pandemic.

London remains badly congested, with cars responsible for nearly a third of journeys in Greater London in 2018, as much as bus and underground combined. In comparison, helped by bike lanes, cycling has doubled since 2000 but still only managed to make up fewer than 3 per cent of pre-Covid journeys. Roadworks, including to instal bike lanes, also hit road traffic, not least buses, whose usage fell significantly in 2014–19, while their average speed fell.

Yet, cities also present the greatest opportunities for addressing major problems, not least due to the availability of finance and human talent, as well as the most significant pressure for doing so. While London's past may serve as a reminder of the persistence of some problems, it is also a testament to adaptability and change. The considerable number of industrial estates, factories, power stations and transport depots that were found in much of London in the 1970s have gone, but much of the land has been used for other purposes. The decay of the inner city has been replaced by prosperity and change. As another instance of adaptability, the Millennium Dome eventually was repurposed as the O2 arena while, for every fiasco, such as the rebuilding of Wembley Stadium – which cost far too much and was delayed – there is a success, for example the Emirates Stadium, while Wembley itself now is judged a great success. Time heals many wounds – especially financial ones and delays – if the outcome works. This may be the case with the over-budget and much-delayed Crossrail.

In some respects, the diversity of the city is part of its global identity, one seen from the 2000s with the spread of grime music from East London. In the 2010s, London adopted Chicago's drill music but gave it a particular slant with the use of Multicultural London English (MLE), a London dialect that incorporates street language, notably Jamaican patois. MLE has then gone round the world. As an instance of a different identity, London was a centre of homosexual activity; in 2017, 134 gay and lesbian organisations were listed in inner London and nineteen for outer London, compared to forty-four for Manchester and thirty-eight in Brighton.

Yet, there are also rises and falls among global cities and room for querying aspects of contemporary London's situation, not least with reference to other cities. Today it is not clear whether or not London can remain in its current position relative to other global cities. *The Road to Wealth: How to Know London,* the title of an early nineteenth-century board game, no longer appears so pertinent. In part, London would be affected by a continuing relative decline of Britain.

There was also much discussion of the extent to which Brexit would lead to a decline in London's financial role and, with it, a crisis for Britain, as the financial sector contributes 7 per cent of Britain's GDP and 11 per cent of its taxes. In the event, despite efforts by Amsterdam, Frankfurt and Paris, the loss of jobs and business following Brexit was far less than predicted. In the late 2010s, there were 190,000 financial services jobs in the City and 67,000 in Canary Wharf and the overwhelming majority remained in Britain by 2022, in part because modern exchanges are now largely online platforms. London's derivative trading platforms have lost much of their euro business and London's abilities to perform financial functions for EU clients have been considerably restricted but, as yet, the situation has remained stronger than anticipated. Prior to the pandemic, 542,000 people worked in the City but fewer than 10,000 lived there.

The Covid pandemic led to much talk of the collapse of cities, while London was hit hard by a major fall in purchasing as commuters and tourists stayed away. Office vacancies increased. Employment, rents and revenues all declined markedly. There was discussion of the possible effects on population size and composition as well as on commuting.

Thus, prior to Covid, the future of the railway termini looked promising, with redevelopment scheduled for the ugliest – Euston

– and the prospect of rising passenger numbers, not least due to the Crossrail and HS2 projects. Whether passenger revenues and the office rents so important to redevelopment projects will recover is far from clear. The chance of a new system with a small number of central stations appears less likely and the long-established pattern will probably continue.

9

Conclusions

....

'London is the metropolis of Great Britain, the seat of her monarchs, the greatest, richest, most populous and most flourishing city in Britain . . . This city is the greatest part built on an hill, with an easy ascent no less pleasantly than conveniently situated on the River Thames, where it forms itself into a crescent or half moon, which makes it much longer than broad, and has the advantage of being sweetened on one side by the fresh air of the river, and on the other by that of the fields.'

Anon, *The Foreigner's Guide*, 1740, 2nd edition

London's history has often provided opportunities for making sense of the present by means of looking at the past. That is not always fashionable at the moment, but the use of the past has been frequent in London's history, just as its impact has been variously presented; for example, through property ownership, buildings and war damage. Thus, the Peasants' Revolt of 1381 provided the opportunity for radicals to cite it, as in 1794 in response to the French Revolution and in 1849–50 when a pantomime, *Wat Tyler: or Jack Straw's Rebellion*, was regularly performed at the Royal Victoria Theatre, Lambeth. It was also a reference point for those who were anxious, such as Charles I in 1642. In 1765, Richard Gough referred to demonstrating weavers in Green Park 'under a leader who gave out his orders from a lofty tree, like any Jack Straw or Wat Tyler of old'. They were complaining about the cost of food and competition from French silks.

Any history of the city that underplays both England's and London's intertwining with world history misses the point. The first London was founded by conquerors, the Romans, who served their purposes and fell into marked decline soon after they left. So total a relationship between city and outside forces was not to be repeated but the continuing relationship was important in the account of London's politics and its economy, one that was particularly driven home when it was under the control of foreign troops or overawed by fortifications.

A city that relied heavily on trade, both domestic and international, could not but be greatly affected by these external links. To foreign eyes, this trade used to be regarded as a cornerstone of the burgeoning success of the British economy and nation. Whereas, in the seventeenth century, few tourists ventured into the business end of London and those that did were often critical, in contrast, by the late-eighteenth century, a trip into the City was a must, including for foreign aristocrats. The Exchange was believed to symbolise positive features of British society, the Bank of England was a tourist site and particular awe was reserved for the new West India docks opened in 1800, a key facility for the Atlantic world.

Communications have been crucial elements in the city's history, helping explain why it was able to take a global role. Conversely, the decline of London's relative international position in recent years has even more clearly been matched by that of the city's docks, as well as of the country's merchant fleet and shipbuilding, although these criteria are not relevant for London's financial position which, instead, relies on electronic communications with which the city is well provided. Controversy over the future of Heathrow takes on part of its weight from the question of London's future as a world city in the sense of a key nodal point in the world's web of communications and transport.

As with New York in the twentieth century and Shanghai more recently, it was the London of the new that was of interest in the eighteenth and nineteenth centuries, and that was pursued by a society that was heavily investing in the future. In turn, the

Victorians disliked much of the Georgian town building, but themselves built for new, a process dramatised with the destruction that accompanied the building of railway stations and lines, as well as with their department stores, hotels, clubs and neo-Gothic churches. The damage done by such work can be better appreciated as a result of our ability to see and understand the devastation wrought by 1960s' planners and buildings. As the recent proposals for expanding Heathrow indicate, many schemes for change are not without serious costs in terms of disruption and deterioration in living conditions.

Various themes can be noted when considering the last sixty years. On the one hand, there is the continued search for change and the new, a search that brings together the entrepreneurial quest for profit with the desire of authority to plan and build. Yet, the legacy of the new is mixed. This is the London of the Westway and Centre Point, and of the slab towers of housing estates and the Millennium Dome. The question that emerges, one already seen in the 1970s with its strong sense of malaise, is whether London, and indeed Britain, is any longer capable of solving its problems.

Looked at from a national perspective, investment in projects such as Crossrail as well as in the city's healthcare could be seen as highly disproportionate. The benefits that London receives over the rest of the country are certainly highlighted by considering what such sums could achieve if spent on the rest of England. Alternatively, the overweighting of the parliamentary representation of Scotland, Wales and some English areas ensures that the South-East, especially Greater London, is relatively under-represented.

Frequent reference to London as a whole is only partially correct for, although the city as a unit has an impact on the outside world, it is experienced by Londoners (and indeed by many visitors) as a complex assemblage of districts and communities, each and all affected by the shifting substratas of class and ethnicity. This point has been true from the inception of the city and underlines the extent to which its history is different for outsiders and inhabitants. This point also affects the coverage of the city's history. Inhabitants might anticipate due attention to their own suburb but, to an Argentinian interested in London's role as an exporter of capital in the nineteenth century or a Newcastle reader aware of the city's past as the major market for north-eastern coal, the history of Hendon or Clerkenwell as distinct areas is of scant relevance.

The same point about the ambiguous value of change can be made about self-consciously new developments in the arts that focused on London. Thus, by 2009 critics had become increasingly very disillusioned with Britart, while Altermodern, the Tate Triennial 2009 exhibition that claimed to offer an alternative to postmodernism, was widely criticised as lacking cohesion or aesthetic content. Yet, instead of any easy classification of change and continuity or the drawing of any simple relationship between change and disruption, tensions involving different strategies for both change and continuity can also be noted. These differences and tensions can be seen in the visual image of London and also in the lived experience of Londoners and those outside who deal with London.

All have a perspective on London today and contributing to that come perceptions of its past and views about its future. Many are very particular to the moment, but there are also repetitions of note. These cover all dimensions, from environment to politics and society to culture. Recurrent issues within London include pressures and anxieties arising from development, migration, poverty, crime and taxation. Those opposing 'London' or, rather, an image of London, to the rest of the country focus on the disproportionately significant role of the capital in politics, mores and the economy. Indeed, part of the history of London is that of imaginations about Britain or England without the capital; imaginations in which Londoners sometimes join, although with different contexts and arguments. These speculations reflect the

love–hate or need–anger relationships that have been there probably from the outset, relationships complicated by those of reac-
tions to government. Part of the problem of the 'London Question'
is that it relates both to the power of London-based government
and to the other varied sources of London's authority and influence. These can combine, as with hostility to the BBC – which is
based in London and perceived (including by its current Director-
General) to have views alien to those of much of the country. It is
an autonomous aspect of government supported by what in effect
is taxation.

In 2016, the journalist Simon Jenkins complained about 'capi-
talis': 'the long-standing centralisation of Britain's political economy caught between a dependence on London and an aversion to
its magnetic avarice'. At the same time, there can be a significant
contrast between London-based government and what are
presented as the views and/or interests of Londoners. There were
many medieval instances, but the most famous was the breakdown of Charles I's position in London in 1641–2. More recently,
although much of London did not support the GLC in this, the
argument was used in its clash with the Thatcher government,
and has more recently been reprised in the Brexit contention.

Drawing deep for continuities is an attractive way to shape a
history and provide coherence, but such an approach appears
particularly problematic due to varied contexts and different
places. In the case of the first, the recurrence of similar issues; for
example, migration, traffic or sanitation, is affected by the politics, society and technology of the age, in terms both of the subject
and the responses. In the latter, there is the role of a cityscape,
much of which was far from urban in 1900, let alone 1850 or
earlier. London's history is that of Southgate as well as the Strand,
or Loughton as well as Ludgate. That dimension is underplayed,
not least due to the end of a Middlesex consciousness, but also as
the consequence of an imperialising character to London's history.
Yet, as with most empires, London's involved symbiosis, one, in

part, expressed by the more Conservative character of the outer boroughs, much of the population of which has a reluctant engagement with supposed metropolitan culture. And this is even more so with the Greater Metropolitan Area. This includes many who have sought to 'escape London', 'leave the city' or who have chosen not to live there.

Like 'Londoners', London is both a series of realities and a set of abstractions. Given that this is the case in the present, it would be wrong if its past was presented as fixed and obvious or its future foreordained. It is this very variety, complexity, contention and lack of fixedness that makes London's history so interesting. Pierre Egan noted in 1820, 'The Extremes, in every point of view, are daily to be met with in the Metropolis.' That remains the case, as does an energy and variety that contribute greatly to the experience of the city.

Selected Further Reading

....

Ackroyd, Peter, *London: The Biography* (London, 2000)

Ansari, Humayun (ed.), *The Making of the East London Mosque, 1910–1951* (Cambridge, 2011)

Archer, Ian, *The Pursuit of Stability: Social Relations in Elizabethan London* (Cambridge, 1991)

Auerbach, Jeffrey, *The Great Exhibition of 1851: A Nation on Display* (New Haven, Conn., 1999)

Baker, Philip, *London, City of Cities* (London, 2021)

Barber, Peter, *London: A History in Maps* (London, 2012)

Barron, Caroline, *London in the Later Middle Ages: Government and People, 1200–1500* (Oxford, 2003)

Barron, Caroline and Sutton, Anne (eds), *Medieval London Widows, 1300–1500* (London, 1994)

Bayman, Anna, *Thomas Dekker and the Culture of Pamphleteering in Early Modern London* (Farnham, 2014)

Beerbühl, Margrit, *The Forgotten Majority: German Merchants in London, Naturalisation, and Global Trade, 1660–1815* (Oxford, 2015)

Brenner, Robert, *Merchants and Revolution: Commercial Change, Political Conflict and London's Overseas Traders, 1550–1653* (Princeton, NJ, 1993)

Brooke, Christopher, *London, 800–1216: The Shaping of a City* (London, 1975)

Brunsdon, Charlotte, *London in Cinema: The Cinematic City Since 1945* (London, 2007)

Campbell, Bruce et al., *A Medieval Capital and its Grain Supply* (London, 1993)

Cassis, Youssef and Bussiere, Éric, *London and Paris as International Financial Centres in the Twentieth Century* (Oxford, 2005)

Copelman, Dina, *London's Women Teachers: Gender, Class and Feminism 1870–1930* (London, 1996)

Corton, Christine, *London Fog: The Biography* (Cambridge, Mass., 2015)

Crawford, Hannah, Dustagheer, Sarah and Young, Jennifer, *Shakespeare in London* (London, 2015)

De Grey, Gary, *London and the Restoration, 1659–1683* (Cambridge, 2005)

Dobbin, Claire, *London Underground Maps: Art, Design and Cartography* (London, 2012)

Egan, Pierre, *Life in London* (London, 1820)

Ford, Mark, *London: A History in Verse* (Cambridge, Mass., 2012)

Fox, Celina (ed.), *London: World City, 1800–1840* (New Haven, Conn., 1992)

Freeman, Janet (ed.), *The Epicure's Almanack: Eating and Drinking in Regency London* (London, 2012)

Freist, Dagmar, *Governed by Opinion: Politics, Religion and the Dynamics of Communication in Stuart London, 1637–1645* (London, 1997)

Gauci, Perry, *Emporium of the World: The Merchants of London 1600–1800* (2007)

Green, David, *Pauper Capital: London and the Poor Law, 1790–1870* (Farnham, 2010)

Green, Nile, *The Love of Strangers: What Six Muslim Students Learned in Jane Austen's London* (Princeton, NJ., 2016)

Griffith-Jones, Robin and Park, David (eds.), *The Temple Church in London: History, Architecture, Art* (Woodbridge, 2010)

Griffiths, Paul, *Lost Londons: Change, Crime and Control in the Capital City, 1550–1660* (Cambridge, 2008)

Guard, Richard, *Lost London: An A–Z of Forgotten Landmarks and Lost Traditions* (London, 2012)

Halliday, Stephen, *London's Markets: from Smithfield to Portobello Road* (Stroud, 2014)

Hanawalt, Barbara, *Growing Up in Medieval London* (Oxford, 1993)

Hinds, Peter, 'The Horrid Popish Plot': Roger L'Estrange and the Circulation of Political Discourse in Late-Seventeenth-Century London* (Oxford, 2010)

Hitchcock, Tim and Shoemaker, Robert, *London Lives: Poverty, Crime and the Making of a Modern City, 1690–1800* (Cambridge, 2015)

Hollis, Leo, *The Phoenix: St Paul's Cathedral and the Men who Made Modern London* (London, 2008)

Hotson, Anthony, *Respectable Banking: The Search for Stability in London's Money and Credit Markets since 1695* (Cambridge, 2017)

Inwood, S., *A History of London* (1998)

Jackson, Lee, *Dirty Old London: The Victorian Fight Against Filth* (New Haven, Conn., 2014)

Jackson, Peter, *George Scharf's London: Sketches and Watercolours of a Changing City, 1820–50* (London, 1987)

Judah, Ben, *This is London: Life and Death in the World City* (London, 2016)

Kelly, Debra and Cornick, Martyn, *A History of the French in London* (London, 2015)

Knight, Caroline, *London's Country Houses* (Chichester, 2010)

Lancashire, Anne, *London Civic Theatre: City Drama and Pageantry* (Cambridge, 2002)

Levene, Alysa, *The Childhood of the Poor: Welfare in Eighteenth-Century London* (Basingstoke, 2012)

Lincoln, Margarette, *London and the Seventeeth Century* (New Haven, Conn., 2021)

Lindley, Keith, *Popular Politics and religion in Civil War London* (London, 1997)

Linebaugh, Peter, *The London Hanged: Crime and Civil Society in the Eighteenth Century* (Cambridge, 1992)

Merritt, J. F. (ed.), *Imagining Early Modern London: Perceptions and Portrayals of the City from Stow to Strype, 1598–1720* (Cambridge, 2001)

Merritt, J. F., *The Social World of Early Modern Westminster: Abbey, Court and Community, 1525–1640* (Manchester, 2005)

Merritt, J. F., *Westminster, 1640–60: A Royal City in a Time of Revolution* (Manchester, 2013)

Neal, Lynda, *Victorian Babylon: People, Streets and Images in Nineteenth-Century London* (New Haven, Conn., 2001)

Nightingale, Pamela, *A Medieval Mercantile Community: The Grocers' Company and the Politics and Trade of London, 1000–1485* (New Haven, Conn., 1996)

Nurse, Bernard, *London: Prints and Drawings before 1800* (Oxford, 2017)

Orlin, Lena (ed.), *Material London, ca. 1600* (Philadelphia, Penn., 2000)

Pennybacker, Susan, *A Vision for London, 1889–1914: Labour, Everyday Life and the LCC Experiment* (London, 1996)

Picard, Liza, *Victorian London: The Life of a City 1840–1870* (London, 2005)

Pierce, Patricia, *Old London Bridge* (London, 2001)

Port, Michael, *Imperial London: Civil Government Building in London, 1851–1915* (New Haven, Conn., 1995)

Porter, Roy, *London: A Social History* (London, 1994)

Porter, Stephen, *London's Plague Years* (Stroud, 2005)

Rasmussen, Steen Eiler, *London: The Unique City* (London, 1948)

Raven, James, *Bookscape: Geographies of Printing and Publishing in London before 1800* (London, 2014)

Rawley, James, *London: Metropolis of the Slave Trade* (Columbia, Missouri, 2003)

Reinke-Williams, Tim, *Women, Work and Sociability in Early Modern London* (Basingstoke, 2014)

Reynolds, Elaine, *The Night Watch and Police Reform in Metropolitan London, 1720–1830* (Stanford, Calif., 1998)

Rosenberg, David, *Rebel Footprints: A Guide to Uncovering London's Radical History* (London, 2015)

Rule, Fiona, *The Worst Street in London* (London, 2008)

Schofield, John, *Medieval London Houses* (London, 1994)

Sheppard, Francis, *London: A History* (Oxford, 1998)

Shore, Heather, *London's Criminal Underworlds, c. 1720–c. 1930: A Social and Cultural History* (Basingstoke, 2015)

Sinclair, Iain, *Hackney, That Rose-Red Empire: A Confidential Report* (2009)

Stevenson, Christine, *The City and The King: Architecture and Politics in Restoration London* (New Haven, Conn., 2013)

Sutton, Anne, *The Mercery of London: Trade, Goods and People, 1130–1578* (Aldershot, 2005)

Sweet, Rosemary, *The Writing of Urban Histories in Eighteenth-Century England* (Oxford, 1997)

Thick, Malcolm, *Sir Hugh Plat: The Search for Useful Knowledge in Early Modern London* (Totnes, 2010)

Tindall, Gillian, *A Tunnel Through Time: A New Route for an Old London Journey* (London, 2016)

Ward, Joseph, *Faith and Philanthropy: Londoners and Provincial Reform in Early Modern England* (Basingstoke, 2013)

Ward, Joseph, *Metropolitan Communities: Trade Guilds, Identity and Change in Early Modern London* (Stanford, Calif., 1997)

Warner, Malcolm (ed.), *The Image of London: Views of Travellers and Emigrés 1550–1920* (London, 1987)

White, Jerry, *London in the Eighteenth Century* (London, 2012)

White, Jerry, *London in the Nineteenth Century* (London, 2008)

White, Jerry, *London in the Twentieth Century* (London, 2001)

White, Jerry, *London: Story of a Great City* (London, 2010)

Wilson, A. N., *London: A Short History* (London, 2004)

Wise, Sarah, *The Blackest Streets: The Life and Death of a Victorian Slum* (London, 2008)

Wohlcke, Anne, *The 'Perpetual Fair': Gender, Disorder and Urban Amusement in Eighteenth-Century London* (Manchester, 2014)

Zahedieh, Nuala, *The Capital and the Colonies: London and the Atlantic Economy, 1600–1700* (Cambridge, 2010)

The Museum of London richly deserves a visit.

Index